SAGE was founded in 1965 by Sara Miller McCune to support the dissemination of usable knowledge by publishing innovative and high-qual ty research and teaching content. Today, we publish more than 850 journals, including those of more than 300 learned societies, more than 800 new books per year, and a growing range of library products including archives, data, case studies, reports, conference highlights, and video. SAGE remains majority-owned by our founder, and after Sara's lifetime will become owned by a charitable trust that secures our continued independence.

Los Angeles | London | New Delhi | Singapore | Washington DC

ADVANCE PRAISE

"Sid's memoir shows readers that he *did it the right way* and offers much needed encouragement to others to fight every day to do the same."

**—Jeffrey T. Cuthbertson, Mayor,
City of Rochester**

"This is not simply another rags-to-riches story, but one fraught with unbelievable hindrances that few, if any of us, could surmount."

**—Edward J. Wolff, Professor Emeritus,
University of Detroit**

"Few people have managed to write with such emotion, clarity, and deliberation as Sid has about poverty, adversity, and a dogged determination to overcome seemingly insurmountable obstacles to succeed. I strongly believe that by reading this memoir, all of us can benefit from [it]."

**—Joseph Knollenberg, Member of the
US House of Representatives, 1993–2009**

"This is an exemplary story of an emigrant who rises from personal and economic hardships, almost receives a Fulbright scholarship, and eventually flourishes in academia and the business world . . . readers whose perspective may be irreversibly impacted by the strength of Mittra's vision and willpower."

**—Virinder Moudgil, President and CEO,
Lawrence Technological University**

to BEE or not to BEE

WINNING AGAINST ALL ODDS

Sid Mittra

SAGE | Response Business Books

www.sagepublications.com

Los Angeles • London • New Delhi • Singapore • Washington DC

First published in 2015 by

SAGE Response
B1/I-1 Mohan Cooperative Industrial Area
Mathura Road, New Delhi 110 044, India

SAGE Publications Inc
2455 Teller Road
Thousand Oaks, California 91320, USA

SAGE Publications Ltd
1 Oliver's Yard, 55 City Road
London EC1Y 1SP, United Kingdom

SAGE Publications Asia-PacificPte Ltd
3 Church Street
#10-04 Samsung Hub
Singapore 049483

Published by Vivek Mehra for SAGE Publications India Pvt Ltd, typeset in 11/13 Berkeley by Zaza Eunice, Hosur, India and printed at Saurabh Printers Pvt Ltd, New Delhi.

Library of Congress Cataloging-in-Publication Data

Mittra, Sid, 1930–
   To bee or not to bee : winning against all odds / Sid Mittra.
     pages cm
   1. Success. 2. Motivation (Psychology) I. Title.
   BF637.S8M584   650.1—dc23   2015   2015024101

ISBN: 978-93-515-0314-9 (PB)

The SAGE Team: Sachin Sharma, Sanghamitra Patowary, Apeksha Sharma, Rajib Chatterjee, and Vinitha Nair

*Dedicated
to everyone inspired by this book
to reach
his or her full potential*

Bulk Sales

SAGE India offers special discounts
for purchase of books in bulk.
We also make available special imprints
and excerpts from our books on demand.

For orders and enquiries, write to us at

Marketing Department
SAGE Publications India Pvt Ltd
B1/I-1, Mohan Cooperative Industrial Area
Mathura Road, Post Bag 7
New Delhi 110044, India

E-mail us at **marketing@sagepub.in**

Get to know more about SAGE

Be invited to SAGE events, get on our mailing list.
Write today to **marketing@sagepub.in**

This book is also available as an e-book.

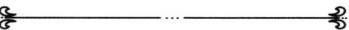

CONTENTS

FOREWORD

I was intrigued when I learned that Dr Sid Mittra, who had permanently settled down in America decades ago, was in the process of publishing his memoir *in India*. But what truly amazed me was that he also decided to donate all of his book revenues to charity, earmarked for training ostracized Indian women so that they could become useful members of our society. To the best of my knowledge, this is the first time anyone settled down in a foreign country has demonstrated his lifelong commitment to his motherland in such a unique fashion.

I came to know Dr Mittra several years ago when he started raising substantial sums of money in the US (approximately ₹65 lakh at today's exchange rate, of which a large portion of the contribution represented his personal funds) for financing the nursing educational program instituted by our Ramakrishna Mission in Vrindaban. Subsequently at our special invitation, Mittra visited our Mission, investing a fair amount of time learning about our multidimensional programs and conducting his independent, in-depth due diligence of our nursing program. It was in this context that I got to know him at a personal level, and that gave me the opportunity to discover what truly inspired him in life. I believed then, perhaps naively, that after making it big in America, he had decided to send a small charitable contribution our way. But when I read his memoir, *To Bee or Not to Bee*, I realized that I could not have been more wrong in my assessment of this man.

Mittra's big successes in many areas of life, both professional and personal, present a compelling life story. I was intrigued by his insatiable desire to set insurmountable goals in life and then invent creative, and often unbelievable, ways of achieving them. But what really caught my attention was his discovering a novel way of simultaneously applying life's four principles, or as he puts it, the four Ps. Soon curiosity got the better of me, and I delved into our holy Indian scriptures to see if these documents contained any traces of his principles. I then discovered that he tries to lead his life thinking of the whole world as one unified family. In fact, *Vasudhaiva Kutumbakam* in Sanskrit means that the whole world is one single family.

Our scriptures go further. In one instance it says:

"अयंबन्धुरयंनेतिगणनालघुचेतसाम्‌| उदारचरितानांतुवसुधैवकुटुम्बकम्‌"

pronounced as:

> *ayaṁbandhurayaṁnētigaṇanālaghucētasām*
> *udāracaritānāmtuvasudhaivakuṭumbakam*

This implies that discrimination based on the feeling that one person is a relative, while the other one is a stranger is mean spirited. For those who hold on to higher principles, the entire world constitutes just one family.

Any person who adopts this valued principle of treating it as *one world* is poised to make his/her best contribution to the society. *Dāna*, or the act of charity, leads a person to be reborn as a happy person and in a state of affluence. Conversely, the absence of charitable giving leads him/her to be reborn in a state of unhappiness and poverty. Even more important, a charitable-minded person encourages and inspires others to follow that noble path, thereby multiplying the gains for the whole society.

These powerful thoughts are beautifully articulated by Swami Vivekananda's advice to all. Says he: "Arise! Awake! Stop not till the goal is reached." I feel that this passion to go forward until the summit is reached is what took Dr Mittra to these present heights. "To succeed, you must have tremendous perseverance, tremendous will. I will drink the ocean," says the persevering soul, "at my will mountains will crumble up." Have that sort of energy, that sort of will, work hard, and you will reach the goal," says Swamiji. Sincerity, sacrifice, and dedication—when these three come together, there is nothing that one cannot achieve.

Swamiji further says,

> him I call a Mahatman (great soul) whose heart bleeds for the
> poor, otherwise he is a Duratman (wicked soul).... This is the
> gist of all worship—to be pure and to do good to others....
> He who sees Shiva in the poor, in the weak, and in the dis-
> eased, really worships Shiva; and if he sees Shiva only in the
> image, his worship is but preliminary. He who has served and
> helped one poor man seeing Shiva in him, without thinking
> of his caste, creed, or race, with him Shiva is more pleased
> than with the man who sees Him only in temples.

With the spirit of these lofty ideals, Dr Mittra is trying to set an
example for others in doing unselfish service for humanity.

It is with enthusiasm that I urge you to read Dr Mittra's memoir,
To Bee or Not to Bee. In reading his memoir what I found most
fascinating was that Mittra first presented the four principles that
created the foundation for his success in life. While you may have
a different way of looking at his life's incidents as they unfold,
chances are that you will be drawn into his life story instantly and
will not be able to put the book down until you have finished
reading it.

In closing, I would be remiss if once again I do not draw your
attention to Dr Mittra's decision to donate all of his book revenues
to charity, helping our ostracized women. In addition to personally benefiting from reading his memoir, which I have no doubt
you will, by buying the book you would also be financially helping these unfortunate women become useful members of our
society.

Swami Suprakashananda
Secretary
Ramakrishna Mission Sevashrama, Vrindaban

PRELUDE

D‌ear Reader,
This prelude has an exciting message for you. *I urge you to read it with anticipation and delight.*

To Bee or Not to Bee is neither a rags-to-riches tale nor the chronicle of an exceptional person or celebrity. In fact, instead of writing about myself, I wrote this book especially to demonstrate the following theme: How YOU can set for yourself seemingly unachievable goals and then, by following a set of designated principles, succeed in reaching them.

About the Book

Years ago, I published my autobiography by using my life as a chronicle. In the process, however, I discovered a unique pattern. Without realizing it, instinctively I applied to my life a set of *simple, but universal. principles.* These are the secrets that revealed how a mediocre person like me, seemingly destined to fail from birth, came to lead an extraordinary life. And since these principles worked even for someone like me, I am convinced *they will work for you.*

Conveniently called *The Four Ps Principles*, these universal principles comprise the following:

- Persevere with passion.
- Pursue professional, family-oriented, social, and spiritual goals.
- Persuade family and friends to help.
- Promote a culture of giving back.

To Bee or Not to Bee captures the spirit of an ordinary man with a life story that sounds unbelievably hopeless. I began my life in India, born under crossed stars. I experienced many failures before I succeeded at anything. I was a dunce. I was constantly punished for poor performance and inattention. I was a high school student who had graduated late after nearly dying of life-threatening illnesses. I was a bank clerk seemingly trapped forever in a dreary dead-end job. I was a research assistant who fumbled at the US Fulbright Scholarship and lost it forever. I was a foreign graduate student in the US, thrown in a rural jail by a formidable Georgia cop for accepting a ride to Washington, D.C. generously offered by a white woman. This was in a place and at a time when such an event was unheard of, with potential penalties too gruesome to consider some 50 years later.

And yet, defying all odds, I eventually became an emeritus professor, authoring hundreds of technical articles and more than a dozen books published by prestigious publishing firms. I also became an international personal finance expert and a philanthropist, living out my goal of making a difference in the world.

At first blush, these achievements may sound like a dream, *but they are not*. I miraculously discovered a secret that, despite repeated failures, *anyone* sufficiently disciplined to persevere can master. As this book clearly demonstrates, each time I met a seemingly insurmountable obstacle, I used *The Four Ps Principles* to create an out-of-the-box solution. That's even though I had to fail multiple times before I found it. For many years, I have been an octogenarian; yet I still follow these principles to achieve new, seemingly unachievable, goals.

In fact, following these principles is allowing me to give back to Indian society in a meaningful way. I have decided to donate *all of my revenues* generated by the sale of this book to an Indian charitable foundation, Ramakrishna Mission in Vrindaban, U.P. (office@rkmsvrind.org). These funds will be earmarked for providing nursing education to improve the lives of women who are ostracized in Indian society.

My Valued Coauthors

It is *unusual* to talk about coauthors of a single-authored book, but that's because it is an *unusual* book. My sole objective in publishing this book is to remain in the background and make *you,* the reader, the centerpiece of this book. Of course, the book is far more inclusive than that, which requires an explanation.

Ralph Waldo Emerson once said, "What lies behind us and what lies before us are small matters compared to what lies within us. And when we bring what is within us out into the world, miracles happen." As you begin to read the book, keeping Emerson's observation in mind, please forget that you are reading my life story. Instead, try to believe that I am narrating an interesting story, and you and I are in it together. Also, if in the process of reading this book you finally realize that this in fact is *your story*, then that will essentially make it "your book," and we will have successfully coauthored this unusual book.

Platform to Achieve Our Objective

In order to facilitate your gaining knowledge of how to apply *The Four Ps Principles to your own life*, and make you a bona fide coauthor in the process, for you I have created a platform with four pillars. These are presented as follows.

- *Pillar One:* At the end of every chapter in the text, I have presented a matrix identifying the principle(s) covered in that chapter. An example of this matrix is presented as follows:

> The following Ps marked with (X) identifies the principles covered in Chapter 5:
>
> [X]   Persevere with passion.
> [   ]   Pursue professional, family-oriented, social, and spiritual goals.
> [X]   Persuade family and friends to help.
> [   ]   Promote a culture of giving back.

- *Pillar Two:* In order to help you appreciate how people around the world have used (albeit unknowingly) the Four

Ps Principles with remarkable success, for your exclusive use I have created a special website (www.tobeeornottobee. org). In this website, for every chapter I have presented one unbelievable success story to demonstrate the true power of these Four Ps Principles.

- *Pillar Three:* In order to assist you in effectively playing your new-found coauthor's role, I have created a special section in the website. Once you have become fully socialized and feel the urge to share your, or someone else's, story of struggles and success, you will be able to post your own life story (subject to editorial approval) in this section and share it with other readers.
- *Pillar Four:* Henry Ward Beecher once said, "There are two ways to reach the top of an oak tree—you can climb it, or you can sit on an acorn." In order to help you climb to the top, I invite you to become a member of the *BCF* (*Bee Can Fly*) *Club* (by following the membership rules presented in the website), and then continue your climb to the top by encouraging others to join the ever-growing BCF Club.

Welcome Aboard, Dear Coauthor

Once I read a story (Ziglar, *Born to Win*) in which a lost traveler asked a farmer where the road they were on would take them. The reply was philosophically profound. "This road will take you anywhere you wish to go," replied the farmer with complete confidence, "but only if you are moving in the right direction." I am confident that by joining me as a coauthor of *To Bee or Not to Bee* you have already embarked upon your journey *in the right direction.* And I am fully confident that if you continue your journey with passion and perseverance, you will undoubtedly reach your full potential in life.

I wish you Godspeed.

Sid Mittra
Rochester, Michigan
August 10, 2015

ACKNOWLEDGMENTS

To say that this book is the product of a single author would be a gross understatement. Many people have contributed to this book in so many ways that it is difficult to acknowledge everyone.

Robert Mittra

My son, Robert, is responsible for planting the seeds for writing my autobiography. Here's how it all began.

The year was 1997 and the place was Rochester, Michigan. On a wintry morning, Robert and I were chatting about our trip to India following his high school graduation. Suddenly, Robert blurted out: "You have lived a life that is far different from anything I can possibly imagine. I know I'd enjoy reading your life story and I'm sure your grandchildren would love it even more."

With that, the idea of writing my autobiography was born. For the next several years, I tried to write about my life, but went nowhere. And when Robert questioned my lack of progress, I retorted: "Since I am not a Gandhi, Martin Luther King, John F. Kennedy, or Dilip Kumar, my life story couldn't possibly be of interest to anyone."

That's when I got a lecture from my beloved son. Said Robert, "No one is saying you are a famous person like the ones you mention. All I am saying is that you've lived a colorful life under diverse conditions in India and America. Your family members would be interested in knowing about all your trials and tribulations." I found his reasoning compelling. In 2006, on New Year's Day, I began writing my life's story, and truth be known, I didn't stop writing until I finished my first draft on the last day of that same year. Clearly, the passion I experienced during this period was both gut-wrenching and exhilarating.

First, reliving 77 years of one's life, in and of itself, is a challenging task. But the pain and embarrassment of documenting my past predicaments, misdeeds, indiscretions, and repeated failures were wrenching. Second, I discovered that there were significant gaps in my story. The only way to remedy that situation was to relive the past. So in January 2007, I traveled to India, visiting the places where I was born, grew up, and worked before migrating to America. That visit jogged my nostalgic memories and gave me the opportunity to take photographs and conduct interviews with family members and friends. I also collected material that helped me close the gaps in my story.

Copy Editors

This book has been heavily edited by several outstanding editors, each making a significant difference to the way the book has finally evolved. I take great pleasure in recognizing each of them.

Roger Wingelaar: Roger was my editor when I published a regular finance column in *The Oakland Press*. And since he had a deeper understanding of Indian culture than most Americans (his wife is from India), I requested Roger to edit the manuscript I had prepared solely for distribution among my family and close friends.

It didn't take Roger long to discover that, while I was a well-published author of technical books, I was a novice at telling stories. So it is no exaggeration that it is he who brought my personal story *to life*.

Edward J. Wolff: Upon deciding to prepare the *family book* for commercial publication, I was fortunate in finding Dr Wolff (Emeritus Professor of English, University of Detroit) as my editor. He literally accepted the manuscript as though it was a PhD thesis. He worked incessantly at meteoric speed, and demanded instant results that could be expected only from a desperate PhD student anxious to graduate. I must confess that Dr Wolff helped produce an *entirely new book* for publication.

Katy Koontz: I soon discovered that in order to improve my odds for publication, the book had to be rewritten as a compelling life story. That's when Katy Koontz (an exceptional editor) came on board.

Katy performed a miracle by changing the quality of the book while still narrating the story in my voice. In addition, she helped me verbalize a lot of memories and stories that had remained buried inside of me for a long time. Her contribution is truly remarkable.

Gregory Bresiger: While the memoir was well-written, I still had difficulty finding a publisher. Then one day, I was advised that I should complete the story of my life before seeking its publication. I took that advice to heart. After working at it for several months, I produced a vastly expanded manuscript with a completely new message.

Once again I ran into the now-familiar dilemma. The newly drafted chapters as well as the old, revised chapters needed to be professionally edited, but by now Katy Koontz had become unavailable. So I reached out to Gregory Bresiger, who had published an article in the *Financial Advisor* magazine highlighting my achievements in the personal financial planning field. It was a long shot, since I did not know him and had no reason to believe that he would oblige.

Fortunately, this time good luck smiled on me. After he learned about the history of my efforts to get this book published, Gregory surprised me by agreeing to cheerfully edit the *entire manuscript* (both new and old chapters covering 300 plus pages). And there was yet another surprise waiting for me. When he learned that I had planned to donate all the book revenues directly to charity, he categorically refused to accept any compensation for this valuable service. Perhaps, the highest compliment I can pay to him is to say that for me it is a rare privilege to have known someone like Gregory Bresiger as an editor and as a true friend.

Once ready, I submitted the manuscript for consideration to a prestigious publishing company with worldwide presence. The fact that you are reading this acknowledgment suggests that you know the publisher is none other than SAGE (India).

Help from Extended Family

The support of my family and close friends was critical in writing this book and putting it in its present form. They include (in alphabetical order): Shantanu and Namita Bose, Subir Guha, Sudipto Guha, D. Kandasamy, Minati Mittra, Robert Mittra, Samir Mittra, Ashok Sapre, Binita Sarkar, Natasha Sarkar, Simkie Sarkar, George Seifert, Mahendra Shah, Rita Sherman, Ramesh Shishu, and Robert Skubic. But the editorial, administrative, technical support, and counseling that Dr Anandi Sahu provided went far beyond anything I had any right to expect. I am grateful to all of them for their various contributions.

Invisible Helping Hand

During all the years I have spent publishing a dozen books by prestigious publishing companies, nothing has even come close to the special treatment I have received from Mr Vivek Mehra, CEO and Managing Director of SAGE (India).

As mentioned, while my memoir was well-written, I still had difficulty finding a publisher. Then one day, as a kind gesture and without any expectation of SAGE's involvement with it, Vivek graciously agreed to browse through the book. He then pointed out that since it abruptly ended just when my life (both professional and social) was about to begin, he would recommend that I first complete the story *before* seeking its publication. I took his advice to heart, and, after several months of research and writing, produced a substantially expanded manuscript with a completely new and powerful message.

And now that the book has been accepted for publication, I can say with confidence that without Mr Mehra's caring involvement and powerful criticism, this book would never have seen the light of day in its present form.

The Commissioning Editor

In my professional life, I've had the privilege of working with many book editors working for such prestigious companies as Prentice Hall, Random House, Harper & Row, and Harcourt Brace. But I must admit that my experience in working with Sachin Sharma, the Commissioning Editor of my autobiography, has been vastly different. Sachin acts as if he is the coauthor of this book. His demeanor, attention to detail, direct involvement with every stage of the publication process, willingness to bend over backward to provide all the help I need, and cheerful disposition, all speak volumes about him as a dedicated professional, while still having fun working on this project.

Bani Mittra

It was my wife, Bani Mittra, who had to pay the whole price of the long hours I spent over a decade in writing, revising, and then rewriting the entire book. But that is only a part of what she has done for this project. Bani's creative, thoughtful, and constructive criticism provided over a long period of time had a major impact on the overall quality of the book. She critically read numerous versions of the manuscript and helped minimize and smooth out my biases in dealing with people, places, and events.

Although I cannot promise my wife of 54 years that this would be my last book, I know that the publication of this book would free some very welcome time for both of us.

Let me conclude by sharing with you the following poem that I received from Bani on January 1, 1988. It is no exaggeration that Joanne Domenech's poem literally planted in my head the seed for this book:

> *May your dreams*
> *never disappear with age,*
> *but may they continue*
> *as alive and as beautiful as you*
> *with the knowledge that they*
> *will someday come true.*
>
> —Joanne Domenech

Sid Mittra

INTRODUCTION: BEHOLD THE BEE

The sky is not the limit. I am.
—T.F. HODGE

On an early-October morning in 1957, I woke up in the dorm room of the University of Florida, sweating and nervous. It was an ordinary Thursday, except for one thing. Even though I was a student, on that day I was scheduled to present my first lecture on Economic theory to our graduate economics class, and that was making me uneasy.

My professor, John Webb, a white-haired man around 70 years of age, was regarded as an outstanding and popular professor. He believed that students are best educated when they reflect on the information presented, digest it, and then (if they find it useful) internalize it. Based on that philosophy, Dr Webb structured our weekly economics class in a unique fashion.

Each class began with one selected student lecturing the class on the key topic assigned for that day. After that initial presentation, Dr Webb took over and asked questions from the entire class. He ensured that we understood the topic. So, ours was a knowledge-based class, with no rote memorization.

Our class of 10 was decisively international in composition, with more than half of us from outside of the US. For instance, my classmates included U Nu from Burma, Jon Valgann from France, Moon Pak from Korea, Susilo Sukarno from Indonesia, Yamaru Jutsi from Japan, and myself from India. Without a firm command over English, the six of us struggled to present thorough and comprehensible lectures. The last two weeks' presentations by Nu and Valgann were problematic. The class was understandably critical of them. Because everyone knew I was educated in India through

English medium, I felt my fellow students would be even less tolerant of any ambiguities in my presentation. I was fearful and edgy.

After remaining agitated for most of the morning, I tried to calm myself. "Isn't it true," I argued with myself, "that our professor has always been kind and respectful of his students and has never been critical of our language deficiency? Besides, I trust that Dr Webb will help me if I need it—he always preaches tolerance and helping others." Reminding myself that I'd survived much worse than this, I decided to improve my odds by practicing my lecture in front of a mirror.

The title of the chapter that Dr Webb had selected for my lecture was "What Modern Economic Theory Really Is." It covered classic publications by three immortal economists: *The Wealth of Nations* (1776) by Adam Smith; *Principles of Economics* (1910) by Alfred Marshall; and *The Theory of Employment, Interest and Money* (1936) by John Maynard Keynes. This was a tough chapter, but I managed to master it. Delivering my lecture in front of the mirror bolstered my self-confidence.

After lunch, I sprinted over to Matherly Hall and went to room 202. I reached half an hour early there, so that I could write my key points on the blackboard before anyone showed up. I was ready by 1 pm, when Dr Webb entered the classroom carrying a glass jar that he placed on the table in front of me without any comment. Then he walked over to his chair and sat down as my fellow classmates began to arrive. I glanced at the jar and inside it saw an insect continuously knocking its head against the lid. I knew there'd be a story behind this because Dr Webb was known for sharing his diverse philosophical thoughts in ways designed to penetrate the psyche.

One day, for example, in an attempt to bolster our confidence as we struggled to master complicated economic theories without external assistance, Dr Webb shared the story of a boy who thought he was helping a struggling butterfly emerge from its chrysalis by cutting the chamber open with a pair of scissors. The butterfly emerged but its wings remaining forever shriveled and twisted, and it was never able to fly. What the well-intentioned boy didn't realize was that the butterfly's struggle was nature's way of helping the butterfly develop its wings so they'd be strong enough for flight.

But on this day, instead of launching into a story about the insect in the jar, Dr Webb simply signaled me to begin. I was able to outline the concepts of Smith, Marshall, and Keynes in a fairly smooth manner. After the class discussion that followed, I had almost forgotten about the insect when Dr Webb suddenly asked nonchalantly, "Okay, boys and girls, what do you see inside the glass jar?"

"An insect trying to fly out of the jar," I answered meekly, "but not succeeding because the lid is blocking the opening."

"That's right Sid, but it is only a partial truth," the honorable professor replied. "So allow me to fill in the blank." And with that, Dr Webb cautiously opened the lid. To our amazement, the insect (which appeared to be a fly) did not even try to escape.

The professor stared at it for a moment and then explained, "After trying multiple times and failing repeatedly, the insect is so heartbroken that it has completely given up, even when freedom is knocking on its door." After pausing to give us time to digest, he added, "I hope this convinces you that the best course of action in life is to adopt a 'pluck until luck philosophy.' That is, if you wish to succeed, never, ever give up, no matter how many times you've failed." We were mesmerized but Dr Webb was not yet through with us. After a long pause, he spoke again.

"By the way, what probably looks like a fly from where you are sitting is really a bumblebee," he explained. "And while it's not moving now, if I tease it a little, it *will* fly out of the jar." And with that, he picked up a stick and started poking the bee. At first, the bee barely moved, as if it were fast asleep; then suddenly it woke up, started moving, and finally flew away through the top of the jar to freedom. Then Dr Webb dropped another bombshell:

There's a legend about a biologist asking a Swiss aerodynamicist to determine if a bumblebee with its tiny body and small wings should be able to fly. Given the bumblebee's body weight and the size of wings, the engineer made some calculations to see if theoretically the creature should be able to glide at the speed it generally flies. His unequivocal determination based on the evidence was that it should be impossible for a bumblebee to fly.

Dr Webb let that sink in a moment before continuing. "I just told you that according to the theory of aerodynamics, the bumblebee *shouldn't* be able to fly. But the creature doesn't know that; so it defies the laws of physics and flies anyway." To the best of my recollection, Dr Webb continued to elaborate on that theme, but I was so overwhelmed by everything I had just experienced that I missed the rest of his story. A few minutes later, he dismissed the class.

As I walked out of the classroom, I had to admit that the professor's "pluck until luck" message was certainly powerful. But the story about the bumblebee's ability to fly even though it was supposedly impossible touched me even more deeply. I simply couldn't get it out of my mind. I sprinted to the library, picked up the appropriate volume of *Encyclopedia Britannica* and read an article entitled "Can Bees Fly? Insect Aerodynamics" with intense curiosity. The article confirmed that an airplane with the size and weight of a bumblebee moving at its speed wouldn't be able to glide. Instead, it would drop like a stone!

"The bumblebee has invented a few tricks to get around this seemingly insurmountable obstacle," the article said. Initially, the bee rapidly flaps its wings, moving them through the air faster than it normally flies. That helps, but still does not produce sufficient power for flight. Undaunted, the bumblebee then uses another trick: when its wings change direction they hit their old wake. This converts some of the momentum of this moving air into *extra lift*, thereby enabling it to fly.

This newfound knowledge started me musing. I confess that initially I felt sorry for the bumblebee. After all, I asked myself, "What crime did it commit in order to deserve a disproportionate body that would normally prevent it from flying, thereby denying it a useful and a productive life?"

It started to dawn on me that, in many ways, my own life was similar to the bumblebee. I began reflecting on my history. My family folklore claimed that I was destined to be born into a superrich family in India, continuing to bask in the glory of a *royal* family for the rest of my life. Unfortunately that never came to pass. Instead, a few years before my birth, due to a cruel hoax, my family's good fortune was abruptly reversed. My father unexpectedly died when I was only seven, reducing us to rock-bottom economic status. The family was then uprooted. I was sent to live with my older sister and her husband. I suffered multiple physical ailments—including one that threatened to become fatal. Educational challenges continued to dog me throughout my school years and well into college. Upon my eventual graduation, I got shoved into the lifeless existence of a faceless, nameless petty clerk working in Bombay. Everyone around me had predicted that I would never be able to get off the ground, and at the time it seemed as though they would indeed be right.

As I continued to reflect, again I began pondering the bumblebee. I wondered whether the bumblebee is able to fly because it is determined to invent the tricks necessary to achieve its goal or does it just continue displaying pluck until luck favors it, its success being the result of relentless trial and error. Maybe it can fly because in its optimistic ignorance, it simply doesn't know it can't.

Many of these theories, I realized, applied to my own story. Like the bumblebee, I ignored my shortcomings. I had never stopped trying to escape the vicious circle of my abject failures, no matter how hopeless my circumstances may have seemed at the time. And now I was not far from receiving a doctoral degree from a US university, half a world away (both geographically and ideologically) from where I had started. Perhaps I had engaged in a relentless pursuit of impossible dreams because I did not have the smarts to recognize my limitations—and so I just ended up getting lucky.

Here's how I did it.

Epilogue: Life's Lessons

It's fall 1957, and I am a first-year graduate student in the US. My professor brings a glass jar with a bumblebee inside it to class and eventually explains that according to an aerodynamic theory, a bee with its large body and small wings should *not* be able to fly. But the bee, unaware of its limitation, manages quite well.

I reflect on the bee story and realize that I am rather like the bee itself. Providence placed me in an environment that made it virtually impossible for me to succeed in life—I was poor in school and was considered a dunce growing up. I had physical disabilities, my family suffered a series of misfortunes and downright tragedies that made it impossible to give me much help or encouragement. And I was constantly dealing with crushingly restrictive rules prevailing in both India and the US. But obstacles that at first seemed insurmountable have proven no match for my insatiable desire to prevail. This book narrates the story of how I did it.

The following Four Ps' list identifies the P(s) that I have covered in this chapter:

[X]   Persevere with passion.
[   ]   Pursue professional, family-oriented, social, and spiritual goals.
[   ]   Persuade family and friends to help.
[   ]   Promote a culture of giving back.

1

HOBBLED BY A HOROSCOPE

*When you are inspired by some great purpose, some extraordinary
project, all your thoughts break their bounds. Your mind transcends
limitations, your consciousness expands in every direction, and you
find yourself in a new, great and wonderful world.*
—THE YOGA SUTRAS OF PATANJALI

I wasn't supposed to amount to much, according to my family's astrologer who also predicted that I might not live long. Not that anyone could blame me. Apparently, the stars were misaligned on the summer day in 1930 when I was born in Banaras, a holy city in northern India.

This wasn't my only rude awakening. A mere two years before I came into the world, my family had been superrich. My father, Kashi Mittra, achieved the rare distinction of being the first Indian president of the prestigious British-owned Imperial Bank of India. He was assigned a 10,000-square-feet mansion with 20 elegantly decorated rooms in Amritsar, a prominent city in the northwest of India. He and my mother, Taru Dutta Mittra, had two cars at a time in India when only millionaires and the most senior government officials had access to automobiles. Father also had a personal chauffer and a coterie of servants, including a gardener, a gofer, and a night watchman. This was indeed a superrich family.

But then disaster struck. For frivolous reasons involving his honor, Father voluntarily resigned his lofty position with the bank when he was only in his mid-50s, and he permanently retired. And with that, the family suffered a meteoric fall from ultra-rich status to the lower middle class, turning its fortunes upside down virtually overnight.

By the time I made my appearance, the world was already in the middle of the Great Depression; so the thought of adding an eighth child to a family that was already financially strapped might have made my father a bit nervous. Still, everyone took that event in stride and made preparations for welcoming the newborn.

By that time, my family was living in an old, four-storied brick building in which the top-floor room had been designated as the *heir-port*. In those days, babies were routinely born at home, and only the most risky births (such as cesareans) occurred in the hospital—and even then with much reluctance. Our heir-port was casually furnished: one queen-size bed for my mother, a small bed (not a crib) for the newborn, and a decorated platform for a woman priest who would bless the birth.

Conspicuously absent were the essential delivery tools that the midwife, known as the *dai*, was expected to bring with her, and the usual amenities birthing mothers are used to today, such as TVs, radios, and reading material. Men were forbidden to enter the heir-port, and only specially designated family members, such as my grandma and my sisters, were permitted. Even then, for sanitary reasons they were required to take a shower and change clothes every time they left.

On Tuesday, May 13, shortly after midnight, my mother began experiencing labor pains and was promptly shifted to the heir-port. It was a typical mid-summer night—hot, humid, and unbearable—and with every advancing hour the temperature was expected to climb. By midday, it had reached the 125F-degree mark. Because there was no air conditioning or even a cooling system, grandma sat on a stool next to Mother's bed and fiercely waved a hand-held fan (or *pankha*), holding Mother's hand as she tossed and turned with pain.

By 1 pm, my grandma felt it was time to send for Preeti, the *dai*, who knew our family well, having already delivered several of my siblings. While one messenger was sent to get Preeti, another was dispatched to bring back a woman priest, whose main task was to bless the newborn. Soon thereafter, both Preeti and the priest entered the heir-port, and the priest promptly occupied the decorated platform waiting to receive her. Preeti immediately checked Mother's condition and announced gleefully, "Let's get the baby out!" Moving swiftly, Preeti eased me out of my mother's body and into the world at 3:20 pm. At that precise moment, using the universal shell called *shankh* (conch, traditionally used in India to symbolize the celebration of auspicious moments), the priest blew the welcome sound.

That's how I began my existence, undoubtedly feeling happy that my long struggle was finally over. And by all known accounts, I remained oblivious to the serious challenges that lay ahead.

Following the traditional Indian practice, I lived in the heir-port for a month, after which I was ceremoniously shifted to the master bedroom on the second floor. As part of that celebration, our family astrologer, D.N. Chatterjee, presented my family with a neatly bound, 13-page booklet in which he had handwritten my horoscope. Noting that I was born on a Tuesday at 3:20 pm under the astrological sign of Taurus, the horoscope predicted that I would always remain dissatisfied (regardless of how much I achieved), I would demonstrate clear signs of hubris, and I would stubbornly refuse to give up until I achieved my constantly shifting goals (whether or not they were achievable). Because the stars did not align properly at my birth, the horoscope also warned that I was condemned to live in poor health and might die young.

These were ominous predictions, which understandably did not sit well with my family. Still, they were pleased to learn that the horoscope also predicted that I would go out of my way to help others, even when that required huge personal and financial sacrifices.

Father's pension from the Imperial Bank was sufficient to permit him to live with a large family in a fairly decent neighborhood. The cost of raising a family was low at that time in India because children did not get involved in extracurricular activities and parents did not buy expensive toys and gadgets—amenities most children today take for granted.

India was still struggling to enter the twentieth century in 1930. As in other cities around the country, most homes in Banaras did not have electricity. Items such as radios and electric stoves were not available. To compensate, people living in the same neighborhood knew one another well and behaved as though they belonged to a large, happy family. The city lacked public transportation, so most walked, rode bicycles, or hired one of the ever-present two-wheeled, horse-drawn carriages known as *tongas* or hand-pulled rickshaws.

Our beds consisted of mattresses on the floor, buttressed by long pillows. Our toys were pots, pans, and rag dolls. Our clothes were simple and always handed down to the next child. We did not have central heating and air conditioning, let alone refrigerators. We improvised by creating hand-held fans with banana leaves for cooling off during the hot season. We used a clay pot with a long, slender neck called *surahi* for cooling drinking water. In the winter, we heated our rooms by burning charcoal in earthen pots. The practice fouled the air and was dangerous, but no one questioned it. It was useless to complain. That's the way it was done then.

Since hardly anyone owned a telephone, friends and relatives felt no need to notify us before visiting. Indeed, they came over for a chat anytime that suited them. And when invited, they did not hesitate to join us for lunch or dinner. This custom of treating everyone as family was part of the Indian tradition.

We didn't have TV programs, creative books, and DVDs that are an integral part of a Western child's learning experience today. Instead, I learnt mostly from Mother, and, to a certain extent, from our caregiver Rima Bai, by listening to their stories.

I still remember how Mother put me to sleep, gently rocking me sideways on her knees and telling me a story that almost always began with, "Once upon a time there was ... a king, or a lion, or a rabbit." Mother intended to teach me honesty and truth in simple ways. Unfortunately, I always fell asleep long before the stories ended, so they did not then impart the morals Mother hoped I would learn. Fortunately, she continued her story-telling practice, eventually teaching me many lessons that shaped my character.

Still I was earmarked early as a dunce because of something I said repeatedly when I was three years old. Whenever I got into a fight with my next older brother Bishu, and my mother had to physically separate us, I'd blurt out, "I don't want to stay here. I want to go to my own home where my wife and children live. I have a lovely home and a beautiful garden filled with flowers in many colors." The first time I uttered those words, only Mother heard them, and she dismissed them as harmless baby talk. But when these outbursts continued, Mother got frightened because of the prevailing superstition that anyone remembering his previous birth would have a short life. Fortunately, this superstition proved to be untrue, although I carried the title of "dunce" for a long time.

When I was barely four years old, Mother was diagnosed with beriberi, a paralytic numbness of the lower extremities that causes oppressed breathing. Owing to the seriousness of her illness, doctors advised that we move to another city. So in early 1935, we moved to Allahabad, another large town in northern India. Despite our limited financial resources, Father managed to rent a red-brick ranch house with a lawn, a flower garden, and a vegetable plot. We also had electricity, indoor plumbing, and running water— luxuries in those days. Since Father was then retired and frequently talked about the importance of living within our means, all this was more than I had expected.

Until that time, I had seen Father only as the head of our family, a man whose main role was to set the ground rules for us to follow and to mete out punishments when we violated them.

But all that changed once we had settled down in Allahabad. Father started spending quality time with us, and I really got to know him. For the first time, he actually seemed jovial. He always wore *dhoti* and *kurta* (a native Indian dress). I never saw him in a formal three-piece suit and matching tie that he wore in the picture mounted on the wall, taken when he was the president of the Imperial Bank.

Like most people living in northern India, our family spoke Hindi (but Bengali at home) and I remember well Father taking pains to teach me English—and then recognizing my alleged intellectual failings. Once when I was five, he asked me to read the address on an envelope to test my proficiency in English. I sat comfortably on his lap and tried to read the whole address. But I succeeded in reading only the first line, "Babu Kashi Nath Mittra." (*Babu* is the Indian word for mister.) Father laughed and let me off easy with a friendly pat, saying, "*Aaro bhalo korte hobe*" (You must perform better). I wonder if he would have treated me so gently before his retirement.

Every day Father would take a morning walk in our flower garden. At his invitation, I would often hold his hand and walk with him—truly precious moments. It was during these walks that he shared some of his ideas about life through interesting stories and anecdotes.

One day he drew my attention to a bunch of ants, saying, "Look how these little ants are working together to carry on their backs loads that are heavier than their body weight, even though no one is asking them to do it. You can be successful in life if you work together and work hard." On another day, he pointed to a lame man walking with a crutch and said,

> This man has lost one leg, but instead of sitting at home and crying, he is going about his normal business as if nothing terrible ever happened to him. Bad things do happen in life, but we must learn to deal with them and go on.

During one morning walk, Father pointed out a bird's nest at the corner of our balcony, which had become an eyesore. "Since the nest appeared to have been abandoned by the birds, Mother asked me to climb up a ladder and destroy the nest," he told me. That seemed like a reasonable request and I expected that he would oblige her, as he usually did. But after thinking about it for a few days, Father told me he had decided against Mother's request.

"Why would you say no to her?" I asked him.

"Because it is not nice to destroy anyone's home, even if it happens to be an abandoned bird's nest," he answered with a commanding voice. "Remember, it's good to build; it is bad to destroy."

"But what are you going to do about this eyesore?" I asked, still nettled, "Mother hates it!"

"It may be an eyesore to you and to Mother, and it does appear to be empty, but it still is someone's home," he answered with a smile. "So I have asked Ramu [our servant] to build a nice bird's nest on the tree and carefully move the old nest from our balcony to the new nest." That satisfied Mother and me, and I guess it satisfied the birds, too.

While Father was the sole breadwinner and disciplinarian, my mother was the homemaker and the one who took care of the children. She received no help from my father in domestic affairs, as was the custom of the day. What I remember most about her is how she comforted me. Every time I received a light spanking from Father for neglecting my studies or initiating a fight, I would rush to her and she would hold me tight in her arms and kiss me, making the pain disappear.

Once after Father had spanked me for ignoring his repeated plea to do my homework, Mother hugged me and explained that Father simply wanted me to grow up strong and successful in life. Another time when Bishu angrily reprimanded me for damaging his writing board, Mother held me in her arms and explained that Bishu was actually asking me to be careful in handling delicate objects so that I would not hurt myself if they broke.

I never saw my parents argue either in front of us or outside our home. Father was always in command, the one who directed us. True, Mother was 18 years younger to Father, which may have had something to do with the way Father ruled the roost. But even so, it was the Indian custom at that time for wives to be subservient to their husbands. I never realized until much later that Mother had a profound effect on Father's thinking and that her ideas (always discussed with Father in private) oftentimes prevailed.

Mother raised 10 children—seven boys and three girls. She was only 43 years old when Father died, and she lived as a widow for another 35 years. She more than atoned for my father's shortcomings. Until the time she passed away in 1972, Mother remained my guiding star and admirably played her role as the matriarch of our family. It is no exaggeration that Mother remained my moral compass for life.

✍

The good life I enjoyed in Allahabad proved to be short-lived. When I was seven, a tragedy, stemming from what seemed like a minor incident, changed our lives forever.

Father followed the sacred practice of picking flowers from his garden every morning to use as an offering during his morning prayers. Men in India believed that such a practice empowered them to follow the right path and purified their soul. Carrying the flowers, Father would enter his prayer room and close the door behind him. Father's prayer room was unusual because it had neither statues of gods and goddesses nor objects such as bells or candles that were an integral part of traditional worship. Instead, the room had only a small table placed in a corner with the following words scripted on top: "Lord, give me the wisdom and the courage to make right decisions." After entering the room, Father would place the flowers on this table, sit down on a small carpet facing the table, close his eyes, and pray.

One beautiful morning of June in 1937, after taking his shower and dressing in traditional worship clothes, Father went to the garden barefoot to pick his flowers. But a thorn pricked his toe, traveling deep inside his flesh. He tried unsuccessfully to get the thorn out, and the injury eventually turned into gangrene. Although he didn't know it at the time, he was severely diabetic and so was especially vulnerable to such wounds. Medical science was primitive in India at that time, and even the leading surgeon from the best hospital in Delhi, who was flown to Allahabad to attend to my father, had access only to limited knowledge and resources.

Under these circumstances, the surgeon had little choice but to try to save Father's life by amputating his leg. In doing so, he could use only local anesthesia because Father's diabetes prevented the surgeon from putting him to sleep. When the doctor asked Father if he could withstand the pain of amputation while conscious, he remarkably replied, "I have faced many crises in my life; I'm sure I can withstand this pain. You do your job, and I'll do mine."

The doctor amputated his leg on the morning of June 28, 1937. By that evening, my mother at his side, Father started to talk. It seemed as if, anticipating his death, he was giving Mother instructions on how to handle the family once he was no longer there. Unfortunately, everything he said came out garbled; Mother could not comprehend a single word. Then he lost consciousness. A few hours later, my father passed away.

The financial situation created by Father's death was devastating. He had no savings in the bank and only a few rupees in the cash box at home. His single life pension (the typical retirement package employees received from private companies in India) was terminated the day he died, leaving our family with virtually no source of income. Biru, my oldest brother, was the only one of my siblings who was working at that time, but his monthly income of ₹100 (about US$20) was barely sufficient to support his own family. My three older sisters (Leela, Usha, and Bibha) were already married and living separately with their spouses. However, Sailo, the next brother in line, was in medical school in Agra. My third brother, Jogu, was a sophomore in college. Bishu (two years older than me), Raj (two years younger), and I were in elementary school, and my youngest brother Braj was only three. Basically, Father had left our family destitute, totally unprepared for his death.

The day after Father died, Biru, Sailo, and Jogu cremated his body and scattered his ashes in the River Ganga. For the next several days, as my brothers were making arrangements to take care of the family, a stream of strangers began stopping by our home. We soon discovered that although Father had been receiving a monthly pension of only ₹180, he somehow found it possible to financially help scores of poor people. It was customary for needy people at that time to go door-to-door asking for handouts. My father was apparently known to be the most generous of all. These people had no knowledge of father's death, of course, and so they continued to appear to collect their regular monthly handouts. Sadly, we had to refuse them.

At that time, however, all of these troubles were lost on me. I was oblivious to the precarious nature of both my short-term future and how the loss of Father would affect the rest of my life. I was, after all, only seven. As a result of the commotion following Father's death, I suddenly lost all warm feelings for him and could remember only the punishments he meted out. As I watched Father's body being taken away for cremation, I turned to nine-year-old Bishu and gleefully screamed, "Thank God, they are taking Father away. Now he won't be able to punish me."

I wasn't supposed to amount to much, especially because stars were misaligned when I was born. In addition, two years before I was born, my father, who was superrich, suddenly resigned from his lofty position and permanently retired. As a result I was born in a lower middle class family.

Epilogue: Life's Lessons

On May 13, 1930, on a hot, summary day, I was born as a happy child, oblivious to the serious challenges that lay ahead, However, my horoscope predicted that I would always remain dissatisfied, demonstrate clear signs of hubris, and would stubbornly refuse to give up on my constantly shifting goals. The horoscope also warned that I was condemned to live in poor health and might die young.

I grew up in a lower-middle class family. India was still a poor country; so I had none of what today's children take for granted.

My character was clearly shaped by my mother who instilled in me a deep sense of honesty and truth. Still, I was called a dunce simply because of the way I behaved.

When I was four years old, Mother was diagnosed with a serious illness, which forced our family to move to Allahabad. There I got to know my father well as he started spending quality time with me.

The good life I enjoyed in Allahabad proved to be short-lived. When I was seven, a tragedy changed our life forever.

One day, while walking in the garden barefoot, a thorn pricked Father's toe, traveling deep into his flesh, and eventually it turned into gangrene. Ultimately, Father's leg had to be amputated and that proved fatal.

Following his death, we discovered that he had left us no savings to fall back on and his pension was discontinued. That left us virtually penniless, and the family was totally devastated.

The following Four Ps' list identifies the P(s) that I have covered in this chapter:

[   ]   Persevere with passion.
[X]   Pursue professional, family-oriented, social, and spiritual goals.
[   ]   Persuade family and friends to help.
[X]   Promote a culture of giving back.

2

WHISKED AWAY AND CANED
IN CALCUTTA

*Anger is an acid that can do more harm to the vessel in which it stands
than to anything on which it is poured.*
—MAHATMA GANDHI

For days following the cremation of my father, our house was turned into a whirlwind of change. All day long, scores of strange people kept coming and going. I recognized none of them and had no idea what they were doing at our home. I asked Bishu what was going on, but he told me to go play outside and keep my big mouth shut. About the only time I felt comfortable was when our cook served my meals; even then, I was too disturbed to really enjoy them.

My mother was cooped up in a corner bedroom, and not once did she come out to talk to me. I found that most troubling, since I felt she had abandoned me. I saw women going in and out of that room, sometimes carrying food and other items, but no one told me what they were doing for Mother or why she seemed to be hiding from me.

Although I had no idea what was going on at that time, I subsequently learned that my relatives were following the old Indian custom of preparing my mother for her new life as a widow. In those days in India, a widow was blamed for the death of her husband and was, therefore, condemned to a life of simplicity, depravation, and isolation. Widows were required to wear nothing but a white sari made of coarse material, cut their hair, become strict vegetarians, spend much of the day in prayer, remain silent most of the time, and reject all invitations to participate in parties and festivities (including the marriages of their own children).

Since such complete lifestyle changes did not come easily or quickly, a widow would be secluded in a room for a while until her relatives were satisfied that she was properly acclimatized and was ready to live her condemned life as a second-class citizen of Indian society. Although this cruel practice has completely changed today (now widows continue to live the way they lived before, and in many cases they remarry without any stigma), this was what my mother was enduring for several days after my father's death.

One day Mother finally came out of the room, restrained by a group of women and crying her heart out. She was wearing the widow's white cotton sari, and her beautiful long hair had been closely shorn in an ugly, uneven cut. At that moment, I wished I had not seen her. I was crushed when she walked past me without so much as a glance my way.

Before I could recover from this shock, a woman I had never met before took me aside. She identified herself as Leela, my oldest sister who lived with her husband in the faraway city of Calcutta. "Father is no longer here to take care of you," Leela announced matter-of-factly, "so I am taking you and Raj with me to live in Calcutta."

"But what about my mother and my other brothers?" I whimpered fearfully.

"We live in a very small apartment and can hardly handle even only you two boys," she said. "But don't worry. This will only be a temporary move. Once everyone settles down, we will bring you back to Mother and all of you will live together again." I was not consoled and continued crying.

What no one bothered to tell me was that the rest of the family would be scattered as well. Mother, Bishu, and Braj were going to live with my oldest brother, Biru. Sailo was in medical school in

Agra, and Jogu had been directed to move in with a close relative living in Allahabad to attend college there. I felt abandoned and alone.

On a rainy afternoon, I packed my clothes and my favorite game of Ludo, a small blanket-pacifier, a toothbrush, and hair oil. I tightly grabbed Raj's hand, and we walked out of our home, trailing Leela and a strange-looking man, who I later learned was my brother-in-law, Santosh Majumdar. He was tall and slim, with a thin mustache and unruly hair that he combed backward. He wore a mean, ferocious expression, and I disliked him from the moment I saw him. What galled me the most, though, was that I did not even get to say goodbye to Mother or to any of my other brothers.

An hour later, the four of us arrived at the railway station and boarded an overcrowded, shabby, third-class compartment on an overnight train bound for Calcutta. After Santosh seated Raj and me across from where he and Leela settled down comfortably, I felt I was traveling with complete strangers who did not love me, and did not want me to be there. Suddenly tears started rolling down my cheeks again. I blamed myself for everything bad happening to our family.

By the time the train left the station, our compartment was overpacked. Passengers squeezed so tightly that there was hardly any space to sit comfortably, let alone lie down at night. I tried to sleep sitting up, but I succeeded in dozing off only sporadically.

The next morning, as our train pulled into a station, I heard a lot of noise. Peering outside, I saw a young boy not much older than myself who was dressed in tattered clothes pulling close to the window of my compartment. With his left hand, he began playing a one-string instrument as he sang a sad song; the lyrics went like this: "An orphan's home is always dark, but if you light it, God will bless you." In his right hand he held a tin cup, and as he sang, he extended it toward me, begging for money. Since I had none, I just stared back at him until he gave up and moved on to the next passenger. Strangely, instead of feeling sorry for him, I envied the beggar boy. I felt that he was free to sing to his heart's content and go wherever he wanted, whereas I felt like a prisoner.

After an arduous journey of 24 hours, our train pulled in to Calcutta. We soon boarded two hand-pulled rickshaws with our baggage and fought the city traffic for an hour before finally arriving at an old, dilapidated apartment complex—Raj's and my new home. Our second-floor apartment had two bedrooms, an open area used as a family room, a kitchen, a bathroom, and a toilet. But it had no living room and no storage facilities. So our baggage and other possessions had to be stored under our bed or on makeshift shelves built near the ceiling.

None of this mattered to me. All I could think about was that I had been uprooted from my family, and no one in this place seemed to care much about me. And I doubted that they cared very much about Raj, either.

The buildings were so close to one another in this overcrowded city that our apartment was virtually blocked from natural light. The one interesting feature, however, was a movie theatre across the street that regularly broadcast music over its outdoor speakers. At first I disliked the noise, but eventually that music became a source of inspiration for me.

In my confinement to this lightless, heartless place, I brooded about what I had done to bring about such punishment. I did not fully realize that Father was gone forever. I was bewildered at my banishment from Mother and my siblings.

Santosh took on some of the roles that Raj and I associated with Father. He gave us orders and punished us for what we did wrong. What we missed, however, were the love and reasonableness with which Father used to hand out his punishments as well as the presence of Mother, who always comforted me when I was hurt. It was apparent to me, even as a child, that Santosh assumed his duties unwillingly, granted us sanctuary grudgingly, and punished me arbitrarily. In my new home, I was still a dunce.

Nowhere was this more evident than in our home schooling. Santosh was not a natural teacher, nor was he interested in becoming one. He had no money to send us to school, so he himself took on the onerous task of teaching us lessons in English, math, and history. Raj responded favorably to Santosh's rote-memorization drills, but I had great difficulty learning when I could not understand the reasons behind the facts. Thus, Santosh was constantly criticizing me and punishing me for failing to regurgitate my lessons.

To teach English, Santosh would pick an English word, tell me how to spell it out loud, how to pronounce it, and finally how to match it with the Bengali word that had the same meaning. (India has 15 languages, with Bengali being the one used in Calcutta.) I would then repeat the spelling, pronunciation, and translation of the chosen English word a hundred times before moving on to the next word that Santosh had selected. I found this endless process to be utterly boring.

One day, after I thought I had mastered the art of learning by rote, I unwittingly got into serious trouble. Santosh had picked the word *elephant*, so following the established routine, I first learned how to spell the word, I then pronounced the word the way I was taught, and then I said out loud, "'Elephant' means *hathi*," its equivalent in Bengali, repeating this cycle a hundred times. The process was not difficult, but it was tedious, and often my mind wandered.

I was so bored that somewhere in the middle of the cycle I mistakenly started repeating, "'Elephant' means *sathi*" (Bengali for *friend*) instead. When Santosh tested me on my newfound knowledge, I repeated with complete confidence that the English word *elephant* meant *sathi*. The result was predictable: I was caned twice, which Santosh decided was the normal punishment for such mistakes. But while caning did focus my attention at the moment on my pain, unfortunately it was ineffective in teaching me to pay attention to my lessons, and hence it did not cure my mind of wandering. I learned little and was caned often.

Learning basic arithmetic was even more challenging. After I learned how to count to 100, both forward and backward, I was introduced to the mysteries of multiplication. No flash cards here— the method was oral repetition, 100 times per multiplication.

"Repeat after me," Santosh would say. "Three times eight is 24. Say it one hundred times." When I completed that cycle, I would go to the next one—four times eight is 32. But no one ever explained that by shifting from "three times eight" to "four times eight," I was merely adding eight to 24. As a result, I learned few mathematical concepts by oral repetition—but that wasn't Santosh's point. I was directed to memorize the multiplication table from "two times two" through "20 times 20." Then, on the day of testing, I would have to instantly recall whatever Santosh demanded.

"What's 13 times 19?" he would ask sternly. "No answer? Hesitation? Can't recall quickly?" I received two canes.

I dreaded the history lessons even more because I had to memorize long names. Chhatrapati Shivaji, a famous seventeenth-century Hindu warrior, was one of the easy ones. The saints were more difficult. We called them saints even though they were always fighting, and that was part of the problem. I could remember neither their names nor the names of their opponents. Perhaps it would have been easier if someone had explained to me why they were always fighting, who was winning or losing, and what was happening to the losers and winners. But again, that wasn't Santosh's focus. I had nightmares trying to remember these odd names, what all these people did, and when. In the morning I would wake up wet. More caning would follow.

My errors with the lessons weren't my only infractions. An odd rule that Santosh made got me into more trouble. During study time, I was directed to sit erect on a mattress. Since I felt more relaxed if I rocked forward and backward, I would break Santosh's rule if no one was in the room—but he always seemed to know. One day, I was able to solve this mystery. Although Santosh was sitting in the next room, he could still see my shadow moving through the open door as I rocked, and that was all he needed to establish my guilt. Luckily, no caning followed, and I was let go for once with only a stern warning.

All these problems with rote memorization and the punishments that followed convinced me that I was indeed a slow kid—slower than anyone else—and, therefore, I deserved all the punishments I received. Perhaps it was this realization that prevented me from blaming Santosh for all of my troubles and helped me tolerate the pain and humiliation that I felt during this period of my life. *Dunce* was my name for years afterward.

Eventually, I got used to expecting failures in my studies and accepted punishment as inevitable. In fact, these things became an integral part of a lacerating early life. Harder to tolerate was the loneliness and boredom I experienced in Calcutta. So to keep myself entertained, I started listening to the music coming from the loudspeakers outside the movie theatre across the street. Hearing the same soundtrack day after day ultimately taught me the dozens of songs each Indian movie typically featured. While I could not seem to memorize much of my history and math lessons, I quickly learned the words and melodies of the songs those loudspeakers poured into the air every day. This accomplishment helped me realize that I wasn't as dumb as people said I was. My repertoire of songs was proof that I could learn about something I enjoyed and *wanted* to learn. Miraculously, this routine turned out to be my salvation.

When Raj and I first moved in, Santosh had a steady job with a German firm. But even before Great Britain formally declared war against Germany in September 1939, the firm closed its branches in India, and all Indian employees, including Santosh, were thrown out on the streets.

The sudden loss of his job almost ruined Santosh, but he soon had a plan. He knew how to manufacture batteries on a commercial scale, so he decided to obtain a patent to manufacture them. Unfortunately, the patent had already been issued to his friend Chandra, who had apparently stolen his idea. With that betrayal, Santosh's last hope of running a successful business vanished.

He was forced to move us all to a small hut in a rural area outside Calcutta, with no running water, electricity, adequate toilet facilities or any other basic services we had in the city. As our financial situation continued to deteriorate, Santosh desperately tried to find odd jobs merely to stay afloat.

Understandably, this series of disappointments affected Santosh's mental health and he started behaving erratically. Although I did not realize it at that time, he started taking out his frustration by mentally and even physically abusing Leela and me. For reasons I could never understand, Raj was spared completely. True, Santosh always gave his reason for punishing me, but his often-repeated justification was that compared to Raj, my behavior was despicable. I would complain to Leela that Santosh was not being fair and that I was sure he wanted me gone, but she maintained silence.

Although in those days in India, caning children as punishment for mischief and lack of attention to studies was not unusual, what Santosh did to me was excessive. At one point, I had developed a severe infection in my left ear that required a doctor's attention. Instead of taking me to get help, Santosh directed Leela to treat my infection with home remedies, which did not work. The infection left me with permanent loss of hearing in my left ear. Perhaps Santosh did not have the money for a doctor, but I blamed him anyway.

Over time, I adjusted to Santosh's neglect and arbitrary punishments. Getting out of the house and partaking in the normal activities of young boys certainly helped. I explored as often as I could. Our home was close to an all-purpose village pond that residents used for bathing, fishing, washing laundry, and getting a daily supply of drinking water. One day I snuck out of the house, slowly stepped up to the bank of the pond and looked down. Noticing a school of small fish, I extended my hand as I stooped down to reach the water, but I lost my balance and fell into the pond.

Because I had never learned how to swim, I would very likely have drowned had a woman, approaching the pond to collect her daily supply of water, not seen me tumble in. She jumped in and pulled me out. When I revived, I pleaded with her not to mention my misdeed to my brother-in-law. She obliged, and to my immense relief the incident was never reported to my family. I escaped a severe caning.

It soon became apparent that the neighbors were not the only ones becoming aware of the difficulties in our family. Somehow the news of Santosh's unbalanced mental condition and erratic behavior reached my mother and brothers, as well. One day after Santosh had abused Leela, she sent a message to our oldest brother Biru, who was living in Calcutta, pleading with him to rescue her soon. While it would be some years before Leela permanently left her husband at Mother's urging, Biru did show up one day when Santosh was out and took Raj and me away. Unlike Leela, we were saved and back in Mother's arms after two long, heartbreaking years.

At that time, Sailo was attending Agra Medical College. Since Biru had a transferable job with the Reserve Bank that required him to move from one city to another, he advised us to rent a house in Agra so that my mother, Sailo, Bishu, Raj, Braj, and I could all live together. What joy I experienced when I moved out of Calcutta and was finally reunited with Mother and the rest of my family! In the embrace of family life once again, I learned to suppress all the unhappy memories of Calcutta. Leela had promised that living with her and Santosh was going to be temporary, and I was thrilled that her prediction was fulfilled.

Those two years left me with two long-ranging handicaps, one physical (the loss of hearing in my left ear) and one psychological (the certainty that I was inferior to Raj in every way). My serious inferiority complex would haunt me for ages, and I indeed felt like the family dunce more firmly than ever. Although I harbored deep resentment against Santosh for years to come, miraculously I never had any hard feelings toward Raj. We always remained great friends.

Eventually, not able to tolerate Santosh's abuse any more, Leela left him. With Biru's help she moved in with us. But in those days, divorce was a taboo, so Santosh and Leela were never legally separated. Ironically, about 10 years later, Santosh appeared at our doorstep in Kanpur, seriously ill and penniless. He had not contacted my family, including Leela, since she left him. Everyone was caught by surprise when he showed up. To my family's credit, Sailo took him in and then got him admitted to the Kanpur Medical Hospital. Eventually, Santosh's health improved somewhat, and he was invited to move back with us. He never fully recovered, however, and he died two years later.

While I was still angry with Santosh, I recalled one of Mother's stories, which helped me formulate (at least outwardly) a decent reaction to his reappearance. In her story, a young boy named

Ramu bore a grudge against his uncle for inflicting constant pain and suffering on him for a long time. But one day Ramu recognized that by continuing to harbor such resentment he was permitting his uncle to continue torturing him. With that realization, Ramu forgave his uncle, buried the past, and started living happily thereafter.

It took time, but I eventually forgave Santosh and treated him civilly. Way down deep, however, I still bore the emotional and physical scars he inflicted on me.

Epilogue: Life's Lessons

The entire Mittra family is displaced, and I am shunted to Calcutta and placed in the care of my older sister and a brother-in-law who is ill-equipped to handle children. The result is disastrous, if predictable. I am regularly caned, prevented from going to school, and subjected to constant verbal and psychological abuse—all leaving me with deep scars of insecurity and inferiority.

But when I teach myself the songs I hear coming from the loudspeakers mounted outside a nearby movie theatre, I eventually realize that I have more capacity for learning than I thought. When the news of my brother-in-law's excessive abuses reaches my mother, she arranges for me to return to her and my other siblings.

The following Four Ps' list identifies the P(s) that I have covered in this chapter:

[X] Persevere with passion.
[ ] Pursue professional, family-oriented, social, and spiritual goals.
[X] Persuade family and friends to help.
[ ] Promote a culture of giving back.

3

OF PACHYDERMS AND PARADISE

When I was five years old my mother told me that happiness was key to life. When I went to school, they asked me what I wanted to be when I grow up. I wrote down "happy." They told me I didn't understand the assignment, and I told them they didn't understand life.
—JOHN LENNON

After spending two miserable years in Calcutta as a nobody, I was overjoyed to return to my mother and brothers. They showered me with love. But life got even better. Our family was soon transported to a storybook village where brother Sailo was revered as *the* village doctor. I, as his brother, basked in his light. In the rest of my life, I have never enjoyed as much freedom, respect, and pure fun as I did during the year I lived in Banpur, a remote village in northern India.

After graduating from Agra Medical College, Sailo obtained a job as a chief medical officer in Banpur's medical facility. That he was appointed to such a high position even though he was only a recent medical graduate was not surprising. His performance in medical school was superb. In his letter of recommendation for Sailo, the principal of the medical college wrote: "[Sailo] Mittra is the most distinguished graduate of the college ... he was the most meritorious student of this college [since its inception] ... he [earned] honors in all subjects, both theoretical and practical." Sailo was young, handsome, competent, and a highly motivated medical professional. He was ready to assume the director's role in the village hospital. But as a nine-year-old, I wasn't much concerned about Sailo's medical abilities. All I cared about was that he was taking my mother, three of my brothers, and me to an *exciting* place.

Soon after we arrived in Banpur, Sailo discovered to his delight that the doctor was the second-most respected and revered member of the community, just after the land baron who owned all the land and whom the villagers revered as a god. As the village doctor and the land baron's personal physician, Sailo enjoyed special privileges. Whenever he walked down the street, everyone bowed to him reverently saying, "*Salam dagdar saheb*" (Greetings, doctor). He had two servants, a gardener, and a night watchman, attending to the family's every need. The only exception was that Mother preferred to do her own cooking, even though we could easily have hired a cook. I was ecstatic with her decision. I loved her meals (particularly her mutton curry with cauliflower and potato, served with rice pilaf).

Our new home had several rooms and was built entirely of refined clay, a construction usually reserved for the wealthy. Our front door did not even have a lock. No one dared to break into the home of the revered doctor. The backyard contained a large vegetable garden sufficient to provide the entire family with potatoes, beans, cauliflower, tomatoes, oranges, and bananas.

A milkman brought his cow to our doorstep each morning and milked her before Mother's watchful eyes. (Everyone in the village was suspicious of milk suppliers. They routinely cheated their customers by adding water to the milk; Mother stopped that.) We bought everything else—food, clothes, and household items—from the local market. Our servants did all the shopping and other household work, and the gardener attended to our lawns and garden. We enjoyed a life of luxury, with no chores, and I became accustomed to being part of the esteemed doctor's family—so different from what I had experienced in Calcutta.

A week after we arrived in Banpur, I had the pleasure of meeting the village's esteemed land baron. He was such a powerful person that no one in the village dared call him by his real name. So, out of reverence, he became universally known as *badka bhaiya* (big brother). I would never have come in direct contact with such an august person had it not been for his desire to meet the honorable doctor's family.

But when the land baron wanted to personally meet our family, no one volunteered. According to the prevailing Indian custom, my mother, being a widow, could not be expected to meet him. My two younger brothers, Raj and Braj, were too young. And my older brother, Bishu, was too shy. That left only me—the dunce—so I agreed to accept the invitation, albeit with understandable fear.

When I first entered the huge double gate, almost 50 yards from the front door of the baron's palatial residence, I saw a young man—tall, handsome, and baron-like—waiting for me at the entrance. He had a fair complexion and a neatly trimmed beard and mustache, and he was wearing breeches like those the British wore when they rode horses. I was speechless and frozen in my tracks, so he hurried to shake my hand.

"Welcome to Banpur," the land baron intoned in English. "I am glad you are here." His deep, rich voice so resonated in my ear that it silenced me.

"Do you understand English?"

"Yes," I replied meekly when my voice returned.

"Tell me, how do you say in English, *mai jata to hun*."

"I go," I replied timidly.

"That's not quite correct," he answered, smiling. "You should have said, 'I *do* go'."

I quivered and bowed my head, wishing my father had taught me more. But even though I failed the test and felt like a dunce again, the land baron rewarded me with a gift beyond my wildest dreams.

"This afternoon," he said with a grin, "I will send you my personal elephant with its *mahut* [trainer]. He will take you for a joy ride for as long as you like. If this is your first ride on an elephant, I'm sure you'll be thrilled."

I stood there, mouth agape, and forgot even to thank him for what was surely the gift of a lifetime. He looked at me, smiled, mounted a beautiful horse that had been waiting nearby, and rode off majestically. He was my image of a god.

And as *my god* predicted, my first ride on an elephant was something I would never forget. At first, I was afraid to come near the huge animal. But the mahut assured me that the elephant was very friendly.

"All his trunk waving is his way of letting you know that he is happy to see you," the mahut explained. I had my doubts. After he ordered the elephant to sit down, the mahut helped me, shaking, to get on the seat perched high on the elephant's back, and then he himself climbed up and sat behind me to steady me.

"*Chal chal*" (Come on, let's get going), he said next, and the elephant rose to its feet. As soon as the beast started walking, I slowly began to relax into the rhythm of his movement. Sitting and swaying so high on the elephant's back, I viewed the world—the field around me—as tiny and strange. As I got used to the lumbering ride, I had great fun watching the elephant uproot a bamboo stalk with his trunk, shove it into its mouth, and quickly swallow the entire stalk. It seemed odd to me later that even though my elephant ride lasted a whole hour, all I could remember were the blue sky, the bamboo trees, and the cornfield we tromped through. It was as though I had been transported into another world.

This elephant ride, I was certain, was going to be my last—but I got lucky. Bishu complained that he was unfairly left out. So Sailo arranged for a second elephant ride, this time for both of us. I acted like a pro by then. I was no longer afraid when the mahut put Bishu and me on the elephant's back, then ordered the monster to pick him up with its trunk, and gently place him on his seat.

The second ride was different. Instead of going through the cornfields, the mahut led us through the village streets. With Bishu beside me, I felt like a king, taking a ceremonial elephant walk through my own kingdom. The elephant greeted onlookers by wildly waving its trunk and blowing loud, ghastly shrieks. The older people greeted us, reverently saying, "*Salam huzur*" (Greetings, Sir), while the children stood there and stared at us, awestruck. Women inside their huts gazed at us in amusement, perhaps, I imagined, in fear. I was indeed the king of the world. This ride lasted only 20 minutes, but memories of those precious moments became indelibly etched in my psyche.

Village life was not all elephant rides, however. Shortly after we arrived in Banpur, I was admitted to the village school. That was different from anything I had ever seen. It was merely a large open area, surrounded by several poles that held up a thatched roof to shade the students from the sun—with no walls, no furniture, no blackboard, no electricity, and no toilet. At one end of the covered area stood a raised platform, which was the seat for our teacher. The students sat on the packed-earth floor facing him. The teacher, who wore only a dhoti (a long loincloth traditionally worn by many Indian men), gave all his instructions orally, sternly, and sometimes even pontifically. A long, one-eighth-inch thick, white cotton string wrapped around his shoulders marked him as a Brahmin, the highest rank in India's caste system.

As a teacher, this man had absolute power over his students. We could speak only when he said so. And we *had* to answer him anytime he called on any one of us. He sat on his platform with his cane by his side. He used it on the students whenever he wished. Our classes started at about nine in the morning when our teacher arrived, and they ended promptly at three when he left. We were allowed to have breaks only when the teacher signaled. No one dared to object when he dozed off—a daily occurrence.

On my first day of class, I discovered that our teacher, whom everyone called *Guruji* (meaning teacher), taught his classes the same way my brother-in-law Santosh had taught me in Calcutta. But Guruji seldom posed a question to me, presumably because I belonged to the revered doctor's family. If I failed to answer correctly when he did call on me, he did not cane me; he instead caned another boy, as my surrogate, whom he chose randomly. The surrogates took the punishment silently, as if they deserved it, and never publicly expressed any resentment toward Guruji or me. Although years later I came to think of that practice as deplorable, I was then immensely thankful.

Although life was good for all of us, there was one notable exception. Sailo's assistant, Akshay Kumar, suffered from a serious drinking problem. When sober, Kumar was a diligent pharmacist but he often mixed various drugs for himself to produce intoxication. Sailo soon discovered that drugs were missing from the pharmacy. But whenever he threatened to fire Kumar, the assistant got down on his knees and pleaded, "*Peeth me lath mariye, pet me nahin*" (Please kick me on the back, but not on my belly), implying that if Sailo fired him, Kumar would starve. Because he felt sorry for Kumar's family, Sailo could not fire him, but he also could not prevent Kumar from stealing the medicine needed to treat patients. This intolerable situation continued for almost a year. At that point, Sailo felt that the only way he could solve this problem was to resign and move to another city.

Kumar's drinking problem was only one of the reasons we left. After a year's stay in Banpur, Sailo felt he needed to get back to Agra to practice medicine in an environment where he not only had access to a wider variety of medicines and surgical procedures, but he also could consult with other physicians and specialists. He also realized that we learned little in school, and the poor educational environment and the sleepy teacher in Banpur were holding us back.

Sailo's decision to leave the village for Agra did not sit well with badka bhaiya, the land baron. He pleaded with Sailo to stay, asking him what he could do personally to make our lives more enjoyable. Sailo tried in vain to assure him that never before had we been treated with such grandeur and goodwill, that we would never forget this joyful experience. But the land baron remained unconvinced. He insisted that his village had a lot to offer and could not understand why we thought another town would be better.

Despite our decision, badka bhaiya was a man of grace. One day before we left Banpur, as a special gesture, he asked the mahut to bring his elephant to our house to wish us bon voyage. When the elephant passed our house, it reared up on its hind legs and let out a loud scream in greeting. As the great beast walked by me, I saw tears rolling down his eyes. I was sure he was sad because the mahut had told him we were leaving. The elephant could not understand why we would leave him when he loved us so much—and that's why he had made that loud sound to plead with us to stay, so that he could take us for joy rides through the cornfields, the bamboo trees, and the village for adulation. I felt helpless. All I could say to my elephant friend was that I loved him very much and that I desperately wanted to stay with him forever. What irony that just a short time before I could not even remember what the word meant in our native language.

I was mad at everyone for forcing me to leave Banpur, mad at Sailo for deciding to leave the village, especially after the land baron himself pleaded with him to stay, and mad at badka bhaiya for failing to convince my brother that it was in his best interests to settle down there. But most of all, I was really mad at my elephant friend and the mahut for not taking me for a ride and running away with me to a faraway place so that no one could ever find us.

But nobody seemed to care how I felt. When I asked Mother why we had to leave, all she said was that we were leaving because it was good for us. Of course she was right, but I did not realize that until much later. I still kept asking what was so good about leaving this idyllic place where we had everything—a big house, a huge garden, lots of servants, and the respect of the whole village, not to mention the fact that I was never caned in school no matter how many times I failed. Why could no one else see that there was no other place like Banpur in the whole wide world?

Regardless, in January 1941, my family returned to the northern city of Agra, the location of the medical school from which Sailo had graduated two years earlier. But I got lucky once again, although only temporarily. Sailo thought he should go ahead of us to find and prepare an apartment for the family, but Mother did not feel comfortable with the idea of living alone in the village once Sailo resigned and left town. So they compromised and decided that everyone would leave for Agra except for Bishu, then 13, and me, 11. We would stay back in Banpur with a friend and join the rest of the family in two weeks. Even if I could not understand the reason for the two of us staying behind, I was eager to accept that arrangement because it allowed me two more glorious weeks in the village I saw as paradise.

Those two weeks went by very fast. I did not have to go to school or do chores. I could run in the fields, play with Bishu and our neighbors' children, sit on the porch watching cows and goats pass, or take long afternoon naps. At times, I did miss my mother and my younger brothers, but what I longed for was to see my elephant friend one more time. I very much wanted him to come by and take me for a ride, but I also knew that was wishful thinking.

All too soon, it was time to go. Bishu and I, with our servant guide, began our journey before dawn on foot toward the train station. The trip was incredibly long, covering 12 miles of a dirt road with numerous potholes, some of them so large that they were difficult to navigate even on foot. Bishu and I also had to carry our essential belongings in heavy backpacks, which made the effort even more arduous. And since our family had never expected us to have to walk for so long on a wintery night with the temperature hovering around 25F degrees, they never bought us winter clothes. We were poorly dressed for our trek. Even though the going was rough, the servant guide yelled at us whenever we slowed down. Soon he started walking faster, and when we got too far behind, he repeatedly shouted: "Chalo chalo!" I guess since our brother was no longer the revered village doctor, he felt no compulsion to be nice to us.

As we continued to walk on the poor, dirty road in that bitter cold, dawn began to push back the darkness. As it got lighter, the servant guide turned around and screamed, "We can't walk on this nice road anymore, because the station is too far and we will miss the train. We will just have to start walking across the cornfield, which will cut the distance by two miles." Then he turned around, and, without waiting for our response, started walking through the field.

At first, I was afraid to enter the cornfield because I saw something crawling in there that looked like a snake. But Bishu grabbed my hand and started pulling me so hard that I had to follow him. As we trudged through the field, terrified of being lost, frozen, or bitten, we tried harder and harder to keep up with the servant guide.

We finally arrived at the Basti train station at about 6 pm. By then, the sun had already set, and I was afraid I would faint from exhaustion. But I was so happy to see Sailo, who had arrived at the station from Agra a few hours earlier and was waiting for us there. Relieved that we had made it, he paid our guide as the man muttered, "Salam huzur," and moved off quickly. I watched him disappear and prayed that I would never see him again. God must have heard my prayers.

That evening, the three of us boarded the train bound for Agra. We were the only passengers in our compartment, so we could use it as we pleased. Sailo climbed up to the top-level wooden bench and stretched out. Bishu decided to use the middle level as his bed, offering me the use of the lower level, which I gladly accepted. When the train left the station at 9 pm, it was pitch black outside— exactly my state of mind. Instead of going to sleep, I chose to look out of the window and into the night. Despite being with my loving family, I feared that my life in Agra might be like the life I left behind in Calcutta. I tried to recall my idyllic life in Banpur, but failed.

I lay there brooding.

Epilogue: Life's Lessons

My elder brother Sailo is appointed as the chief medical officer of a clinic in the village of Banpur. As a member of the revered doctor's family, I suddenly enjoy freedom, respect, and pure fun. By a stroke of luck, the land baron invites me to take a *king's ceremonial walk*, riding on the land baron's personal elephant through the cornfields and the village streets, where people line up to salute me. Unfortunately, because the village lacks educational facilities and Sailo finds his clinic too limiting, my stay in the village is cut short, and the family returns to the overcrowded city of Agra.

The following Four Ps' list identifies the P(s) that I have covered in this chapter:

[X]   Persevere with passion.
[X]   Pursue professional, family-oriented, social, and spiritual goals.
[X]   Persuade family and friends to help.
[   ]   Promote a culture of giving back.

4

A DUNCE NO MORE

Courage doesn't always roar. Sometimes courage is the quiet voice at the end of the day saying, "I will try again tomorrow."
— MARY ANNE RADMACHER

At 4 am, our train arrived at the Agra Junction station. The few dim lights burning around the platform did little to fight the darkness. As we got off, Saila hired a *tonga* (a horse-drawn cart) to take us home, an hour's ride from the station. Once we arrived, I was disappointed to find that, compared to our palatial home with its beautiful garden in Banpur, our new house was quite a comedown.

The old and decrepit two-storied building looked like a make-shift shack that had been haphazardly erected in the middle of a crowded bazaar. A living room and two bedrooms made up the first floor, while the second floor held a large family room and kitchen. The upper floor also had an open space with four walls but no ceiling. We would use this as a bedroom for the better part of the year, sleeping under the sparkling stars. The house was big enough to accommodate all six of us, but it was a far cry from our Banpur home. And unlike Leela and Santosh's place in Calcutta, there was no movie theater across the street broadcasting Indian music.

Living in the inner city was both difficult and depressing. Our home stood near a busy intersection, close to a barbershop, a cigarette stall, and a variety of other stores. Roaming cows and heavy traffic flowed by our house day and night, creating an unbearable racket. Although Sailo had joined the Agra Medical College as a full-time physician, money was tight, owing to the rampant inflation caused by India's participation in (through Great Britain) the World War II.

Our life in Agra was, thus, a constant source of struggle. We had running water only for two hours or less each day, between 2 am and 4 am. So someone had to wake up after midnight to fill water buckets for the day. Like most houses in Agra, ours had no electricity too. But even if we had had it, we still could not have afforded electrical appliances, such as a radio, refrigerator, or even a vacuum cleaner. So we went without.

Most essential household goods, such as food and clothing, and even medical care, were rationed owing to the war. And the archaic and wasteful distribution system that the city government used made things worse. Transportation was another problem. Because the British were constantly moving thousands of army personnel, public trains allotted limited space for transporting the masses. All trains invariably ran late without notice. In fact, if a train arrived on time, everyone joked that it was 24 hours late.

With Mother's help, our family found creative ways to lessen the strain on our budget. We ate meat only on the last Sunday of the month. That's when Mother prepared a traditional spicy feast of mutton curry, fried rice, fried vegetables, and desserts, such as *gulab jamun* (doughnut balls in warm, sweet syrup) or *burfee* (a delicious, sweet, solidified pudding).

For lighting, we could afford to use only three kerosene oil-based lanterns—one in the kitchen, one in the living room, and a third in our study room. Each lantern had two vertical metal bars that connected the lantern's top to the base tank used for storing oil. During study time, when Bishu, Raj, Braj, and I sat down around the same lantern, two of us had to sit across from the metal bars, which cast a shadow on our reading materials. As the oldest of the four, Bishu decided that the two brothers who had the lowest grades in school should occupy the seats with obstructed light. We followed that rule to the letter, so during my entire school career, my seat permanently remained in the shadow. I was not happy with this, but because of the inferiority complex I had developed during my stay in Calcutta with Santosh, I did not have the courage to argue with my brothers.

Even though we accepted our limited budget as a way of life, we still continued to be creative in supplementing our finances. Once, during the war, Sailo's medical college directed him to find someone willing to produce rolled-up bandages on spindles. Even though the job was both menial and tedious, we grabbed it because it paid ₹1 for four bandages. That was good money for us. We produced over a thousand bandages and put our windfall to good use by enjoying mutton and chicken dinners more often.

Equally creative was our idea of improvising games that didn't require buying an equipment, such as badminton and cricket. We made up a game called *genatari*, which required only a used tennis ball and tiny bricks. The game was a little like baseball, with a pitcher throwing a tennis ball to scatter a stack of bricks. Ten fielders would then try to tag the pitcher before he could put the stack back together. This competitive game was simple, kept us physically fit, provided a lot of fun, and cost virtually nothing.

During the early years in Agra, no incident had a more profound effect on me than the one I experienced at a Ringling Brothers Circus. After a series of trapeze acts, followed by horse and bicycle riding by expert acrobats, four men wheeled in a platform. On this platform a Russian lady sat in front of a Singer sewing machine with a manual turning wheel. The lady sewed a piece of cloth and gave it to the emcee, who was standing nearby.

When the emcee showed the material to the unimpressed audience, everyone, including me, booed. But then he boldly announced that although the woman had lost both hands during World War I, she had trained herself to use her legs and toes as perfect substitutes for her lost hands. This was certainly a startling revelation, since the way she was placed on the platform made it impossible to tell that she was using her legs and not her hands.

A hushed silence hung over the audience as the woman then whispered into the microphone using broken English, "Every morning, I wake up and thank God for saving my two feet." That incredibly valuable lesson in dealing with adversity stuck with me for a long time, although it would be many years before I would grasp its full power.

Until I arrived in Agra, I had never attended a real school and had not enjoyed the opportunity to socialize with children of my age in a normal educational environment. In Calcutta, and later at the village school in Banpur, I did learn math, English, science, and Indian History, but that learning was casual, sketchy, and of little value. So there I was in Agra, 11 years old and seriously lacking in formal education, social skills, and most important of all, self-confidence. I was frightened witless.

Sailo attempted to get me admitted into grade seven at St. John's High School, arguably the best school in town. But not surprisingly, I flunked the entrance test and the admissions officer suggested that I try another school for a year, go through an intensive study program at home, and try my luck at St. John's the following year.

But we soon discovered that despite the city's large size, it had a few acceptable school choices. Some schools offered only grades three through seven, while others were not accredited as standard schools. After an intensive search, Sailo finally selected Dayanand Anglo Vedic (D.A.V.) High School, primarily because it was willing to admit me to grade seven. The all-boys school was owned and operated by the Arya Samaj religious organization, an offshoot of the Hindu religion.

Unlike St. John's High School, which was close to our house, D.A.V. School was a long bike ride. So one July day in 1941, I biked the 45 minutes to my new school, arriving anxious and scared. The number of students I saw milling around outside over-whelmed me. Once through the doors, I saw a big board in the school's lobby that listed the 10 principles on which Arya Samaj was based. So, like a Catholic school, this was a special denomina-tional school where students were expected to subscribe to its unique brand of religious philosophy.

My goal was to stay in this school merely long enough to improve so I could move to St. John's. But all this exposure to a different religion along with the crowd of unruly students brought tears to my eyes. With some effort, I found my classroom, where I soon discovered that the teachers there used the same rote method that had been employed by Santosh and my teacher in Banpur. I got turned off all over again.

In time, however, I adjusted reasonably well. I did all right in my classes and made a few friends. But not all my relationships were rewarding. Marble shoot was then a very popular game, although I couldn't play because I couldn't buy marbles. One day as I was watching my classmates compete, a tall, handsome, and lavishly dressed older student, whom I had never met before, approached me with a proposition.

"I will give you a few high-quality marbles if you let me kiss you," he said in a commanding voice. His suggestion so stunned me that I froze, stupefied. Immediately noticing my fright, he uttered a stern warning: "If you ever mention this to anyone, I will slaughter you." And then he walked away. I took his threat seriously and did not have the courage to share this incident with anyone.

One day not long thereafter, our teacher asked each of us to write two paragraphs on any subject of our choosing, print our name at the bottom of the page, and hand over our sheet to him. Apparently, while cleaning the bathroom, the janitor had found a note in which a student offered to have sex with another student in exchange for 10 expensive marbles. He turned the note over to the principal, who had then ordered the mysterious writing exer-cise. We all found out about it the next day, when I also learned that the student who had approached me with his proposition had in fact turned out to be the guilty party. He was instantly expelled.

Since I was totally ignorant of sexual matters and fearful that someone else might approach me in this school, I decided to do so well in my studies that I would get into St. John's overnight. It did not happen that quickly, but within a year I did manage to get admitted into the eighth grade of St. John's High School.

Although I was grateful, my academic problems continued to dodge me. I found the eighth-grade course load and the high educational standards of my new school onerous. The fact that I was only 12 years old and scheduled to graduate from high school at the age of 14 (because back then high school ended with 10th grade instead of 12th) did not help.

I envied a fellow student named Ajay Trivedi. Judging by his clothes and demeanor, I could tell Ajay came from a poor family; nevertheless he was very smart and better than I was in every subject except science. I lacked confidence and, hence, hung all my hopes on beating him at least in this one course. Once I did that, I convinced myself, no one would ever be able to call me *dunce* again. I put in so much extra effort into studying science that my teacher repeatedly told me that my performance puts me at the top of the class.

In those days in India, mid-term exams did not exist, and the grade for each course depended only on the final exams. At the end of the school year when I completed the final exam in science, I was confident that I'd earn the top grade in the course. But when the results were announced, I was devastated to learn that even in this class Ajay had beaten me. I was sure that my teacher, Sudhir Lal, had made a mistake, so I thought of asking him to review my grade. But even before I could muster the courage to approach him, Lal sent for me. When I arrived in his office, he placed my exam notebook before me and pointed toward the line on which I had written the title of the course.

"The word is *science*," he said, his voice heavy with sadness, "not *scince*, as you have spelled it. Anyone who misspells the word 'science' does not deserve to earn the highest grade in that course." I left Lal's office with my head bowed in shame. And I wondered why in Calcutta I couldn't have learned to spell *science* instead of *elephant*.

ᔕ

Despite my humiliating defeat, I did complete eighth grade on time and moved up to ninth grade. But the challenges of the higher grade were becoming too stiff for me, and my science teacher's rebuke continued to haunt me. I desperately needed help, but did not know whom to ask.

Providence—although in the form of adversity—rescued me from my academic angst, although in the process it nearly killed me. In 1943, the year before I was scheduled to enter my final year of high school, I was struck by a severe case of typhoid that lasted an unprecedented 128 days. I also suffered from a kidney infection and a skin rash. My days in Calcutta suffering from an ear infection were nowhere near as bad as my ordeal with these illnesses. No allopathic medicines available in India at that time could cure me. And because my sickness lasted for several months, my family—recalling the early death my horoscope had grimly predicted—feared that I would not survive.

As I convalesced, I had a lot of time to think. I used this time to mull over various personal matters since in truth I could do little else. One such matter concerned my Hindu religion. Having been born in the holy city of Banaras in a deeply religious Hindu family, I was destined to remain a devout Hindu. But a powerful experience I had had several months earlier inexorably changed the way I would choose to practice religion, and as I lay in bed, my body fighting the typhoid, I could not get the incident out of my feverish mind.

On the day in question, the local temple of Goddess Kali was having a special celebration. Due to a prior engagement, my mother and brothers could not go, but they felt that I should represent the family by attending by myself. In this temple, the idol of Kali was depicted as a black woman with four arms. In one hand she had a sword, in another the head of the demon she had slain, and the other two arms were raised to encourage her worshippers. Her eyes were red, her hair was all tangled, and her face and breasts were smeared with blood.

I found myself alarmed by the frightening image of the idol and could not understand how a goddess could look that scary. Unfortunately, no one had ever explained to me that a lot of powerful symbolism permeated the idol. For instance, I learned later that Kali's blackness symbolizes her all-embracing, comprehensive nature, because black is the color in which all other colors merge. Similarly, her disheveled hair forms a curtain of illusion. But even if someone had explained all this symbolism to me, I still wouldn't have grasped it at the time, and hence I would have remained terrified by that image. And the dastardly act of the devotees that soon followed destroyed what little respect I might have had for the goddess.

An integral part of that day's ritual was the sacrifice of a lamb to symbolize the devotees' recognition of Kali's prowess at destroying evil. I recall seeing the huge idol of Kali and a shivering lamb bleating for mercy as it stood in front of the idol. Grief-stricken, I prayed that the goddess would show her mercy on this poor creature by sparing its life.

The goddess did not oblige. Moments later, a devotee swung his mighty sword and chopped off the head of the lamb. Blood splattered all over the altar, as the devotees shouted with jubilation, "*Jai Ma Kali!*" ("Hail Mother Kali!"). I found this slaughter so shocking and the jubilation that followed so despicable that I froze and my mind went absolutely numb.

Many months later, as I lay in my bed recuperating from my dreadful illnesses, the horror of that day came back to me, and all the thoughts I had pushed aside at the time came flooding forward. Although I was only 12, at that moment I felt a powerful urge to reject all rituals and tokenism, including repeating unintelligible Sanskrit verses recited by priests as a way of practicing Hindu religion. Yet, I also wisely decided to keep these troubling thoughts to myself.

Fortunately, I did recover from my illnesses, although I just barely survived. By the time I fully recuperated, however, the school year was half over, which compelled me to withdraw for that year. This boon in disguise allowed me to get additional coaching, which made me far more confident and relaxed when I went back to school the next year.

Although skipping a school year allowed me to get help with my studies, it did not cure me of becoming bored with the rote memorization method used by my instructors at St. John's (the same method used by teachers in D.A.V. School and by Santosh in

Calcutta). I still remember an embarrassing encounter with a geography teacher named Avad Bihari Shukla. He had a reputation of spewing information about each country in great detail without explaining its relevance or presenting visuals of the people and places he covered. Nevertheless, the unpleasant experience sowed the seeds for a dream that, at the time, I would never have believed would someday become my future.

Shukla—a short, bald man in his mid-50s—had been teaching geography longer than anyone could remember. In fact, he had become something of an institution, commanding great respect and authority. On that fateful morning, he walked crisply into the classroom, wearing a sharp-looking three-piece suit (unusual for an Indian teacher but typical for him) and wielding his ever-present long wooden pointer. A large map of the world hung on the wall behind him and a small map of India was mounted next to the blackboard. Shukla looked at his students, paused for a moment, and then routinely announced, "Today, we are going to study America."

Then, without even pointing America out on the world map, he started speaking in a monotone: "America was discovered by Christopher Columbus in 1492. It is the third largest country in the world. America has 3.7 million square miles and lies between 38 degrees North and 97 degrees West. America is even richer than England. The famous cities are New York, Los Angeles, Chicago, and Miami." On and on he droned.

His lecture contained endless statistics, dates, and cities, totally devoid of any life. My attention wavered as millions of questions started circling in my mind:

> Why does one have to discover the richest country in the world that everybody already knows about? If only rich people live in America, what have they done with their poor people? Is the capital of Washington more beautiful than Banpur? Do rich Americans like Indian food? Are there tongas in America? Is there some way I could visit America and see for myself if Americans look different from the British people?

"Mittra!" Shukla suddenly yelled, shattering my daydream. Pointing his stick at me, he demanded, "Tell me who discovered America and the year it was discovered!" Clearly, he'd caught me not paying attention.

I drew a blank. Hearing no response, Shukla spoke angrily. "In case you have forgotten, in just a few months you are going to sit for the final exam. If you can't even remember these simple facts, how can you expect to pass?" And then, without forewarning, he dropped the bombshell: "I want you to get out of my class and stay out until you are serious about paying attention to my lectures."

Hanging my head, I left the class, humiliated once again, and in tears as my classmates watched me disappear in shame. I did return to the class the next day, but to no one's surprise, my final grade in geography turned out to be below average.

My loss of a year of schooling had one other consequence—this one undesirable. Ever since I lost my father at the age of seven because doctors couldn't save him, I had dreamt of becoming a medical professional, saving people's lives and treating the sick the way Sailo and other doctors cared for me during my long illness. After I fully recovered, I informed my family that after I graduated from high school, I wanted to enroll in a pre-med curriculum in college. But citing my near-fatal illness and my resultant weakness, my mother and Sailo in concert declined my request. My dream of becoming a medical doctor, following beloved Sailo's footsteps, was dashed.

In 1945, at the age of 15, I graduated from high school and was placed in the second division, a distinct sign of mediocre performance, given the superior grades of my two younger brothers, Raj and Braj. Even so, I felt that for me, my placement was not too bad. Unfortunately, no one else agreed.

Perhaps the greatest contributor to the serious inferiority complex I labored under was Raj's spectacular academic achievements. Raj, who was two years younger but only one year behind me in school, was consistently placed at or close to the head of his class. He graduated from high school with distinction in all the courses offered (equivalent to *Summa Cum Laude*). He was placed in the top fifth percentile of all the high school graduates in the entire state of Uttar Pradesh, India's most populous state, an achievement all of us were extremely proud of.

One of the more dramatic demonstrations of my feeling academically inferior to Raj came when I was in the ninth grade and Raj received a story book from Mother as a birthday gift. He suggested we read the book together, sitting side by side, and I agreed. Whoever finished reading the page last was to turn to the next page. The activity was supposed to be fun, but it soon turned into a huge embarrassment for me when it became clear that by the time Raj finished reading the two open pages, I had not even finished reading half of the first page. I began to fake it by carefully turning over the page whenever I sensed that Raj was finished reading. The experience made me jealous of Raj. That envy made me feel even stupider.

Thus, I graduated from high school thoroughly convinced that I was a poor student with a perpetual learning disability. And despite my many scholastic achievements later in life, I would never even come close to Raj's success as a highly acclaimed, internationally recognized research scientist. Fortunately, my feelings of jealousy eventually faded, and they certainly did not spoil the affection we had for each other as adults.

Once I concluded that I was definitely academically inferior, I began becoming restless. An instinct inside of me kept pushing me to achieve something different to prove to everyone that I was not a complete dunce. Money was a problem, especially since the country's involvement in World War II imposed serious financial hardships on our family. So after much thought, I invented a way to achieve something educational and rewarding that would not cost any money and would impress people at the same time.

In 1943, I joined the Boy Scouts and remained active in that until I graduated from high school two years later. I passed various tests. I received a number of badges, became a King Scout, and was eventually promoted to the rank of patrol leader. But I made one potentially disastrous decision that almost erased all my achievements.

Shortly after I earned my King Scout badge, I discovered that my friend Ramesh Trivedi was struggling to pass the test for a proficiency badge that he desperately wanted. In this test, as part of survival skills, he had to demonstrate the ability to cook out in the field without assistance. Unfortunately, he failed the cooking test a couple of times and was getting disheartened. Since I had already learned how to cook as a prerequisite for earning my King Scout badge, I offered to help him pass by cooking the meals for him, even though I knew such assistance was strictly against the rules.

So with my help, Ramesh received his proficiency badge, but our scoutmaster, who was a conservative Muslim and a strict disciplinarian, suspected foul play. He first obtained Ramesh's confession and then pinned me down. I had little choice but to admit my guilt. That's even though I knew the scoutmaster had the power to strip me off my badges and expel me from the scouting program.

After reflecting for a day, he let me go without punishment, but only after pointing out my character weakness in helping Ramesh cheat. The scoutmaster took away Ramesh's badge and gave him a strong warning, but since the boy admitted his guilt, he gave him another opportunity to pass his cooking test. Ramesh finally learned how to cook, passed the test, and earned his badge. Ultimately he, too, became a King Scout.

With the exception of the Ramesh incident, I was proud of my achievements as a Boy Scout, but I still wanted to demonstrate that I possessed talents that others did not. So I decided next to turn my attention to Indian music.

Ever since I was a little boy, I wanted to be a singer. But my family never had the money for basic musical training. Fortunately, I found an old, unused harmonium—an Indian keyboard with manual bellows—sitting around the house, and I began tinkering with it until I had taught myself how to play. I learned to sing songs by playing the harmonium as an accompaniment.

One day, for a small fee, a man offered to teach me how to play tabla (Indian drums similar to bongos). I was excited about the offer, but I had no way of paying for the lessons. A friend suggested that if I taught his sister Naina Jain how to play the harmonium, he would pay me ₹30 per month, which would pay for my drum lessons. That sounded like a good idea, but I still faced a major hurdle.

In those days, in India—and to a certain extent even today in small cities and villages—boys and girls were not allowed to socialize with one another, either alone or in a group, before marriage. And even though in this case Naina's parents would be present when I taught her, I knew my own family would still object strongly to such an arrangement, especially since Naina was in her mid-teens and came from a highly conservative family.

I felt I should reject the notion that girls should be prohibited from taking music lessons from boys, so I accepted my friend's offer and obtained my family's permission by informing them only that I was going to offer harmonium lessons to *a student* and use my tuition money to pay for drum lessons. Fortunately, Naina turned out to be an excellent student, which made me feel vindicated.

But deep down, I still wanted to become an accomplished vocalist more than I did to be a drum player. So after a frantic search, I found a classical vocal music teacher named Vishwa Nath who agreed to teach me. He was an odd-looking man, with a serious face, a bulging belly, and a completely bald head. Still, I felt he was godsend since he was willing to charge me only ₹10 per lesson, provided I took my lessons with another student.

When I arrived for my first lesson, I was surprised to discover that my fellow student was a blind boy named Atul Prasad who was in his mid-teens. Atul came from an extremely poor family, and he could not afford to buy even the basic *tanpura*, a string instrument with a gourd base that generates a drone sound when the strings are plucked (an integral part of any vocal classical Indian music). He had a physical deformity that caused him to constantly twist his face, making it very uncomfortable to look at him.

What bothered me most, however, was Atul's blindness. In those days, in India everyone—and that certainly included me—was highly prejudiced against blind people, believing that they were destined to be street beggars. Agra had no schools for the blind, who had no opportunity to participate in other social or physical activities. That's why all Atul could do to improve his chances of success was to learn music from a teacher who agreed to charge very little money to help him out.

After the lessons started, I noticed how quickly Atul was learning. Fortunately, for both of us, I began to relax and our friendship grew steadily. Like Atul, I put my heart and soul into learning classical vocal music and practiced as often as time permitted, and I enjoyed my music sessions immensely. As diligent a student as I was, however, Atul could devote many more hours to practicing, and he became a far superior student singer. I fell farther and farther behind, and became progressively more jealous. Eventually, I began to resent him. I could tell that my teacher sensed this, although he didn't confront me.

My problem came to a head one day when I went for my music lesson and Nath told me that Atul was very sick and could not make it to class. At the end of my lesson, he gave me some money and asked me to buy a thermometer and deliver it to Atul's home. He explained that Atul's parents did not have the money to buy the thermometer, but that it was important for them to check his temperature often to see if he needed medical attention. I did buy the thermometer as Nath requested, but my jealousy got the better of me and I did not deliver it.

The next day my teacher went to Atul's home to find out how he was doing. To his dismay, he learned that I had not delivered the thermometer, and he immediately sent for me. When I arrived, I found him raging.

"Did you buy the thermometer for which I gave you the money yesterday?" he demanded to know.

"Yes," came my meek reply.

"You didn't deliver the thermometer to Atul's family because you hate him, don't you?"

Not knowing what to say, I remained silent.

"I have known about your negative feelings for Atul for some time, but I never thought that you'd stoop so low. You should be ashamed of yourself!" he raged.

And with that, Nath demanded the thermometer and expelled me from his music class *for good*. I begged him for forgiveness, but he insisted his decision was final. I sorely regretted my actions, but it was too late. Looking back now, I do hope with all my heart that Atul not only survived but also went on to lead a productive life with music; I know he had more potential to become a successful vocal singer than I.

When I lost the privilege of learning vocal classical music, I was heartbroken. Although I was afraid that my drum teacher might have felt slighted when I refused his generous offer, I decided to revisit him and was delighted to learn that he was still willing to take me on. With that, I took the first step toward starting my professional training in tabla. Partly because of my failure with vocal music lessons, I redoubled my energies to learn Indian drums and was awarded a diploma in tabla by the venerable Gwalior University in record time.

By both being made patrol leader in Boy Scouts and receiving my diploma in tabla, I demonstrated—to myself at least—that my mediocre scholastic performance did not mean I could not achieve modest successes in other areas in my life (my self-sabotage aside). I further proved to myself that I was not a perpetual slow learner, as most people thought—a monumental relief for me. The nickname *dunce* was beginning to disappear from my psyche.

Epilogue: Life's Lessons

In Agra, my family fights poverty and the disruption caused by the ravaging World War II. While living with my mother and brothers again, my inferiority complex blossoms when I am declared *the dunce* of the family. Occasionally, I rebel by acting up, yet I always manage to avoid getting into serious trouble.

At the Ringling Brothers Circus, I am moved by a woman who has lost both hands during the war and brings the house down by claiming that every morning she thanks god for saving her two legs (which she has learned to use as perfect substitutes for hands).

Because of my lack of a formal education, I am shunted from one school to another. My weak educational background and various ailments force me to drop out of school for a year before eventually graduating from high school as an average student. I also earn a diploma in tabla and become a King Scout—thereby proving to myself that I am not a dunce after all. But I remain a rebel. Defying the strict rules, I help my fellow scout cheat to earn a badge, and am eventually caught and reprimanded.

The following Four Ps' list identifies the P(s) covered in this chapter:

[X] Persevere with passion.
[X] Pursue professional, family-oriented, social, and spiritual goals.
[X] Persuade family and friends to help.
[   ] Promote a culture of giving back.

5

GAINING INDEPENDENCE:
INDIA'S AND MINE

Freedom is not worth having if it does not include the freedom to make mistakes.
—MAHATMA GANDHI

Since Mother and Sailo had quashed my pre-med program dreams, I grudgingly declared business administration as my major when I began my studies at St. John's College in Agra. By this time, World War II had finally ended. The economic, social, and political situations in India had just started to improve, albeit at a snail's pace. Big changes were coming for India, as well as for me personally. We were both beginning to take our fledgling steps, simultaneously bold and awkward, toward our independence and our ultimate destinies.

Those two paths intersected in 1945, when I was only 15. With the war's end that year, the British held a national election where the incumbent Winston Churchill famously vowed to oppose any suggestion for breaking-up of the British Empire, and the Labour Party candidate Clement Atlee promised to free India. The result was startling. In one of the most famous landslide elections in British history, Churchill was soundly defeated and the British people gave Labour, pledged to freeing India, a tremendous victory. Following his victory, Atlee appointed Mountbatten, as the last viceroy, to make the arrangements to end British rule on the sub-continent. The Viceroy kept his promise to free India within two years. By 1947, the partition was completed, although the subcontinent was left with two new countries, India and Pakistan, and tens of thousands died in the process, due to tragic communal wars.

Prior to his defeat, Churchill had attempted to stamp out the freedom movement in India and vowed to punish those who resorted to violent means. To that end, the British established special prisons where political agitators would be imprisoned and *lashed*. But to soften negative publicity at home and around the world, they also hired Indian medical practitioners who would attend to the wounds inflicted on the punished Indian prisoners.

One of these freedom-fighter prisons was set up in Agra, where I lived. My cousin Basant Basu was appointed as the prison's medical director. Years earlier, Basant had contracted small pox. It scarred his face and left him feeling conscious. In a manner of speaking, we were like twins—his scars external, mine internal—and so we shared an unspoken bond.

After working at the prison for some time, Basant told me about his experiences with the prisoners, who had been arrested for throwing stones at British soldiers during riots or for urging others to resort to anti-government violence. Their ultimate goal was to fill the British prisons with freedom fighters so that the world would take notice of India's freedom movement and their plight.

These riots were of course in clear defiance of the nonviolence policy that Gandhi preached. That confused me. I did not realize that the Gandhian-style nonviolent rebellion in the form of national civil disobedience against the British Empire required a lot more self-control and discipline than most Indians possessed.

During one of his visits to our home, Basant was overcome with emotions as he described the plight of these young freedom fighters, who passionately wanted their country to be free. Even the Indian jail workers, who meted out harsh punishments by lashing the prisoners, hated to do their job because they, too, were Indians. They never wanted to hurt their own countrymen. In a similar fashion, Basant found it painful to see such wounds inflicted on these young men who were standing up for freedom. I, too, was critical of the British for ordering these lashings, although I also felt that they had the right to curb violence.

One day, when Basant was at a low point, I pleaded with him to let me into the prison so that I could see for myself who these prisoners were and talk to them about why they were inviting punishment. At first, he was unwilling to take the chance. However, since the guards in this prison were not as strict as they might have been in a normal prison (presumably because the prisoners were not typical criminals, in fact patriots, and had little interest in escaping), he agreed.

Even though I was 16, I knew that if my family found out about the plan, they would certainly prevent me from unlawfully entering a prison camp. So on the appointed day, I slipped out of the house unnoticed and met Basant at a prearranged place. He took me to the prison as his personal guest. The guards greeted him with, "*Salam dagdar saheb*" (Greetings, doctor) and let us in. I was extremely nervous. I had never been inside a prison and did not know what my punishment might be if authorities found me out.

From Basant's modest office, I could see an outdoor area surrounded by barbed wire where two dozen shabbily dressed young men, from about ages 15–30, were milling around. Despite being in prison and forced to stand under the scorching sun, they looked surprisingly relaxed and happy, sharing stories and laughing hysterically. They did not appear to be wounded or hurt, and I could not tell by looking at them how long they had been imprisoned.

Basant picked up his stethoscope and suggested that I remain in his office until he returned from attending to his patients. He had to go to another part of the prison, he explained, and he would be gone for an hour. Although he never specifically asked me not to venture beyond that room, I am sure he expected me not to take that chance.

After Basant left, I got up and went to the window to watch the prisoners. I had mixed feelings about the way they acted. I wanted to congratulate them for having the courage to stand up to the powerful British Empire, but I did not appreciate their decision to resort to violence in doing so.

Standing there, I recalled a book I had read in my history class that described a similar situation. The book, *Khudiramer Fansi* [Khudiram's Death by Hanging], immortalized a teenager named Khudiram Bose who in 1908 sacrificed his life for gaining freedom from the British people. Like Bose, these boys were young, spirited, and willing to take lashings for their struggle to gain freedom from the British. Nothing seemed to have changed in India in half a century. Even though I was generally opposed to violence, I admired their bravery while recognizing that I myself did not have the courage to engage in such extremes. I soon could not stand the thought of coming this far and failing to ask the prisoners inside the fence why they had made such choices, and how long were they willing to keep it up. I wanted to know what true bravery was really like.

After hesitating for a little while, I left Basant's office and walked over to the fence. The young prisoners glanced at me strangely, not knowing who I was or why I was there. I decided to direct my question to the prisoner closest to me, a wiry youth who appeared to be in his late teens.

"Aren't you afraid of the lashings, and will you do the same thing again when you are set free?" I blurted out in Hindi without any sort of introduction. The young man exploded, suddenly jumping at me like a wounded lion and pressing his face against the fence.

"I believe in freedom and I am not afraid of the lashing!" he shouted very deliberately. "And I will keep doing it until we are free. *Mera Bharat Mahan!* [My India is great!]"

Before I had a chance to digest all of that, an older boy standing next to him with a meaner, more menacing expression joined in, shouting, "I also will do the same thing again. And if you have the guts and love our country like we all do, you should do what we are doing, too."

Quaking at his rebuke, I rushed back into Basant's office, slumped into a chair, closed my eyes, and almost passed out in fright and embarrassment. I felt guilty because I had violated my cousin's trust by venturing out of his office. But more importantly, I wished that I had the courage to stand with those young boys inside that fence, yet I knew I did not. I had been punished many times in the past and had certainly endured unjust pain. But I had never invited punishment willingly. If I were to join this freedom fight, I would have to find the courage to deliberately commit an act that would result in me being lashed by prison guards. A cowardly rebel, I could not bring myself even to contemplate such an action. I had been spanked enough.

I sat there wallowing in self-pity until Basant returned. He appeared drained by his rounds and did not ask me if I had left his office. I was grateful for that because if he had, I would've had to lie. I did not want to talk about my conversation with the prisoners, and certainly not about their challenging me to join their civil disobedience. Quite clearly, I was a coward—but working ever so slowly toward a lion's heart, if only in my dreams.

I chose other ways to affect change, beginning to more sharply define for myself how I wanted to look at the world around me and in what ways I wished to leave my mark on it. One such way was volunteering at the Mark Memorial Institute, established by the college to give students a chance to serve the needs of the nearby village residents (particularly helping with hygiene, yogic exercises, and child education). Of the available options, I was interested only in child education, but I had no idea what I was up against when I signed on to teach the children of a local village.

On the first day, I found myself surrounded by vast wheat fields, a group of peasants, and little boys who were waiting for help. Contrary to what I had expected to find, the village had no classroom, no tables, no chairs, no books, and no blackboard. In fact, I could find nothing that might even be used to improvise a classroom.

I soon learned that the villagers had no school because they considered teaching children wasteful. After all, such a regimen took them away from working in the field. Moreover, the little girls of the village stood at a distance, since prevailing social customs prohibited them from participating in any programs in which boys were present. Nevertheless, I was impressed with the warmth of these simple-minded, friendly people. As a gesture of goodwill, they offered me samosas and Fresca drinks.

Despite my initial success in meeting these villagers, I returned home somewhat depressed about the uphill battle I was facing—particularly about the girls not being able to attend my classes. Ultimately, I had to accept that girls were out, and I had to create the educational facilities myself if there were to be any at all. In time, I set up an open-air classroom, and I even improvised a number of creative educational games that made learning fun for the boys. While it upset me that my pleas to teach the village girls forever fell on deaf ears, I was delighted to note that no one ever complained that my services took the boys away from doing *useful* work.

I had plenty of chances during these years to do what seemed right to me, regardless of how impractical or dangerous it appeared to others. An example was my eagerness to fulfill the wish of a high school friend named Hari Prasad who had been infected with tuberculosis (TB). When I learned from a teacher that Hari, seriously ill and confined to bed, was feeling terribly lonely, I felt obliged to visit him—even though I knew he had a contagious and deadly disease.

Such a visit would not be an easy thing to plan. Hari lived in a village that was far away and not accessible by commercial transportation. It would take a very long bicycle ride to get there. And I knew that Sailo would never approve of my visiting a TB patient anyway. So, after some intense soul-searching, I decided the right thing would be to visit my friend without telling anyone in my family.

I lied to my family, telling them that I was going to a friend's home to study and that I planned to spend the night with him. Since neither house had a phone, I knew that my family had no practical way of checking on me. I took off on my bicycle around

8 am, reaching Hari in his remote village around 3 pm. As soon as I saw him, I knew it was worth the long ride.

"How good of you to come!" Hari said in a warm greeting, coughing all the while. We spent several hours talking about the good times we'd shared and the fun we'd had in school growing up. I reminded him of the time that he and I had compared cartoons we'd drawn of one of our mean-looking teachers. We laughed but agreed that wasn't nice. Then he reminded me about the time we'd challenged each other to see who could win the most Boy Scout badges in a year.

At one point during our reminiscing, Hari started coughing uncontrollably and spit out blood in a spittoon. That scared the daylights out of me. Silently, I blamed his parents for allowing me to come there and expose myself to such a deadly disease. But I kept my mouth shut and didn't let anyone know about my fears.

After we finished an early dinner, Hari's family pleaded with me to spend the night, but I graciously declined, saying I had to get back to finish the next day's schoolwork. So after our long visit, I rode off at 8 pm, arriving back in Agra around 3 am. I waited in a park for several hours before I felt I could safely return home without suspicion. I did feel considerable guilt lying to my family, and also to Hari. I worried about exposing myself to TB. But I also believed that I had done the right thing, fulfilling the wishes of a terminally ill friend. Hari died a few months later. When I heard the news, I felt relieved, justified, and even triumphant.

During my sophomore year of college, the negative feeling I had developed a few years earlier at the Kali temple about traditional Hindu rituals came to a head in a way that I could not have predicted. This gave me an opportunity to redefine what being Hindu meant to me, separate from what I'd always been taught by my family and my culture about my role as a Hindu.

Durga Puja—an annual five-day festival honoring the Goddess Durga—was celebrated in the eastern state of Bengal with the same fervor and enthusiasm as Christmas was in the Western world. Durga, a form of supreme goddess, was depicted as a woman standing on her lion mount and wielding 10 different weapons, one in each of her 10 hands. She is the embodiment of the feminine and creative energy (known as *Shakti*). Naturally, people like myself from Bengal who later moved to other parts of India formed their own groups to celebrate what was for them the biggest festival of the year.

After the shocking incident at the temple of Kali several years previously, I had toyed with the idea of rejecting all religious rituals. But after considering the strong religious beliefs of my family, and still being unsure whether I should make such a unilateral pronouncement, I had decided to continue participating in all of our religious festivals. So every year in the fall, respecting Hindu tradition, I attended the Durga festival along with everyone else. And this year started out just like all the rest.

On a beautiful October morning in 1945, I went to the festival hall in Agra with my family to join in the celebration. People were milling about having a grand time. Unlike the frightening idol of Kali, the beautiful idol of Durga sitting with her children (Lakshmi, Saraswati, Kartik, and Ganesh) mesmerized me. Devotees had surrounded the idol with gorgeous flowers and other essential ingredients needed for performing various rituals. It was an impressive view of the goddess. And yet I had an eerie feeling about her, as if there was a disconnect between the goddess and me.

The priest stood facing the crowd, the idol of Durga behind him, as he lit the traditional incense. Holding a religious text, he then started narrating the prayer verses in Sanskrit. The devotees, clutching flowers, pressed their hands against their breasts, closed their eyes, bowed their heads in reverence, and began repeating the verses after him.

I, too, stood with the crowd and acted as though I was reciting the verses. But after a few minutes, something completely unexpected happened. I suddenly felt an electrical shock running through my whole body—strong enough to make me feel dizzy. It was in that state of mind that I felt Goddess Durga was scolding me for faking my prayers, challenging me to be honest, and directing me to practice what I truly believed in.

After the prayer ritual was complete, everyone dispersed and started socializing again. Still feeling dizzy and confused, I walked away from the crowd and stood alone in a corner, reflecting on my experience. I soon started feeling very weak and after struggling for several minutes to remain standing, I actually fainted. When I regained consciousness a few moments later, I was lying on the floor and the people around me were trying to decide what to do with me. When I finally grasped what had happened, I stood up, paused for a moment, and looked around to see if I could spot any of my family. Seeing none, I slowly walked away from the scene.

Back home, when I told my family what had happened, they attributed my physical weakness to the lingering effects of the long illness I'd suffered in high school. But deep down, I knew that the incident was the goddess's way of empowering me to renounce the *traditional* Hindu religious rituals and practice my religion in a way that was honest and truthful for me.

Even after this incident, it wasn't easy for me to define my own brand of the Hindu religion. I found it difficult to end the familiar beliefs and rituals of my childhood. I couldn't explain to anyone that running from organized religion by no means meant I was running away from a higher power. As a teenager, I could not explain that I was not struggling to invent a new religion, but a new religious identity.

In the end, I convinced myself that the philosophies my mother had taught me—of honesty, truthfulness, and caring for and helping others—constituted the foundation of *my brand* of religion. Over the years, I came to believe that true religion is unencumbered, totally intuitive, and ultimately a personal affair. Equally important, I never lost my reverence for the harmony and beauty of what I believed was the creation of a higher power.

I would like to conclude by saying that I am *not a religious person* by any stretch of the word. I do, however, believe that I am superbly spiritual. And if I had to label my religious beliefs, I would say that to *make a difference, or MAD*, is my religion. I have experienced and witnessed numerous shades of helping hands throughout my life. Many have affected me so deeply that they have truly helped shape who I am.

As the struggle for India's independence was intensifying, widespread communal riots between Hindus and Muslims were undermining that quest for independence. The Muslim community, fearing reprisal by Hindus in an independent India, was fiercely fighting to carve out an independent Muslim country. This fed communal hatred of mega proportions between the two groups.

I found such fears of reprisal ludicrous, based on my own experiences and those of my friends and relatives. While I could do nothing to stop the movement toward the creation of two separate countries, I vowed to do everything in my power to continue maintaining a close relationship with my many Muslim friends. I encouraged all my Hindu friends and acquaintances to do the same.

One of my dearest Muslim friends was a man named Amman Rashid whom I had known since the eighth grade at St. John's High School. Not only did we go to school together back then, but later, we were also both Boy Scouts and had helped each other earn merit badges. I also knew Amman's family. They lived about a mile away from my home in a predominantly Muslim neighborhood. I celebrated the Muslim holy festival marking the end of Ramadan (the month of fasting) with them, and they, in turn, celebrated the Hindu festival of Diwali (the festival of lights) with my family. Over time, Amman and I had become close.

One August morning, in 1946, one year before India was partitioned and Pakistan was born, I was presented with the most death-defying opportunity I've ever had to act on my beliefs. I was home studying for my next class, which did not start until 11 am. All of my brothers were out—at school or in their own college classes—and Mother was in the kitchen with the door closed, cooking for the day.

I heard an impatient knock at the door and opened it to find Amman standing there, looking awfully frightened and panting for breath.

"Mittrabhai [brother Mittra], please save me," he blurted out immediately. "They are coming to kill me." I looked past him, but saw no one.

"What are you talking about Amman?" I asked excitedly. "Who's trying to kill you?"

Amman pushed me aside, jumped past me, and slammed the door behind him. He scooted to the window to make sure the street was empty. He took a deep breath and ducked behind the couch.

"This morning," he whispered, "when I went to the vegetable market, I overheard someone hinting that the RSS (Rashtriya Swayamsevak Sangh) was coming to our neighborhood with their knives and sickles to 'take care of us'. I ran home, but found our door locked and no one there. I could not think of anyone else but you, so I came running. Please don't let these RSS hoodlums kill me."

Amman's mere mention of the RSS sent chills down my spine. In 1942 when the political uprising in India against the British, known as Quit India Movement, was intensifying, this group was at the forefront of that movement. Its political philosophy was to preserve the spiritual and moral traditions of Hindus by resorting to violence, whenever necessary. I had been invited to join the group, but I categorically rejected it because I could not accept its claim of Hindu superiority—never mind that violence should be used to attain it.

I panicked at Amman's story, understanding that he was indeed in grave danger, and knew I must do whatever I could to protect my friend. An idea flashed through my mind. A narrow passageway separated our house from the house next door. No one even remembered that it was there. The door to this passageway was always locked because it was not a usable travel space. There was, however, an exit door from the passageway to the street. I was certain that without my mother knowing, I could open the door, let Amman walk into the narrow space and lock the door behind him. Then when I felt it was safe, I could open the door again and signal for him to escape through the door to the street. That way he would not have to go through our house again, and Mother would not try to stop me if she opposed my plan.

Explaining my idea, I quickly led Amman to the passageway and locked the door behind him. I then waited on pins and needles, having no idea what would happen next or how long Amman would need to stay hidden. About half an hour later which seemed like an eternity, another knock on the front door came, this time a loud rapping. When I opened the door, I found a group of strangers carrying knives and sickles glowering at me.

"Yes, what do you want?" I asked nervously, more than a little frightened.

"Did anyone come to see you this morning?" demanded a boy in his late teens, his expression positively ferocious.

"No, no one has come here," I answered, trying hard to hide my anxiety.

"Are you telling the truth?" he shot back menacingly, tightening the grip he had on his weapon. Before I could answer, another young boy spoke up, using a somewhat softer tone.

"Look," the other boy said, turning to the group, "these people rent the house from the well-respected Bagchi family. Bagchis are Brahmins and they would never rent the house to a Muslim-lover." To my great surprise, without further discussion the group took off, still clutching their deadly weapons.

Waiting a little longer to be sure it was safe, I unlocked the passage door and signaled to Amman that he could leave. Mother, busy all this time behind closed doors in the kitchen, had no idea what had just transpired. She had merely heard me talking to someone and when she asked me about it, I told her that Amman had come by to borrow a book that he needed to study for an exam. She returned to her chores without giving it a second thought.

A few weeks later, I discovered that Amman and his family had vacated their residence and left town. I was saddened because we hadn't been able to say goodbye. I wondered what had happened to him. Sometime after India was partitioned and Pakistan had been born a year later, I received a letter from Amman. He explained that since they felt threatened by Hindu extremists, his family swiftly sold everything in Agra and moved to Karachi, a city that eventually became the capital of the newly formed Pakistan. He thanked me for saving his life and invited me, his friend *Mittrabhai*, to visit him in Karachi.

Epilogue: Life's Message

I enter college as a business major and find academia dull, drab, and colorless. I manage to earn my undergraduate degree in four years, but my performance is lackluster. While a student, I am caught up with a number of incidents involving the movement for Indian independence. I save the life of a Muslim friend chased by hoodlums on the eve of the birth of Pakistan. I also learn the true value of freedom the hard way when I visit a prison where freedom fighters are jailed. These prisoners tell me that they will continue to fight for freedom even when they know they will receive a lashing for their illegal activities, and they challenge me to join their movement. I recognize I am a coward rebel and can never bring myself to be lashed because of committing violent acts. During this phase of my life, I experience a massive transformation. An odd experience where I faint at a religious festival prompts me to renounce all the traditional Hindu rituals and embrace practicing my religion based on faith and not on mechanical religious rites.

The following Four Ps' list identifies the P(s) that I have covered in this chapter:

[X] Persevere with passion.
[X] Pursue professional, family-oriented, social, and spiritual goals.
[X] Persuade family and friends to help.
[   ] Promote a culture of giving back.

6

MY WORLDVIEW WIDENS

When one door of happiness closes, another opens, but often we look so long at the closed door that we do not see the one which has been opened for us.
—HELEN KELLER

In the afternoon of my 19th birthday, I was sitting in our living room, looking out the window, and trying to distract myself from the heat. The temperature topped 120F degrees by noon and was expected to crawl toward the 125F degree mark before the end of the day. The wind was picking up, creating a heat storm, known in northern India as *loo*—a scorching, dry, summer afternoon wind blowing from the west. This was a serious health hazard for anyone foolish enough to be caught in it. Our street was deserted.

Everyone in my family, who was home, was upstairs taking an afternoon nap. Normally on a day like this, I, too, would be taking a long nap to escape from the heat and boredom. But on this day I could not sleep. I sat at the window, fretting about my future. It was May 1949, and just the month after I had received my under-graduate degree from St. John's College. I knew that with only a bachelor's degree from a school that was average at best—and being placed in the second division besides—I would have to settle for a clerical job with little chance of advancement.

Sailo (supported by his wife, whom he had married three years previously) made great sacrifices to take care of me and see that I obtained an education since my return from Calcutta. So I felt I had no right to ask my family for further financial support for graduate school. Yet the more I envisioned my life as a faceless, nameless, dead-end clerk, the more I despaired. I saw no hope for escaping a perpetually humdrum existence. That morbid thought made me feel trapped and, thanks to the loo, unable to breathe in the stifling heat.

I still felt inferior to my two younger brothers. Why was it that only I turned out to be so incompetent? Why could I not be smart as Raj and Braj were, who had graduated from high school with high honors? They continued their high levels of achievement in college, and would no doubt eventually earn doctoral degrees.

I cannot recall how long I remained in that state, staring out of the window, motionless, with tears rolling down my cheeks. The loo now in full force outside matched the intensity of the storm raging within me. As my thoughts tumbled around inside my head, I slowly began to realize that, in addition to the familiar inner voice of my depressed and defeated self, a more sound and upbeat second inner voice with a totally new and different point of view was vying for my attention. This voice was so different from the tone of my usual thoughts that at first I dismissed it. But the relentless duel between the two voices continued to haunt me.

"Why are you so hung up on failure?" asked this new voice. "Why don't you try to change your destiny and become successful?"

"And just how would I achieve that, since I am trapped in this situation?" quipped my other, more familiar side.

"You are trapped by nothing more than a poor attitude, the first side insisted. Find a way to break out of it."

"Raj and Braj can do that, but not me. I'm not smart enough. Everyone says so—and I believe them because they couldn't all be wrong."

"Thinking only the worst of yourself will eventually destroy you. If you wish to succeed, you must believe in yourself and look at everything positively."

"But how can I look at my life positively when I haven't accomplished very much of anything?"

"Are you so sure that's true?"

I paused for just a second, and the memory of living with Leela and Santosh surfaced. "At least I managed to survive that abusive ordeal," I mused. Then thoughts about learning to play the harmonium, and using that skill to earn money to pay for tabla lessons floated into my consciousness. Earning a diploma in tabla from Gwalior University was something no other member of my family had managed to accomplish so far. "True, but so what?" I thought, snapping back into my gloomy mood. "That isn't going to change my future."

"These achievements demonstrate something very powerful," retorted the new side. "Starting with nothing but determination, you managed to beat the odds to overcome many obstacles and realize your goals." Without giving me time to reflect on this, the voice continued making its case for why my depression was without foundation. "And what about helping other people? You helped your friend earn his Boy Scout badge, even though you broke the rules to do it. And you took enormous risks and went to a lot of trouble to visit a dying friend. Surely these are not the actions of a loser."

"Yes, but by breaking the rules, I ended up getting us both in trouble," my more familiar side countered. "And I lied to my family about where I was when I went to visit Hari. Shouldn't I be condemned for that?" Memories of other times I deceived my family came to mind as well, including visiting the prison with my cousin Basant (not to mention actually talking with the prisoners without him knowing) and hiding Amman from the RSS while making sure my mother remained clueless to this potential danger.

"Breaking the rules and lying *aren't* ideal, of course, but you showed great compassion and a determination to help people you care about. That counts for a lot. You need to discover the good qualities within yourself. If you continue to believe people who are critical of you, then you will live up to their negative view of you, and failure will be assured. If you want to succeed, you must believe in yourself and create your own future. It's not a lack of ability but your defeatist attitude that is at the heart of your problem. Instead of focusing on what you think you *can't* do, begin focusing on what you *can* do. Stop feeling sorry for yourself and get to work. Your whole future lies ahead of you."

Stunned, I sat in silence for quite a while. Finally, I drew a long breath and decided to go along with the message of the second, new voice. Going forward, I vowed to think positively, find suitable employment, work hard, and achieve professional success just as my father had. I attributed the dueling voices in my head to the horrendous heat that day, but no matter the cause, the experience had forever changed me. I somehow knew that I would never sink as low or feel as hopeless again.

Even before I could send out resumes seeking a suitable job in Agra, we got the good news: Sailo had been appointed as the superintendent of the prestigious Hallett Hospital (now known as Lala Lajpat Rai Hospital) in Kanpur, 177 miles away in northern India. This was a huge promotion for him. The job came with a large bungalow, detached servant quarters, a gardener, an automobile, a night watchman, a domestic servant, and a telephone system. The exalted position gave our family a new level of affluence.

This got me thinking again: "Should I ask my family to support my graduate education, since they were now in a financial position to do so?" I felt obliged to abandon that idea, however, when I heard that my brother Biru, now a mid-level officer with the Reserve Bank in Delhi, had already arranged a clerical job for me at the Kanpur branch. I soon received a firm offer for a position I felt duty bound to accept. Still, I simply could not resist the urge to get a master's degree, although I knew that a full-time job at the Reserve Bank would automatically ruin any chance of pursing a master's.

As a petty clerk at the bank, all I was asked to do was to count the soiled one-rupee paper notes and bundle them up in batches of 100. The job was demeaning. Making bundles of rupee notes required no brains. Performing such a menial task all day long only reduced my sense of personal self-worth. I will not deny that the thought of asking my family to pay for my graduate degree again crossed my mind. But before I could broach that subject, I committed an act that invited my family's wrath and with that, any hope of asking for educational assistance evaporated.

At 11:30 one night, while everyone else was asleep, I was sitting in the living room, engrossed in a mystery novel, trying to escape my misery. Suddenly, I heard a knock on the door and opened it to find a forlorn Chinese man standing there.

"Sir," he addressed me softly, "I got lost driving from Agra to Lucknow and now can't find a hotel anywhere. With me are my wife and two small children, and I am afraid for us to sleep in our car. Could you please let us stay with you for the night? We won't bother you, and I promise to leave first thing tomorrow morning."

As outlandish as his request sounded, I was so touched by the man's appearance and by the plight of his family that I invited them to come in. Clearly, I did not have the maturity to weigh the risks of such a decision. In those days in India, stories were rampant about strangers entering people's homes as lost tourists and then robbing them. Choosing to dismiss those stories, I quickly set about arranging a place in the living room for the family to settle in for the night.

True to his word, the man and his family made no trouble and left before dawn the next morning, without even saying goodbye. The man did, however, leave me a note that said simply, "God bless you." I was relieved.

Nevertheless, when Sailo heard about the incident later that morning, it did not sit well with him. He reprimanded me for my stupidity in endangering the entire family. I was properly humbled and realized the incident wiped out any hope of my asking for help financing my graduate studies. Clearly, I was not worth such an investment.

Not long after, I became embroiled in another controversial problem—one that seemed virtually impossible for a 20-year-old to solve. Too naïve to recognize my limitations, I became involved anyway. My 25-year-old cousin Jatin Sengupta, an officer at the Reserve Bank in Calcutta, perhaps the most eligible bachelor in his department, became smitten with his junior colleague Riva Chandra. He eventually wished to marry her, although they faced one seemingly insurmountable obstacle: Riva was a widow, who had returned to work when her husband suddenly died, leaving her to support their young daughter on her own.

In the 1950s in India, marrying a widow was unacceptable. Anyone daring to do so ran the risk of being ostracized. For that reason, Jatin was uncertain about proposing. But he also reasoned that becoming a widow was not Riva's fault, and society should not prevent her from remarrying. And that created a dilemma. On one hand, Jatin wanted to give Riva and her daughter a new life. On the other, he did not want to marry a widow with a child without the approval of his family, an approval he was quite sure he would not win; distraught because he could not find anyone to turn to for guidance, he confided in me.

At that time, I had neither the maturity nor the experience to become entangled in such a controversial matter. Still, I told Jatin that as long as he was able to accept Riva and her daughter happily, he had my support. I agreed that initially he would invite the wrath of his family, but I also expressed the hope that over time they would accept Riva. I saw no reason why Riva, as a widow with a daughter, should be classed as third rate, even below widowed women with no children, who at that time were considered second rate.

After months of wrestling with this question, and with my unconditional support, Jatin proposed to Riva, who readily accepted. They were married the following year with predictable consequences. The couple was ostracized not only by Jatin's family, but also by his friends, which hurt them deeply. Early on in their ordeal, I appeared to be the only person who supported their marriage.

Despite the obstacles, the union was a happy one. The couple had two children of their own, along with Riva's first daughter. All three children grew up in a loving and caring environment. After almost a decade, Jatin's family finally accepted Riva as one of their own. My support for the couple gave me heart. I began to see women and prejudices against them in a new way.

I soon received another opportunity to challenge cultural bias. In my department at the bank was a 30-year-old colleague named Prajapat, who was reserved and withdrawn. A loner, he even avoided going to the lunchroom where we all socialized. One day, I learned that Prajapat was a Dalit, thereby considered *untouchable*.

The Indian caste system is made up of four main castes: Brahmin (engaged in scriptural education and teaching, essential for the continuation of knowledge), Kshatriya (responsible for handling of public services, including administration, maintenance of law and order, and defense), Vaishya (engaged in commercial activity as businessmen), and Shudra (relegated as unskilled laborers). Because of their status as the lowest class in society, those in the last group came to be known by such names as Scheduled Castes, untouchables, and even Dalits (which included those in numerous sub-castes both in India and also throughout southern Asia). Over the course of many centuries, these people were condemned to perform only menial tasks, such as sweeping streets and cleaning homes; hence, they were known as untouchables and were forbidden even to stand close to upper-caste people. They were not allowed to enter Hindu temples, and in many parts of the country, the Dalit women were even forced to bare their breasts before upper-caste men as a reminder of their low station.

Prajapat grew up not far from Kanpur in the small, secluded village of Pathaoli, living with 12 family members in a single-room hut and sleeping on a mud floor. His father, an agricultural laborer, drank, smoked, and gambled. As a boy, Prajapat was restricted to certain designated parts of the village. Dalits lived in what was known as the Colony; they were not allowed into the Ur, where the upper castes lived. On rare occasions when Prajapat had to go to the Ur, he was required to get off his bicycle and keep his eyes on the ground.

Although Prajapat was born into abject poverty, his father managed to give him education by sending him to school in Kanpur. To continue his studies, he frequently had to go hungry and study by candlelight. Luckily, after India's independence, he received a government scholarship earmarked for members of his caste. He went to college and earned a B.A. in economics.

Then Prajapat got a real break. The Reserve Bank hired him under a government-instituted quota system. But getting a decent job did not automatically grant Prajapat social acceptance. Because of his lowest caste status, bank employees refused to shake hands with him and shunned him.

My experience with members of the lowest caste had been limited to seeing them from a distance, performing menial labor such as sweeping the street and similar lowly tasks. I did not even recognize that by not treating them as respectable human beings that I, too, was discriminating against them. But seeing how the bank employees were responding to this unfortunate man who was only trying to improve his position in life, I was moved by my feelings about injustice. I decided to make amends by becoming his friend. My efforts did not sit well, either with my fellow employees (who gave me dirty looks that were meant to shame me) or with Prajapat himself, who at first suspected that I had some ulterior motive and, therefore, did not trust me. But over time, we became friends, and he openly shared his thoughts with me.

I learned from him, for example, that it was not only the upper-caste people who felt they were superior to the members of the lowest caste. The Dalits themselves also believed that they were born inferior and were doomed to stay that way for life. I tried to dispel that notion for Prajapat, but he never fully agreed with me.

Prajapat also told me that his family taught him many things that seemed wrong to him. Yet despite his valiant efforts, he never succeeded in changing their views. Prajapat's family had drilled into him that it was sinful for him to touch a girl, for instance. This lesson was so deep-rooted in his psyche that he could not violate it even after he got married. But when he did give in after waiting for a month, he was so guilt-ridden that he offered his blood to God by cutting his finger and asking forgiveness for committing an unpardonable sin. Naturally, I told him that such a notion was absurd; after all, his parents had clearly given in as well. Relieved, he agreed with me, although I don't believe he made much headway in alleviating his guilt.

One day, a colleague casually mentioned that a local college had started offering early-morning classes to enable office-workers to earn a degree while working full time. After excitedly checking into this, I found that the information was indeed accurate. The Dayanand Anglo Vedic College (or D.A.V. College), affiliated with Agra University, offered a full range of morning courses leading to a Masters of Business Administration (MBA) degree. I paused for a moment when I recalled that several years ago I could not wait to get out of D.A.V. High School in Agra because of its perceived low quality. But now, for my graduate studies, I was anxious to get into the D.A.V. College. I knew this was the miracle I had sought. I could not let anything get in the way of making my dream come true. I applied at once and was accepted.

Examining all the obstacles I would have to overcome to put my plan into action, given my situation, I realized only a superman could make everything work. Geography was the first roadblock. The living quarters of Hallett Hospital, where I lived with my family, was far from the city limits, and both the Reserve Bank and the college were at opposite ends of the city. So my home, my place of work, and my school were at three points of an exceptionally large triangle. Since my only means of transportation was a bicycle and traffic was awful, even in the early morning hours, the commute would be difficult and time consuming even in good weather. It would be excruciating, if not downright impossible, in the bitter cold of the winter.

Timing was the next seemingly insurmountable problem. Morning classes started at 5. My residence was a 45-minute bike ride away. So I would wake up at 3:30 am, get dressed, pack my lunch, and head off to class on my bike at 4:15 am. In winter, the temperature dropped below freezing at night and sometimes even touched the 20-degree mark. But since the weather usually warmed up during the day, no one in our family had much cold-weather clothing. I learned how to tie a woolen scarf over my head and ride my bike with both hands tucked in my pockets. I never complained about my hardships. So the family remained oblivious to my weather-related problems and never offered to help.

Classes ended at 10 am, but my bank job started at 10:15 am. And since the bank was at least a 30-minute bike ride from the college, it was impossible for me to get to work on time. With the kindness and understanding of my superiors, I worked out an arrangement that allowed me to come to the office 15 minutes late as long as I agreed to stay 30 minutes longer at the end of the day. So while most employees left the office at 5 30 pm, my day ended at 6 pm.

This meant I would not reach home again until 6:45 pm. After a light snack, I would work on my school assignments until 9 pm. I would then have my dinner and retire for the day at 10 pm. I arose five and a half hours later to start the same routine all over again.

Despite the arduous commute, the tight schedule, and the considerable workload, my crazy plan somehow succeeded. Two years later, in the spring of 1951, I earned my MBA degree. And, for the first time in my academic career, I was placed in the *first division*. Now I had solid proof that I was no longer a dunce.

My family and friends congratulated me for having achieved something meaningful. But at that point, instead of basking in the glory, all I could dream of was a few things. I wanted to donate my textbooks to the university library, lock up my worn-out bicycle, and take a week's leave to do nothing but catch up on my sleep. And that's exactly what I did

Epilogue: Life's Lessons

After earning my undergraduate degree, I land a clerical job in a bank located in Kanpur. But I refuse to accept my fate as a nameless clerk and set on an incredible journey of bicycling between my home, my job, and the university with merely five and a half hours of sleep in between to squeeze in both a full-time job and enrollment in a master's program as a full-time student.

While working at the bank, I become embroiled in a controversial situation dealing with the marriage of a widow, strictly prohibited at that time by the Indian society. Despite my naïveté in such matters, I manage to rise above my own prejudices and openly support this marriage. The experience gives me heart, and I begin to see women and social biases against them in a new light. My horizons widen still further when I befriend a fellow bank employee belonging to the *untouchable* caste and attempt to make amends when I realize I am unknowingly discriminating against this caste. This chapter ends with my earning a master's degree and joining the elite group of students placed in the coveted *first division*.

The following Four Ps' list identifies the P(s) that I have covered in this chapter:

[X]   Persevere with passion.
[X]   Pursue professional, family-oriented, social, and spiritual goals.
[X]   Persuade family and friends to help.
[   ]   Promote a culture of giving back.

7

FUMBLING THE FULBRIGHT

You make mistakes. Mistakes don't make you.
—MAXWELL MALTZ

Now that I had my master's degree, I also had the opportunity to apply for a higher position, according to the bank's policy. Thanks to my first-division status combined with my supervisor's favorable review, I landed a position as an assistant in the research department of the Reserve Bank in Bombay (now called Mumbai). I was thrilled. Not only was I going to live in the premier financial city of India, but I would also be working in the research department of a major bank. This was akin to how my father had begun his professional career.

For me, that was quite an achievement. During these early days of India's independence, good jobs were scarce. Indeed, a recent graduate had little chance of finding a decent position—let alone at the head office of a prestigious institution (the counterpart of the Federal Reserve in the US). And the post was considered permanent. Once I was hired, I could not be laid off for any reason other than for a criminal offense.

When word of my employment in Bombay spread, everyone congratulated me. They predicted that I would continue to rise through the ranks to a senior management position, like my brother Biru. While I was exuberant, I was also nervous about leaving the safety and comfort of my family and the city I loved. Myriad questions arose. Where would I go after I arrived at the Bombay Central Railway Station? Where would I live? How would I travel from my home to the bank? Riding a bicycle would not be an option in such a big city. What would I do if my boss disliked me? Would my income be sufficient to live comfortably in a glamorous city like Bombay? Then there was the problem of having to deal with the new language of Marathi, which was widely spoken in Bombay. I had grown up speaking Hindi almost exclusively.

While considering these questions, a friend of Biru's who was an officer at the bank, invited me to stay with his family until I was ready to live on my own. So, with that question temporarily solved, I planned to leave.

On a muggy summer afternoon in 1951, at the age of 21, I boarded a noisy, third-class train compartment bound for Bombay. Even though I was confident that I had made the right decision, I was aware of the enormous risks I was taking. At 3 pm, the train let out a loud whistle announcing its imminent departure, jarring my nerves and heightening my anxiety. As the train pulled out of Kanpur, I sat motionless, feeling small in the overcrowded compartment.

About 24 hours later, the train screeched to a halt at the Victoria station in Bombay. Although I didn't have a clue what I would do if no one met me, those fears evaporated. I spotted my brother's friend and colleague, Deb Nath Chatterjee. Holding a big sign that read, "S. Mittra, from Kanpur," he stood out on the packed platform. Tall and fit, despite being close to retirement age, Chatterjee welcomed me with a broad smile. He hired a baggage handler to collect my luggage and carry it to another platform, from where we then boarded a local train.

The ride from Victoria to the suburb of Dadar was short, and Chatterjee and I had to stand because all the seats were occupied. At Dadar, Chatterjee hired yet another baggage handler and we walked more than two miles to get to his cozy, four-bedroom apartment on the third floor of a tall building in the affluent neighborhood of Hindu Colony. From the time I walked into Chatterjee's home, everyone in his large family—his wife of 40 years, his seven daughters, and his one son—made me feel part of the family. The apartment became my sanctuary, a place where I always felt comfortable, welcome, and secure.

My first day at my new job, however, was bad. From Chatterjee's home, I had to walk the two miles back to the Dadar station to catch the local train to Victoria. By the time the train had arrived at Dadar, it was already overcrowded, and the only way I could ride was to hang on to the people who were themselves hanging out of the car's open doorways. Since it was monsoon season, I found myself not only risking my life dangling on the outside of a fast train, but also getting drenched.

Somehow I survived that 45-minute treacherous train ride. But once at the Victoria station, I still had to make it to my office. The roads were flooded. All buses were packed to capacity. I could not afford to rent a taxi, even if available. So I walked in the downpour, without an umbrella, for more than half an hour to get to the Reserve Bank.

When I entered the elevator and asked the operator to take me to the third floor, he gave me a dirty look. About the only comforting thought I had at that moment was that Chatterjee had assured me everyone at the bank spoke English or broken Hindi, so I would not have to struggle to communicate in Marathi after all.

The elevator's door opened on the third floor. When I stepped out, I found my department to be just one large room. All the windows had been blocked by a series of cubicles constructed for senior officers. Outside the cubicles sat the officers' personal messenger boys, called *chaprasæs*. These boys performed miscellaneous chores—carrying files to various departments, serving refreshments to the officers, and making trips to the mailroom. Hundreds of battered desks occupied by clerks, research assistants, and superintendents filled the rest of the space. These desks were tightly packed, giving the place the chaotic appearance of an open market bazaar.

I asked myself, "Is this the glamorous place I dreamed about when I had first landed a job at the Bombay branch of this bank?

And should I be thrilled that I am destined to spend the rest of my professional life in this place?" I just stood there—soaking wet, bewildered, and dismayed.

One of the messenger boys came over to ask me who I wanted. He was flabbergasted (thanks presumably to my bedraggled state) to hear that I was a new hire reporting for work. Politely steering me through the maze to a desk, he suggested that I sit there for a while and get dry before seeing my new boss, Superintendent Ashok Gogte.

As I sat on my chair, I had a sinking feeling that I was in the wrong place at the wrong time. The dangerous train ride, the 30-minute walk in the torrential rain without an umbrella, and the first impression of a frenzied office—all seemed more like a nightmare than a dream come true. I closed my eyes, took a deep breath, and attempted to think positive thoughts. But the more I tried to imagine brighter days ahead, the more I saw myself as destined to remain a nameless clerk forever, sitting at a shabby desk and soaking wet. My hopes sagged like my drenched clothes.

Superintendent Gogte, a native of Bombay in his late 40s, was demanding of his assistants. But he was also fair, kind-hearted, and willing to accommodate their special needs. Despite his supportive nature, however, I found my new job tedious, boring, and much too clerical in nature for my taste. Patiently, I hoped that after the initial training period, I would be asked to perform more challenging tasks. But that did not happen. I soon realized that my position as a research assistant was merely a fancy title for a nameless petty clerk.

Over time, I got used to the routine: fighting awful traffic in the morning, working a boring clerical job where I posed as a research assistant during the day, and then returning to Chatterjee's comfortable home in the evening. Despite the gratitude I felt for Chatterjee, I trespassed on good manners when I failed to make an effort to find a place of my own. The truth was that living with Chatterjee's family was the only part of living in Bombay that I enjoyed in the beginning. I feared losing that comfort.

At first, the family assumed that I was not looking for separate accommodation simply because I was still getting used to my new life. But after several weeks, when I still unthinkingly displayed no effort to find a home of my own, the family started dropping hints about my moving out. Still nervous about being able to manage on my own, I chose to ignore their hints.

A Sunday morning came when Chatterjee asked me to accompany him to a place he was going to visit. Assuming this was his way of showing me another interesting section of the city, I followed with enthusiasm. We boarded the local train and got off at the Churney Road station. We walked through busy streets for about half an hour before arriving at a place called the Bengal Lodge in the Crawford Market area. It was very busy with hundreds of shops and traffic jams. I had never seen so much traffic before.

Bengal Lodge was a misleading name. It was an old, dilapidated building that reminded me of a degenerated hut in Banpur, ready to be condemned. Still not knowing why we were here, I followed Chatterjee inside. He directed me to rent a room for ₹30 per month. I was shocked because until then he had not said a word about renting a room either in this place or anywhere else.

I indeed rented the room, which at 15 feet by 20 feet turned out to be not much bigger than a cubbyhole with two beds—which meant, I assumed, that I would share the room with another boarder. My new living quarters had no closets and hardly any storage space; I would have to keep my things in a suitcase, slid under my bed. A few nails had been hammered into the wall for hanging clothes. Down the hall was a bathroom with one sink, one shower stall, and one toilet. I would have to share it with 20 other boarders living on my floor.

After renting the room, I returned home with Chatterjee, who then hired a taxi and helped me load my belongings into it. He wished me luck in my new home. I bade goodbye by expressing my deep gratitude to his family. Arriving back at Bengal Lodge, I squeezed my things into my cubbyhole and settled in. All I could say to myself was, "Welcome to the real world of Bombay."

Living in Bengal Lodge was unbearable from the start. Most of the boarders were long-time residents. They did not seem to mind the lack of space, privacy, or cleanliness, nor did they object to the volume of the traffic and the din from the market all night long. I could not share their camaraderie, however. I still felt like a country boy lost in this huge metropolis. When I found myself having fleeting visions of marrying a Chatterjee girl just so I could move back into that comfortable home, I remembered the sting of their abrupt farewell and laughed sardonically.

I did, however, enjoy meeting a young man named Ratan Mukherjee who worked in the building. Ratan had left his home in East Pakistan in search of a better life in Bombay, but was totally lost until someone helped him strike a special arrangement with the lodge. Instead of being officially hired as a bellboy, Ratan was allowed to live in the building in exchange for running errands for the boarders. He never failed to greet me whenever I left or entered the building.

One day when I returned from work, Ratan was not there. No one seemed to know his whereabouts, and I did not press the matter. He finally showed up three days later, severely beaten and weak. He looked like he'd been mauled. He appeared not to have eaten anything for days. I brought him into my room and ordered some food, and as we sat together, he told me what had happened.

Two days prior to his disappearance, a boarder had reported that his wristwatch had been stolen. Assuming that Ratan was the culprit, the police whisked him away and put him in jail. They starved him and beat him mercilessly for two days until he was forced to *confess* that he stole the watch. Once the police got his confession, they beat him some more before finally letting him go. I promised him that I would talk with the management and with the other boarders. I hoped that incident would not be repeated. Ratan was consoled but still bruised. Neither the watch nor the thief was ever found. Still, the incident taught me the value of being a good and caring listener as well as of extending a helping hand whenever someone desperately needed my help.

After three long months, in sheer desperation, I finally decided that I had to find a way out of the Bengal Lodge. The noise, filth, and lack of decent facilities were too much. So I took the advice of a colleague and started looking for suitable accommodation in the "Paying Guests" section of *The Times of India*. After searching for a month, I found a room in the Windsor Guest House, only a short walk from the Colaba terminal bus station. The station was only a 15-minute bus ride away from my office. Since all the downtown buses originated from there, finding a seat on the bus would not be a problem. But the best part was that I would have my own private room with an attached bath. Included was a full breakfast every morning of two fried eggs, hash brown potatoes, toast, and tea with warm whole milk and real sugar—all for a monthly rent of ₹110. Although the expense ate up nearly half of my salary, to me it was worth it. I could finally say, "Yesssssss! I love Bombay."

I had been hired ostensibly to conduct basic research leading up to various bank publications, occasional research papers, and special white papers dealing with major economic problems facing the country. But I soon discovered that my recruiters hired me under false pretenses. Conducting this research was the domain of the research officers. They sat comfortably in their enclosed offices, while glorified clerks like me were called upon to be nothing more than gofers. Under the title of *research assistants*, we were limited to photocopying printed background material, and proofreading the articles and memoranda produced by the research officers. The potential for promotion was small. Even so, the next step up was superintendent, and all superintendents did was supervise gofers. The rank of research officer seemed eons away.

I found my situation so frustrating that I became visibly irritable and impatient. For a while, my fellow slave workers thought that Bombay's heat and humidity was getting to me. They attempted to console me by assuring me that in time I would get used to the climate and accept my place at the bank. We were all there together—like rats in a maze. In desperation, I applied for a scholarship to join the PhD program at the venerable Banaras University in the northern province of Uttar Pradesh, where I was from originally. But my application was rejected.

Like a zombie, I eventually succumbed and began tolerating my incredibly tedious job. And so to compensate, I started developing a social life that would relieve me from the boredom. I not only made some new friends, but also practiced vocal and instrumental music. I even staged some musical programs. In addition, I began performing at Bombay's popular All India Radio. I may have been mired in a mechanical ten-to-six routine on weekdays, but I became a minor celebrity with an exciting social life after office hours and on weekends.

Ironically, my boring job did offer me one thing that I found exciting: lots of girls in various departments of our bank. Women and men freely interacted with one another both inside and outside the bank, if only in groups and in social settings. Western-style dating was just getting started in the progressive-minded Indian–Christian communities of cosmopolitan cities, such as Bombay and Delhi, but the concept was new to me. Given the prevailing Indian custom, my family assumed that I would never socialize with girls, either alone or in groups. With time, my family assumed, I would settle down by marrying a girl with their approval. I knew they expected me to adhere to this hopelessly outdated tradition. So it took four long years before I had the courage to ask a girl for a date. I met Monica David at the celebrations of the Indian Republic Day. She was pretty, friendly, had a great sense of humor, and was a lot of fun. Despite the fact that she was a Christian and I was not, one day I dared to invite Monica for tea in a restaurant near Victoria station. I was surprised and pleased by the smile she flashed me when she said yes.

When we arrived at the restaurant, the waiter seated us in a small booth with a swinging door. It closed only part of the doorway, providing some privacy for those seated inside. Monica and I were there barely five minutes before the door swung open quite suddenly, apparently because the intruder didn't realize that the booth was occupied. Unfortunately for me, the interloper turned out to be Joseph Saldanha, a Christian colleague in our research department. He always seemed to carry a chip on his shoulder. I instantly felt a pang of guilt and knew it would be embarrassing if word of my dating a Christian girl spread. But Joseph appeared so suddenly that I couldn't think of anything to say to him to justify my being there with Monica.

He apologized and started backing out of the room, at which point I blurted out, "Hey, Saldanha, come back and let me introduce you to *my cousin.*"

Joseph indeed turned back, smiling at me mischievously, and said, "Thanks, Mittra, but you needn't take the trouble. Last week, your cousin happened to be *my cousin.*"

Before long, I became chummy with many girls whom I met in the office and as partners in musical programs. But one girl especially attracted me. I met her on May 11, 1953, a beautiful summer day in Bombay, sunny and comfortably warm with a light breeze gently blowing inland from the Arabian Sea.

I was the organizer of a musical extravaganza held that day in the auditorium of the Bombay Concert Hall to celebrate the birthday of India's Nobel Prize-winning poet Rabindranath Tagore. The auditorium was packed to capacity before the starting time. At 7:30 pm, the emcee welcomed the guests, while the artists and their accompanists waited backstage with anticipation, socializing, and having a grand time.

But one artist was sitting apart from the others, lost in deep contemplation. She immediately caught my attention. I had not met this girl before, but assumed that she was Bani Sarkar. A colleague had told me about her. As the program chairman, I had consented to his extending an invitation to Ms Sarkar to perform.

I must confess that curiosity got the better of me, and I trespassed on good manners by repeatedly staring at her. She appeared to be in her late teens and wore a beautifully embroidered sari in a lovely peach color (my favorite). Her long braided hair—a distinct sign of Indian beauty—caressed her body, resting well below her waistline. She had a fair complexion and appeared to be wearing hardly any makeup, unusual for a female performing artist. What touched me, however, was that Bani's serene physical beauty seemed to reflect an inner beauty. Enchanted, I wanted to walk up to her and introduce myself. But even though I was the program chairman, my taking the liberty of approaching her directly backstage without a proper introduction would be violation of our established tradition. So I refrained.

Before long our program started, and I quickly moved from backstage to the stage manager's booth, hoping to see Bani perform very soon. But I had to wait a whole hour before she was invited to present her item. Introducing her to the audience, the emcee noted that Bani had a superb musical voice and mastery of numerous singing styles and compositions. As I waited with anticipation, she began her program with a prayer in slow, invocation style. Then she followed it with an artfully selected group of Tagore songs interspersed with enchanting classical-based songs. I was mesmerized by her personality on stage, and her hypnotic voice kept ringing in my ears even after she had concluded her performance and received thunderous applause.

At the end of our program, I went backstage and again found Bani sitting in a secluded corner. After hesitating for just a moment, this time I did take the liberty of introducing myself.

"Miss Sarkar," I said in a voice filled with admiration, "this is the first time I have attended a performance of yours, and I must say I was mesmerized both by your voice and your artistry."

"Thank you," Bani responded in a barely audible voice, saying nothing more and, thus, shattering my hopes for starting a meaningful conversation.

That night, I left the program somewhat disappointed, but undiscouraged. I was confident that soon I would find a way to establish a friendship with Bani. Unfortunately, my confidence turned out to be largely misplaced. Bani was such a shy girl and her family members were so protective that I hardly ever was allowed to speak with her during the four additional years I lived in Bombay.

Since I gave everyone the impression that I was thoroughly enjoying my new life, my family and friends advised me that I should marry and settle down. But beneath this facade, I still feared that I would spend the rest of my career as nothing but a glorified clerk. My supposedly *glamorous* life paled next to this fear, and slowly I sank into the doldrums. In spite of my social prominence and my contacts with girls, I became disgruntled. It was like having a nagging headache—I was not sick enough to stay in bed, but I didn't feel good enough to enjoy life.

One day this annoying frustration overwhelmed me. I broke the long-standing office rule about not going over the head of an immediate supervisor. Superintendent Gogte was certainly kindhearted, but he did not have a research bent. He showed no inclination to become a research officer. Because he lacked ambition, I feared he would denigrate mine. I wanted to produce research papers to convince the bank that I deserved to be promoted directly from a research assistant to a research officer, bypassing the intermediate rank of superintendent.

To skirt Gogte, I would have to violate the bank's established rules by directly approaching his boss, a research officer named M. Narasimham. Punishment for such an act was normally severe—at worst, an on-the-spot firing from what was otherwise considered a permanent job, and, at the very least, a delay of no fewer than five years for the next promotion. Although I knew the move was risky, Narasimham, a graduate of Cambridge University, was bright, aggressive, and articulate; and I suspected he was too smart to blindly follow the bank's stifling bureaucratic rules.

One evening, I discovered that Narasimham was still in his office, even though it was after quitting time and everyone else had left for the day. Hesitating for just a moment, I found the courage to knock on his door, and when prompted, I entered.

Seeing a research assistant standing there—and after office hours, no less—Narasimham looked somewhat surprised. "Yes?" he blurted out in response to the interruption.

"I am Mittra, a research assistant in your department," I answered meekly.

"I know who you are," he replied impatiently. "What can I do for you?"

I paused for a moment, as if to remind myself of the serious consequences of my action. But realizing that I had already crossed the point of no return, I gathered up what courage I could muster and began to speak.

"After spending a lot of time as a research assistant and studying carefully what research officers produce, I believe I am almost ready to begin producing these research papers myself," I said in a quivering voice.

"You do?" Narasimham replied, flabbergasted. After a brief pause, he then continued, "I have never heard this before. Can you explain to me why you feel this way, so soon after you were hired as a research assistant?"

That was certainly the opening I was looking for, and with his tacit permission (and gaining confidence as I proceeded), I began to lay out for him my plan for directly becoming a research officer without first being promoted to superintendent. Narasimham listened intently, his facial expressions alternating between bewilderment and fascination. When I finished, I held my breath for a second or two, hoping that I hadn't just committed a serious error in judgment.

Silence hung in the air between us for a moment. Suddenly, Narasimham stood up and looked around the room, as if he were searching for an answer amidst the beautiful paintings of South Indian temples hung on the walls and the cricket tournament trophies proudly displayed on the side tables. After a couple of minutes, he sat down again and looked straight into my eyes. I waited nervously, not knowing what would come next.

"Mittra, I'm glad you spoke up," he finally said. "I admire thoughtful, aggressive assistants who are anxious to get ahead. Go on and start writing research papers, but instead of going through your superintendent, send them directly to me. I make no promises, but I'll see what I can do." Music to my ears!

During the next year and a half, I produced a sizeable number of signed research papers and dutifully sent them on to Narasimham. Without my knowledge, he forwarded my work along with his favorable comments to P.S.N. Prasad, the bank's economic advisor and the head of our research department. Narasimham's willingness to violate the department's protocol enabled me to impress Prasad with my research skills. What happened next was phenomenal.

On a beautiful day in January 1953, a very surprised Gogte informed me that I had been selected as the bank's nominee to the US Fulbright Committee. Since he had no knowledge of my directly approaching Narasimham or my subsequent direct contacts with him, he had no idea why the bank would even consider someone with no seniority whatsoever. I, too, acted surprised. I certainly didn't say anything to him about what I'd been doing. I realized Prasad must have played a major role in my selection, since, without his direct and strong support, the bank surely would have chosen someone further up the chain of command. Decades later, Prasad showed me his letter recommending me for the Fulbright scholarship. "Mr Mittra's work is characterized by precision and objectivity," he'd written. "He has a good analytical mind and a capacity for clear and effective exposition."

The nomination, I soon discovered, was just the beginning of the process. I was then faced with the nightmare of filling out a lengthy and challenging fellowship application. In India, college admission forms were merely two pages long and requested only factual information. In contrast, the Fulbright application contained more than two dozen pages, accompanied by long, explanatory notes and comments. The forms also asked many complicated and involved questions, such as, "What, in your judgment, is the true value of higher education?" and "How would you be able to help your country upon your return?" The request I found the most formidable was this: "Explain in your own words why we should award you the fellowship."

The pressure to complete such an outlandish application became almost unbearable. Sometimes I wished I had the will to stop the agony and remain a gofer, but the prospect of going to Harvard and earning a master's or a PhD, distant as these goals were, pushed me. On April 16, the deadline for submitting the application, I said a prayer to Saraswati (the Hindu goddess of learning) and hand-delivered my application to the Fulbright office in Bombay.[1] The receptionist receiving the application looked at me rather strangely, but I was too relieved to be concerned.

Two days later, I received a phone call from that office, asking me to meet the officer-in-charge immediately. Could it be that they thought my application needed further work? Or could the officer be confused about the way I answered one of those enigmatic questions? Or maybe they were calling to tell me that I had already won the fellowship! My anxiety mounted.

As I arrived at the Fulbright office precisely at 10 am the next day, I was escorted into an executive-style office, where I was surprised to see an Indian woman, working in the American Consulate, sitting behind a beautifully crafted mahogany desk. As I approached her, I noticed a plaque with her name, Novart Parseghian, and instantly recognized it as Parsi (Persians who settled in India). A zillion frightening questions started circling in my head: "What was this Indian lady doing in an American Consulate office? Was she especially assigned to my case because my poorly written answers were confusing to an American? Would she summarily reject my application because Indians don't like to support other Indians?"

Fortunately, I did not have to dwell on these questions for too long. Parseghian greeted me with a smile and invited me to sit down in the chair facing her. On her desk, I could see a manila folder with my application peeking out. After exchanging the usual formalities, she asked me how I felt about my chance of winning the fellowship.

"I feel very good about it," I answered nervously, "especially since I have been nominated by the bank. Many of the questions on this application I found very hard to answer," I added, "but I hope I gave good responses to all of them." Mentally, I crossed my fingers.

"I liked your answers," Parseghian agreed. "In fact, I believe you'd have an excellent chance of winning this fellowship, since we generally award a fellowship grant to *the Reserve Bank's nominee.*" Then her expression suddenly turned grim. "Mr Mittra," she asked, "do you know the deadline for submission of this application?"

"I sure do," I replied, gaining confidence. "It was April 16. I reminded myself of that date every morning when I woke up. I made sure that I completed the application by the due date, and I hand-delivered it to your receptionist that same afternoon."

"Yes, we did receive your application on April 16," she replied, the sadness in her voice unmistakable. "Unfortunately, you missed the deadline by almost a week." Then, as if to make sure that I heard her correctly, she said forcefully, "The deadline for the application was the 10th of April."

For a moment I thought Parseghian was joking. But when I saw the serious look on her face, I began suspecting they had another candidate in mind and that they were cheating on me. My heart stopped beating and my mind turned numb.

"I remember carefully noting the deadline when I first received the application," I protested once the initial shock wore off. Parseghian picked up my application, turned to page one, and put it down in front of me. The official deadline of April 10th jumped out.[1]

I do not recall how long I sat there, motionless. But the next thing I remember was hearing Parseghian whisper, "Mr Mittra, from the look on your face, I gather you want me to ignore this slip on your part and assume that we received your application in time. I can't blame you, because, as I have already said, you would have had an excellent chance of winning. But since you did miss the deadline, I must regretfully *disqualify your application*." She then took a deep breath.

"It might be difficult for you to fully recover from this terrible blow," she added, "but I sincerely hope that this devastating experience will make you more determined to find another way to get to America for higher studies." She went on talking, but my mind didn't register anything else she said after that. As I walked out, I couldn't help remembering the time in eighth grade when I'd penned *scince* instead of *science* on a test and lost getting the top grade in the class.

I left the Fulbright office in a daze. I was expected back at work before noon, but I could not return and behave as if nothing had happened. I needed to be alone. I kept asking myself how I could have been so irresponsible and downright stupid. "Some things never change," I told myself despondently.

I walked to the nearest train station and boarded a train bound for Churchgate. From there, I started walking toward my guesthouse, an hour's walk from the station. I was sure I had permanently lost any opportunity for receiving the fellowship in the future, because under the rules, I would have to be re-nominated by the bank to reapply. I was sure the bank would never give me a second chance.

When I finally reached home, I was too upset to sit and stew about it all by myself. So I walked back to the Colaba station and got on the upper deck of a slow double-decker streetcar. I occupied the front seat facing the street, closed my eyes, and almost passed out with pain and disgust.

I rode the double-decker all the way from Colaba to its final destination at King's Circle, a three-hour journey. Then I bought a return ticket and rode another three hours back to Colaba. Still angry with myself, I was no more ready to go home than I had been before, but I had exhausted all the places where I could go to lick my wounds. Frustrated, I returned home and went to bed fully clothed. I passed a sleepless night brooding over the disaster I had brought upon myself.

The next morning, I went to the office at the usual time, still in my wrinkled clothes. On the outside, I tried to behave as if nothing had happened. Inside, however, I was a totally changed person. During the course of the previous night, I had made a firm decision to do whatever it would take to win a fellowship grant to study at an American university—*any* American university. I had no idea exactly what that would entail, but I was determined to get to the US, one way or another.

When I left work at 5:30 that evening, I went straight to the US Information Services library, which contained volumes of information on the US universities. I pored over various documents, finding the world of American universities utterly confusing. I could not differentiate among the universities of New York, Purdue, California Lutheran, and Stetson. I was not too sure, for example, if I could assume that any direct relationship existed between the size of a university and its national ranking. I was just too ignorant and ill equipped to choose, and so I spent weeks trying to figure out how to start a new application process.

Finally, in the absence of a more rational plan, I arbitrarily divided the US into four zones: east, west, north, and south. I then picked one university from each zone, and during the summer of 1953 sent a request to each for both an admission application and a fellowship grant application. I then waited patiently to receive these forms, promising myself never to miss an application deadline again.

In time, I received four applications. Like the Fulbright, these applications were bulky and they asked numerous difficult questions. Although I had gone through a similar set of queries earlier, I still found the task quite daunting. Several times I wished I had saved a copy of my Fulbright application for reference.

When I finally finished them all and went to the post office to mail them, I was shocked to learn that it would cost ₹100 to send the four applications by first class, registered airmail. Even then the post office would not guarantee their delivery before three weeks. Mailing the four packets would cost two-fifths of my monthly salary, but what other choice did I have if I wanted to earn a fellowship grant to study in the US?

I put myself on a near-starvation-level budget, but it didn't pay off. Several months later, I received four rejections. By then, I had made up my mind to continue this bizarre application process until I got what I wanted. So in 1954, I returned to the USIS Office to pick eight more universities to write to—double the number I had originally selected. This time, I felt compelled to send the applications by surface mail, even though I realized that it would take at least three months for them to be delivered. Ultimately, I received eight polite rejections.

In 1955, I again doubled the number of picks, from 8 to 16, and repeated my routine. Unfortunately, I failed this time as well. Heartbroken, I refused to give up. Toward the end of 1956, I mailed out 16 more, hoping to somehow get lucky.

One evening in the spring of 1957, I returned home from work and routinely opened my mailbox. As had been the case so many times, one of the letters was from an American school, the University of Florida (UF). Of the 16 fellowship applications I had most recently sent out, I had already received 15 rejections. I had no reason to believe that that this response would be any different.

Still, I was puzzled when I looked at the return address on the envelope. All the previous rejection letters had come from the universities' admissions offices. But this one was sent from the school's Economics Department. Since I had applied only to business departments and had no background in economics, this didn't make sense. I wondered out loud if I would be compelled to reject a fellowship grant if in fact it came from a different department than the one I had applied to.

I don't remember how long I stood there with the sealed envelope clutched in my hand, but eventually I mustered enough courage to tear it open. I stopped after reading only the first six words: "We are pleased to inform you ...."

After that I squeezed my eyes shut, afraid to open them again for what seemed like an eternity. Cautiously, I opened one eye and read on to learn that indeed I had been awarded a fellowship by the Economics Department of The UF in Gainesville. But instead of feeling ecstatic about winning a fellowship after trying for four long years, I was terrified that this might turn out to be some kind of hoax. I spent that night tossing and turning in bed, wondering if somehow I could persuade the University to transfer this fellowship from the Economics Department to its Business Department. I knew that was wishful thinking, but I couldn't just give up without trying *something*.

The next day I went to the US Consulate office and asked to see a consulate officer. Since I had no appointment, I was turned away but was able to schedule an appointment for the following day. I went back to my office but could not concentrate. My supervisor, noticing my distraction, asked if I was sick and needed to take the day off. I politely declined his offer, since I felt that in my mental condition staying home would be even worse.

The next day, my 15-minute meeting with US Consulate Officer Roger Smith turned out to be a pleasant surprise. After reading my fellowship letter, Smith assured me that I had no reason to worry.

"Mr Mittra, this letter originated from the Economics Department simply because that department (instead of the Business Department) happened to have the fellowship grant money," he explained. "But there is no reason for you to worry. It is the University's graduate school that is responsible for deciding what graduate courses you'd be required to take and which of their schools would award you a PhD degree. So if you have a degree in business, then it would be the Business Department that would grant you the PhD degree." Smith wrapped up our meeting by advising me to accept the offer without delay and to begin making preparations for attending the UF. I was so excited that I left without expressing my gratitude. I hope that appreciating my mental condition, he forgave me for my indiscretion.

One of the preconditions for admission was that I had to provide proof of my proficiency in English. I was advised that Dr John Kirkland in USIS's Bombay office was authorized to issue me an English proficiency certificate. I learned that he was in fact a tenured professor of English at the UF who was in Bombay on a one-year assignment at USIS. I made an appointment to see him, with hopes that he would go easy on me, recognizing I was headed for his school, and quickly issue me the necessary certificate.

I liked Dr Kirkland the moment I saw him. With his well-trimmed beard and mustache, and his shiny three-piece suit and tie, he looked like quite a distinguished businessman. He gave me a big smile as he ushered me into his office, making me feel totally relaxed. He had, as it turned out, devised an unusual way of testing my proficiency in English. He would share with me an interesting story and he promised that if I could effectively relay the story back to him, then he would grant me the required certificate. And with that, Dr Kirkland began narrating the following story:

> Two friends, Dick and Harry, lived in a small town. Dick was a mediocre student, while Harry was brilliant. Both had vowed to help each other whenever either one faced difficulties. One day, a respected teacher informed Dick by phone

that in order to pass the final exam, he would have to answer three difficult questions, giving him one week to prepare for the exam. Dick panicked when he heard that, and because he *had* to pass the exam, he pleaded with Harry to take the test on his behalf. Fortunately, the teacher had never met either Dick or Harry, so Harry agreed to act as an impostor and take the test, hoping that the plan would work.

On the appointed day, unsuspecting of any foul play, the teacher asked Harry (posing as Dick) the following three questions:

What is the distance around the world?
What is the depth of the Atlantic Ocean?
What am I thinking right now?

Without batting an eye, Harry answered these three questions this way:

The distance around the world is the distance a point on the equator travels around the sun in a 24-hour period.
The depth of the Atlantic Ocean is the distance a heavy metal object would travel from the surface of the water to the bottom of the sea.
Right now you are thinking that I am Dick answering your questions. But for your information, I am Harry posing as Dick.

Despite the fact that Dick had cheated, the teacher was impressed with Harry's answers, and as a special favor, gave Dick a passing grade.

I repeated the story back to Dr Kirkland and received my certificate of proficiency in English from the distinguished professor with no trouble. Leaving the language issue behind, and since it was too late to go back to work, I decided to take the rest of the afternoon off to reflect on what lay ahead. I climbed into a cab and asked the driver to take me to Cuffe Parade in the southern part of Bombay. Once there, I found an empty bench and sunk into it, very happy but still juggling many conflicting thoughts.

The day was sunny and beautiful, and gentle sea breezes caressed my face as I surveyed my surroundings. To my left was the upscale neighborhood of Colaba Causeway, which appeared way too busy for my tastes, with scores of families and tourists milling around the commercial area. Straight ahead was the vibrant Arabian Sea, its rough waves beating down on the white sand beach, which was covered with seashells. Scores of birds were circling overhead, looking for scraps of food that people often threw for them. As I watched the roaring waves, I fell to brooding again, realizing that the restless waves reflected my prevailing mood.

My language requirement was out of the way, but a lot of hard work was yet ahead of me. I had to get busy, preparing for my long journey. But how would I manage to get to the US? And how would I pay for such a trip? Thinking about the virtually insurmountable financial and logistical problems I faced, I felt completely overwhelmed. I closed my eyes and slumped down a bit on the bench, letting the warm sun wash over me and listening to the crashing of the waves, as relentless as the questions surfacing in my mind. I was emotionally exhausted, and my body's defense mechanisms soon took over.

I dozed off, still facing the US—and my future.

Epilogue: Life's Lessons

I move to Bombay as a research assistant in the country's central bank, which I soon discover is merely the position of a glorified clerk. Dismayed, I attempt to compensate by trying to become popular in social circles, and even date a girl by defying the prevailing social custom. Unfortunately, nothing works for me.

After much effort, I get to apply for a Fulbright grant to study in the US, but I am rejected when I carelessly miss the submission deadline. Instead of giving up, I embark on a preposterous plan of applying for grant after grant for years, until I succeed. This bizarre strategy leads to 43 rejections in four years, but the 44th application brings results: I am awarded a grant to study at the UF and prepare to travel to the US.

The following Four Ps' list identifies the P(s) that I have covered in this chapter:

[X]   Persevere with passion.
[X]   Pursue professional, family-oriented, social, and spiritual goals.
[X]   Persuade family and friends to help.
[   ]   Promote a culture of giving back.

Note

1. This date represents my best recollection. Contacts with USIS in India and the State Department in Washington, D.C. in the US failed to confirm this date.

8

SLOW PASSAGE TO THE LAND
WHERE DREAMS COME TRUE

*Losers live in the past. Winners learn from the past and enjoy working
in the present toward the future.*
—DENIS WAITLEY

For the next several weeks, I walked around as if in a dream. I
shared my exciting news with no one because I assumed no
one would believe me, and I made no initial preparations for traveling abroad. Two months later, on May 13, 1957 (my 27th birthday), I decided that it was time to visit an international travel
agency.

I discovered that travel to America by ship would be the most
affordable. But such a journey from Bombay to New York would
take about three months. Even if I sailed at the earliest time possible, I would not reach the University until late October—too late
for the start of the fall session on September 1st. The alternative,
however, flying from Bombay to Gainesville, would cost nearly
$800—the equivalent of my total salary for 16 months. I left the
travel agency in dismay.

Ludicrous as it may have been, I came up with a desperate idea.
I had once been introduced to a girl whose father was a mechanic
with Air India. The airline then offered employees a free plane
ticket for each family member to any city in the world where Air

India flew. For a moment, I imagined marrying into that family, but fortunately the fantasy (along with my cloudy memory of the girl in question) quickly evaporated. As clever an idea as it may have been, I was not up to such chicanery.

My savings amounted to about $100—only a fraction of what I needed. And I'd also need money to buy personal articles for living in the US. I doubted my family would give me a loan, since my plan would involve giving up a permanent job at a premier government institution to chase a doctorate degree in America. At that time, getting a degree in a foreign country was arguably of dubious value in India. An advanced degree from England would be respected, but not so with one earned in the US, especially by someone who's overall scholastic record was mediocre.

True, Raj had done something similar several years earlier, but he had first established a brilliant academic track record at a premier Indian institution (Calcutta University). So when he easily won a full four-year fellowship grant from the University of Toronto to work toward a PhD, the family enthusiastically supported his plans and quickly offered to absorb his travel costs. Clearly, I had none of those things going for me. My family would surely think me insane to entertain such a scheme. Indeed, I believed they could be right.

As I left the travel agency, I needed time to reflect. So I took a bus to the Gateway of India, a celebrated landmark by the Arabian Sea built in 1924. It commemorated the visit of King George V. Facing this memorial to the British Empire was a statue of Shivaji, a great seventeenth-century Indian warrior who endured every obstacle in his life with great determination and courage. I came here because I wanted to face my seemingly insurmountable obstacles in similar fashion. I hoped the statue would inspire me. I sat on a bench facing the ocean, looking out in the direction of Florida. I watched the waves breaking on the retainer wall.

I'd spent four long years applying for fellowships, and I finally got one; but I would lose it if I could not come up with the money to pay for my trip. This predicament was even more painful than my Fulbright failure. True, it was I who missed the deadline with the Fulbright. But misguided or not, I still could blame Parseghian because she had the power to accept my application despite my mistake. But now, I couldn't blame anyone, not even my family, whom I did not have the courage to approach.

My thoughts shifted to my late father Kashi. I remembered the stories I'd heard about him facing far more impossible predicaments while always finding a way to succeed. Like Shivaji, he never gave up. Although he was born in affluence, my father was catapulted into poverty when his land baron father abandoned his kingdom and migrated to a state that adopted a different language. Kashi was forced to become a street hawker at the tender age of 12. He became very successful at it. Then at 18, he got a job as a night watchman at the central jail, only to resign frightened out of his wits after seeing a strange female who turned out to be the ghost of a woman hanged the day before. Then he became a rickshaw puller, and worked hard to get regular clients. A year later, one of his regular customers, an officer with the Imperial Bank (India's premier banking institution), recognized Father's drive and work ethic. He offered him a clerical position. Slowly, as the years wore on, Father kept moving up the ladder at the bank. Eventually, at the age of 51, he became the president of the Amritsar branch of the bank—a position no Indian had ever held before him. And he managed this with only a sixth-grade education!

Thinking about Father and sitting there in the shadow of Shivaji, I realized that there was *no way* I could get this far and then just give up. There *had* to be a solution to my dilemma, and I *must* find it. And then suddenly, I hit upon a crazy idea only slightly less desperately creative than marrying the Air India mechanic's daughter. I remembered that the bank's director of research, Dr P.J. Pinto, had told us that he had once sailed from Bombay to France. He then journeyed by train to London, and finally flew from London to Washington, D.C., to work for the International Monetary Fund. Maybe I could come up with an affordable hybrid plan, following the Pinto strategy and then ask Raj for additional financial assistance. After all, since Raj had earned his PhD overseas, surely he would recognize how valuable this opportunity could be for me. This seemed like a strategy that might succeed.

When my travel agent, Amrit Singh, saw me return, he assumed that I was ready to buy the plane ticket. But when I told him I needed to get to America for half the price quoted, he maintained his composure while pointing out politely that there was no bargaining on price.

I explained my hybrid plan, suggesting the following itinerary: boat from Bombay to France; train from France to Amsterdam; ferry from Amsterdam to London; plane from London to New York; bus from New York to State College, Pennsylvania (where Raj was a professor at Penn State University), and finally another bus from State College to Gainesville, Florida. Singh, an experienced professional who had worked at various travel agencies for some 20 years and who specialized in travel to the US and Europe, was dumbfounded.

"Mr Mittra," he sputtered. "I understand you have never traveled abroad, and in fact you haven't even traveled much within India. How in the world did you come up with such a convoluted travel plan?" I remained silent.

Singh, looking grim, agreed to work on the details and invited me to return in a few days. He cautioned me, however, that my creative plan might not actually end up being much cheaper. But when I returned two days later, Singh gleefully announced that I could indeed follow such a plan, dropping my travel cost to $595. That $200 reduction might not have been attractive to anyone else, but the 25 percent savings certainly excited me. Singh warned me, however, about unpleasant accommodations that I might find unacceptable.

"I don't care how bad the accommodations are," I shouted with glee. "As long as I can get to Gainesville for under $600, I wouldn't mind swimming part of the way."

"There is a French ship owned by Messagerie Maritime Company that sails in late July from Calcutta to Marseilles, France," Singh explained. "Typically, ocean-going passenger ships have three classes of accommodation, but on this ship, there is also an inexpensive fourth class."

"I follow you so far. Go ahead," I said impatiently.

"Far below the third class, the fourth class is designed to carry Cambodian prisoners captured by France during fighting in

Indochina. This class has no amenities to speak of and is not air-conditioned. It can be extremely uncomfortable, especially for a 14-day journey during summer."

"That's okay, as long as it's cheap," I responded, carefully suppressing my growing nervousness.

"In the fourth class, there are indeed a couple of cheap rooms with four berths in each room that are allocated for regular passengers," he continued. "I can reserve one of these berths for you. Are you willing to travel to Calcutta from Bombay and then for two whole weeks endure the stress and discomfort associated with traveling in the fourth class of this ship?" He paused a moment and added, "I myself wouldn't do it, but I will let you be the judge for yourself."

I was speechless. Traveling with prisoners? No amenities whatsoever? What would that mean? Would I be able to breathe? And would I have to eat with the prisoners? What if a hostile prisoner broke free and killed me? What was I getting into? After recovering from my initial shock, I asked if there were any other problems.

"When you disembark at the port of Marseilles," Singh told me, "you would have to carry your own baggage from the port to the train station. Upon arrival there, you would need to find the train to Amsterdam. In Amsterdam, once again you'd have to carry your baggage from the train station to the dock where you'd catch a ferry across the English Channel to London. In addition, you should be aware that virtually no one speaks English in Marseilles, and this language barrier would continue as you travel through Europe—France, Belgium, and Holland—as the local languages would keep changing."

Singh was surely right, I thought. I could not count on people helping me, I would have little money on me, and I would be forced to carry my heavy luggage on my back. My mind started weighing the benefits of cheap fare on the one hand with the risk of traveling with prisoners and getting stuck in Europe on the other. "Should I say this is getting too crazy and walk out?" I wondered. "Or should I say the heck with my fears and just hope that I make it to America?"

My spirit of adventure—or perhaps my downright stupidity—prevailed. I agreed to Singh's itinerary and made the reservations that included traveling for two weeks in the fourth class of a French ship with prisoners. This would indeed be my journey to the Promised Land or to death. I wasn't sure which.

Next, I pleaded with Raj to grant me a loan of $500. Despite his initial hesitation, he promised to send me the money soon. And when I told my family about my final decision to travel to America and work on my PhD financed by a fellowship grant, to my great surprise, they didn't oppose my seemingly crazy plan. Instead, they actually gave me a whopping $300 to pay for part of my travel cost. I thanked them profusely and told them I'd never forget their generosity. They remained silent, presumably hoping that good sense would prevail and I would change my mind.

Now feeling well-financed, I proceeded to obtain a US student visa. I used some of my savings buying clothes and related articles for the trip. But I still had to overcome one other major obstacle. In the 1950s, because of strict exchange controls, Indians traveling to foreign countries were permitted by the Reserve Bank to carry only $8. I obviously needed to carry more cash than that. That's because I was going to be traveling for almost two weeks from Marseilles to Gainesville. I would need to buy food and pay for a hotel in London, among other expenses.

My chances of asking the Reserve Bank to grant me clearance to carry additional dollars were nil. Strict regulations prohibited the bank's employees from asking for special treatment. Still, I pleaded, and I finally succeeded in getting the bank to allow me to carry an additional $50. It seemed like a lot of money at that time, but only because I did not realize what I was doing. I did not know what it meant to land at a European seaport with $58 in my pocket, then travel through foreign countries on my own for two weeks. Nor did I realize that carrying two large suitcases without wheels through all these ports and stations would be a Herculean task.

All that ignorance and naivety aside, my immediate challenge was to resign from my job. Quitting a position at the Reserve Bank turned out to be much more daunting than I had expected. In fact, in India a permanent position at a government-owned institution was so difficult to obtain that no one before me had ever contemplated leaving. The bank's administrative officer, Sudhir Dhotiwala, assumed that my resignation letter was a practical joke and decided to reprimand me for it. At 350 pounds, Dhotiwala carried a lot of weight—both literally and figuratively—and he behaved as if he virtually owned the bank. When he discovered that I was indeed serious, he tried to save me from my *foolish* action by offering to grant me a leave of absence without pay for two years. And when I refused even that, he used his full power of persuasion to sweeten the pot with a counter offer: the bank was willing to grant me a two-year leave *with pay*, holding my accumulated salary in an escrow account that would be released to me on my return.

I was severely tempted to accept the bank's unprecedented offer. On reflection, however, I decided that in order to succeed in the US, I would need to burn my bridges behind me. So with guarded confidence, I declined the bank's final offer and resigned.

When the news got out, I was universally branded as a crackpot, and no one even thought of arranging a going-away party for me. My colleagues assumed with relief that at the close of business on June 30, I would quietly disappear into thin air.

As usual, when I arrived at the office on that day, Superintendent Gogte gave me a whole bunch of work to do, telling me he expected me to finish my assignment before leaving for the day. The assignment turned out to be far more time consuming than I had anticipated. I suspected that Gogte had feelings of envy when he assigned me this task, but I chose to ignore that. I was still working at 5:30 pm, when everyone started to leave. Gogte waited a bit but when he saw that I would not be done for a while, he left the office. He directed me to place the files on the master shelf of the filing cabinet when I finished and to lock the cabinet before going home. He never even said goodbye.

It was almost 6:15 pm when I finished. Everyone had gone home, and the large office looked like a ghost town. I got up, placed my files in the filing cabinet, and locked it, as instructed. But when I turned around, I was shocked to see a beautiful young lady wearing a colorful sari standing behind my desk, holding a little box. I recognized the woman, whose unusually long braided hair virtually kissed the floor, as a research assistant in our department. But because she worked under a different supervisor, I had never spoken to her directly. And on this last day of my job, and at this late hour when everyone had already left the cavernous office, this young lady was waiting for me—and that made me nervous.

"I am Malti Khade," she whispered sheepishly.

"Yes, I have seen you in this office before," I mumbled uneasily, still standing by the filing cabinet.

"Mittra," Malti said apologetically, "we all know it is your last day at the bank, and I am sorry we didn't arrange a farewell party for you."

"I appreciate your thoughtfulness," I said, beginning to relax a little.

"While I couldn't arrange a farewell party for you, I did bring a gift. It is something small, and I hope you won't be offended by accepting it from me." Before I could respond, she continued, "It is a donkey carrying a load on its back. The space for the load can be used as a pincushion. This gift signifies that in life, a person may have to carry a heavy burden, and society may inflict pain and suffering on him. But if he continues his journey despite his difficulties and sufferings, ultimately he will succeed."

I was stupefied. Then she stepped forward and handed over the gift.

"I hope that you will carry my gift to America," she said, "and that someday you will remember me as a friend who wished you great success in life."

With that, Malti turned around and left the room. Utterly baffled, I whispered, "Thank you," but even I could not hear my own voice.

I had never dreamed of receiving such a thoughtful gift from a colleague—no less from a girl I had never even spoken to. I still have difficulty believing it really happened. Over the past six decades since then, I have traveled through many continents. I have changed homes numerous times, yet this priceless gift still sits on my desk, reminding me that success will come to me if I continue to step up to life's challenges.

∽

I was soon ready to leave with all the proper paperwork in hand. When I was saying my goodbyes to all of my friends in Bombay, I wanted to bid goodbye to Bani Sarkar as well. But I realized that to do that, because she did not have a phone, I'd have to go to her home uninvited, which I did not have the courage to do. Disappointed, I dropped that idea.

During the last week of July, I left Bombay for Calcutta, where I expected to board the ship to Marseilles. But once in Calcutta, I learned that without informing the passengers, the shipping company had changed the departure port from Calcutta to Bombay and had rescheduled the departure for August 10.

I had just traveled 48 hours by train from Bombay to Calcutta; now I would have to travel for another 48 hours to return to the place where I'd started. Not only would I have to bear the additional cost of returning to Bombay, but since I had already moved out of my apartment, I'd also have to pay for a hotel room until the ship sailed. I found this unexpected change of venue and added expenses most annoying, but one silver lining did exist. With this fortuitous change of plans, I felt I could muster sufficient courage to visit Bani and say goodbye.

My visit to Bani's home turned out to be far more pleasant than I had anticipated. I found her parents to be very cordial. I was astonished when they excused themselves for a while so that Bani and I could share a few moments alone. Those were the most precious moments of my long stay in Bombay. When the time finally came for me to leave, defying all established social practices, and to my utter surprise, Bani suddenly whispered, "Will you remember to inform me of your safe arrival once you reach America?"

To say that I was startled by her bold request would be a gross understatement. But before I had time to formulate a proper response, I blurted out: "Yes, but only if I find a letter from you waiting for me when I arrive in Gainesville."

Predictably, Bani's response was silence.

And so I finally sailed from the Bombay pier on August 10, 1957. At that time, none of my family members was living there, nor was it practical for them to make a trip to Bombay merely to see me off. However, to my pleasant surprise, Bani's father came to the port with his son to bid me goodbye. I wondered why her father, who was unrelated to me and whom I had met only once before, had taken the trouble of making this trip to the pier. I also wondered why, if he somehow sensed that I had developed some feelings for Bani, he didn't bring her along to see me off. While I couldn't ask him, still I wished Bani had come, too, so I could see her shy but smiling face one last time before I set sail into the unknown.

The boat trip from Bombay to Marseilles turned out to be much less daunting than I had feared. First, I found that by happy circumstance, a relative of mine named Ashok Ghosh was traveling on the same boat. He was bound for the University of Illinois in Urbana to work toward a PhD in Agriculture. And second, I learned that my fellow fourth-class passengers and I did not have to stay in our quarters, along with the prisoners, other than for sleeping. I could go anywhere third-class passengers could, and could eat with them in the dining hall.

Even so, meals were not a high point. I was used to home cooking. Meat and vegetables were either fried or mixed with Indian spices and served with rice and an unleavened flatbread called chapattis. But the food served on the ship was mostly green salad, roast beef or broiled chicken, boiled potatoes, peas, and carrots (all without spices), dry bread, and cake or pastry. Passengers invariably sprinkled salt and pepper on their food—a practice foreign to

Indian culinary practices. Neither could I understand why so many different types of bread and cheese were served. They were all revolting. But I ate them all, knowing full well that was all I was getting. Even the Western-style breakfast cereals, toast, muffins, and doughnuts were abhorrent. The typical morning meal I was used to consisted of *puri* and *bhaji* (Indian bread and fried vegetables).

On top of all these food trials, I had trouble adjusting to dinner served at 5 pm. I found I was not at all hungry then, but was ravenous by 9 pm, the time I was used to eating dinner. If I wanted to eat then, I had to pay extra for a sandwich. That was impossible considering that the $58 I hoarded was untouchable while I was on the ship. So I ate dinner with everyone else and learned to suppress my late-evening hunger pangs until the next morning.

One evening after dinner as I came up to the upper deck to watch the sunset, I felt a tap on my shoulder. Ashok, looking stern, said that it was his unfortunate duty to tell me that I was disturbing the others at the dinner table. I, who had always taken pride in myself as being friendly and kind, could not imagine what I had done to cause offense. I assumed it must be a language barrier issue, and I asked Ashok to tell what was objectionable.

"It has nothing to do with anything you said," he explained, but rather with your behavior. When dinner is served, you start grabbing more than your share, leaving less food for the rest of us. Everyone thinks that throughout your life you must have practically starved to death, and this is the first chance you are getting to eat a healthy meal. Since I know that is not true, I am puzzled and upset by your rude behavior.

I was aghast. Only then did I realize my meal mates were not that far wrong about why I acted so rudely. I had to admit to Ashok that every evening when I sat down at the dinner table, I was fearful of how hungry I would be for the rest of the night. Without realizing that I was doing it, I took more than my share. This incident, though embarrassing, was also enlightening. I promised him I would cease. I did.

Our first and only stop en route to Marseilles was at the African port of Djibouti. I watched with interest the way the natives performed various chores at the port. While our ship was docked, a merchant standing on the pier sold a passenger named A. Raman a couple of Arrow shirts for a throwaway price of $5 each. Once the bargain was struck, the merchant put the shirts into a bag and threw it onto the deck. Raman picked up the bag and then threw a pouch with the money back to the merchant, completing the sale.

Later that evening, when everyone gathered in the dining room, we asked Raman to show us his new Arrow shirts. Hesitant at first, he finally obliged sheepishly. When Raman opened the package, we discovered that it contained only the front of the shirt—the part that was visible through the package window. The rest of the package was empty, and Raman had been cheated. We all felt sorry for our fellow traveler. I was aware of similar scams prevailing in some parts of India, but I never knew that merchants in other countries also used such shady business practices. I realized that I had a lot to learn about the world beyond India. I was happy that I hadn't had the money to buy such a shirt, even at a throwaway price.

This was a once-in-a-lifetime journey. I wanted to share my travel experiences with my family so I brought on board a thick, leather-bound notebook and a red pen to write about my strange and funny experiences. Each afternoon I would sit on the deck facing the ocean and write about everything that had happened to me the previous day. One day, as I was writing, a distinguished-looking Indian man, who appeared to be in his mid-60s, startled me by sitting down beside me without forewarning. Impeccably dressed in a blue suit and tie, the man did not look like anyone I had expected to meet on this ship.

"Hello. I am Shambhu Verma, and I'm sorry if I disturbed you," he said before I had a chance to say anything at all.

"Hello," I answered, intrigued. "I am glad you came to talk to me. I am S. Mittra, and I am going to Florida."

Looking puzzled, Verma blurted out, "I have been watching you write for some days from my executive suite on the upper deck. I thought you were a writer traveling to France on assignment. But if you are bound for Florida, then why are you traveling on this ship going to Marseilles?"

"My writing is an attempt to share the trip's experiences with my family—left behind and already missed," I explained. Still finding him puzzled, I outlined my intended itinerary, glorifying it a little by describing it as my desire to have a variety of travel experiences. My companion agreed that my plan was certainly unique. Still, as 40 years earlier he had been a student headed for London and was now a successful businessman, he asked if I needed some advice. "How could I be so lucky to be offered advice from a successful businessman and an accomplished traveler?" I wondered.

I told him that my biggest concern was how I would manage my two suitcases from the dock in Marseilles until the end of my trip. He was certain that just carrying my small suitcase would be onerous enough. He predicted that I would likely be forced to abandon the larger one when it became too bulky to carry. Sagely, he suggested I send the heavier suitcase by ocean freight from Marseilles to Gainesville. I told him that was an excellent solution, but that I could not afford it.

Verma knew all about the dollar problem for Indian travelers, so he magnanimously offered to pay for shipping my heavy suitcase to Gainesville. He made it clear, however, this was not a free offer. As repayment for his kindness, he expected me to be generous to others in the future.

"Someday I'd like you to find a way to help someone who desperately needs help, as you do today," he exhorted with a wink. I thanked him profusely and promised to do that.

From the time I set my foot on our French ship, I made every effort to stay away from the Cambodian prisoners. True, I had to sleep in my fourth-class berth every night. But I sprinted out of that area first thing every morning and did not return until I was ready to fall asleep at night.

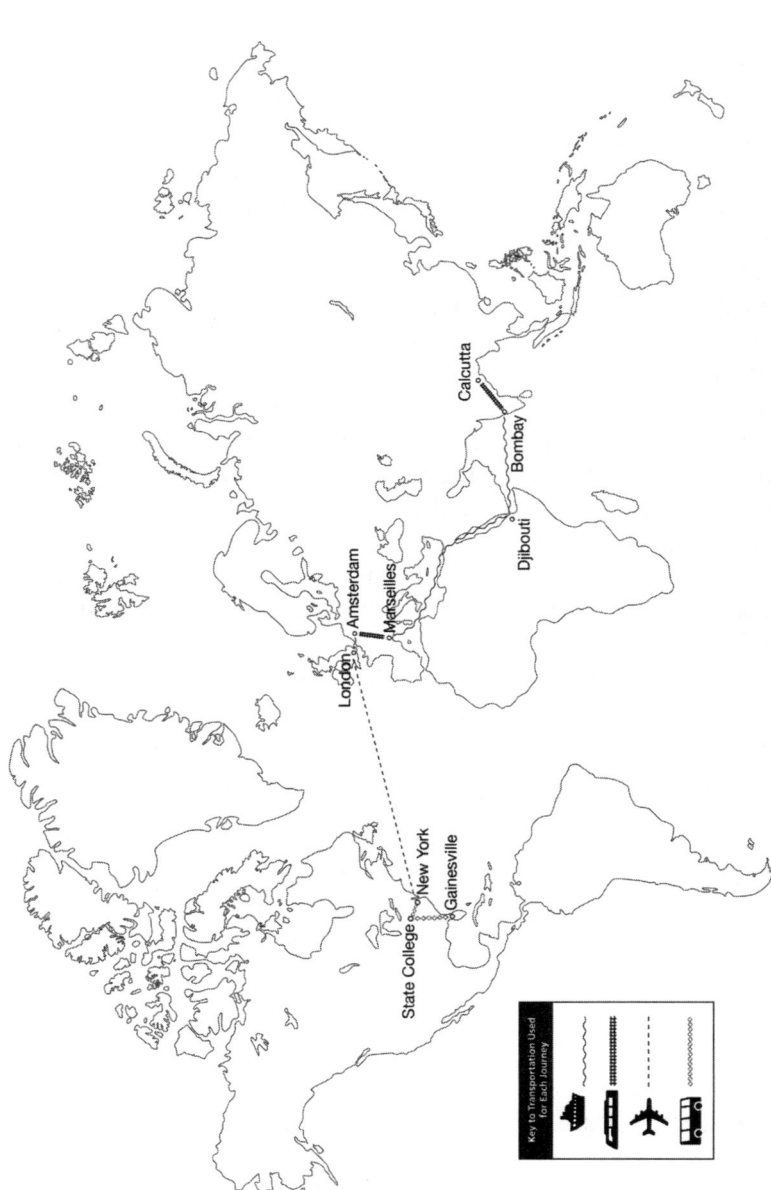

En route my incredible journey to the US. All I had was $58 and a dream
Source: Author.

Curiosity eventually got the better of me, and one day I decided to peek into the prisoners' living quarters. I presumed they were in chains and, therefore, could not harm me, but I also did not expect to be able to talk to them since they spoke a foreign language. When nobody seemed to be around, I snuck past my room and approached the door that led to the prisoners' quarters. As soon as I put my hand on the door handle, my heart started pounding so hard that I thought it would burst. As I turned the handle and peeked through the slit, I saw about a hundred Cambodian prisoners freely roaming about inside a large room with iron bars on the windows. They were not chained, and their movement was not restricted. Neither did they seem to be angry, uptight, or belligerent. Instead, they looked friendly and appeared to be having a good time—in fact, they reminded me in their demeanor of the Indian political prisoners I'd seen in Agra years ago.

Slowly, I got used to the environment on the ship. I spent the rest of the voyage relaxing, exercising, watching the sunrise and the sunset, eating politely, and writing about my experiences. I hardly made any new friends and was mostly stuck to myself. And all too quickly, we arrived at Marseilles.

The port was even more confusing than I had feared. Once the ship docked, we disembarked and went through immigration. Then, we were told to find our baggage, match our ticket numbers to our bags, clear customs, and move on. The baggage area looked as if it had been hit by a tornado, with suitcases thrown in every direction. The only way to locate my luggage was to examine each bag; it took two hours to find my two suitcases. They had been thrown haphazardly into two different piles far apart from each other.

Fortunately, Verma had not forgotten me. When I cleared customs, he was waiting for me, and he directed a porter to haul away my heavier suitcase. Moreover, he delivered me and my small suitcase by cab to the Marseilles train station and even paid for the ride. The man was a godsend. Unfortunately, overseas travel being new to me, I was not as organized as I should have been; at some point I lost the address he gave me before I thanked him profusely for his generosity and bid him fond farewell.

I then used my three-hour wait for the train to figure out how to buy food cheaply in France and in other countries in Europe.

At the train station, menu prices were posted outside the restaurants, so I knew eating there would be too pricey. As I wandered about the station wondering how I was going to survive, I came upon a kind of vending machine I had never seen before. I watched carefully how people dropped in coins and then opened a small door to take out the item selected.

I approached one such machine and studied the offerings and prices posted. I settled on a can of a strange-sounding food solely because it cost only one franc, plus a loaf of bread that cost a quarter-franc. Opening the can was a shock. It contained sardines—a bunch of tiny cooked fish floating in olive oil. I will never forget my first taste of those smelly, bitter, salty fish. But they were cheap, and I accepted them as the meal of my choice.

For the next several days until I reached London, I lived on relatively inexpensive canned food—most of it sardines and bread—and tried to limit my meals to two per day. I had to choose between sustenance and nausea. I never did grow to like the taste of sardines, but each night just before sleep, I repeated to myself, "Hello America, here I come." That, even more than the sardines, kept me going.

I luckily found an English-speaking Frenchman who helped me locate my train when it was time to board. The journey through Europe turned out to be very enjoyable, and I found European trains spotless and relatively uncrowded. I was delighted to notice that, unlike the situation on Indian trains, every passenger was assigned a seat. No one was standing in the aisles clutching the ceiling bar.

Throughout the journey, I sat next to a large window and admired an ever-changing, breathtaking view of green meadows, rolling mountains, flowing rivers, waterfalls, and floating clouds in a blue sky. Even though I had visited several popular scenic areas in India before, in reality, they were not all that scenic. Those sites were generally in disrepair, unclean, and sometimes strewn with litter and garbage. So the pristine, natural environment I witnessed on the train in Europe reinforced my naïve belief in the superiority of white people. I was, after all, a citizen of a very recent former British colony.

At the French border, several passengers disembarked and new ones entered our compartment. Soon after the train resumed its journey, a new passenger sitting across from me, whom I initially thought was British, smiled at me and asked, "Hello! Are you from India?"

"Yes, I am," I answered quickly. The stranger's accent definitely wasn't British, but I couldn't tell where he was from.

"My name is Rick Davis," he said next. "I am from Boston, the eastern part of America. I was in Calcutta during World War II. Unfortunately, we were pretty much confined to army barracks and I didn't get to see your country. I'm sure it is very beautiful."

I nodded my head.

"And what are you doing in Europe?" Rick asked.

"I'm on my way to the University of Florida in Gainesville."

"You don't say!" he replied with surprise. "I myself graduated from Florida State University in Tallahassee, which is not too far from where you are going. What a small world! Florida has a beautiful campus," he concluded, "and I'm sure you'll fall in love with it. Good luck to you."

All this happened so suddenly that for a little while I did not comprehend what was going on. But later, I realized that I was beginning to feel comfortable talking to a white man without feeling inferior.

My excitement grew as the train carried me closer to Amsterdam, where I would hop a ferry to England. I would soon set foot on British soil and visit London itself—it was nearly like arriving at the gates of heaven. Although most Indians who traveled to England back then harbored similar feelings, I can say looking back now that such an attitude is a sad commentary on the submissiveness of people who had been colonized and controlled by Great Britain for around 200 years. Politically, I was a citizen of a free country, but psychologically I was still a slave—a delusion I would still operate under for years.

I suppose the process of breaking free started the moment I arrived in London. I had longed to get to England so that I could speak in English to everyone around me. And people in London did speak English, but to my chagrin, I had difficulty understanding what they said. To make matters worse, they could not understand me, either. The communication gap was never more obvious than when I asked a policeman for help in what I thought was good English. He gave me a puzzled look and countered, "Do you speak English?"

Despite my language problem, I was able to track down a long-time Indian friend named Subir, whom I had helped get established in Bombay. He was now working in London. In return for that favor, he put me up in an inexpensive YMCA, generously paying my room and board for my three-day stay so that I could conserve my dwindling American dollars. After I told him of how I lived on sardines and bread, my friend was so touched that he took me to a famous Indian restaurant in central London then-named the Bombay Grill. He treated me to a gourmet Indian dinner.

Aaaah ... the sweet aroma and the spicy tastes of tandoori chicken, basmati rice, *ratankorma* (a spicy meat dish), *aloogobee* (cauliflower and potato), chutney, *rasgolla* (a cheese-based, syrupy dessert), and Darjeeling tea. Indian food in England was just like the food at home. Full to the brim, I thanked him for his generosity, and we agreed to keep in touch.

Subir also bought me a three-day transportation pass for unlimited travel within London. I then spent most of my time there navigating the subway trains; sightseeing at landmarks such as Buckingham Palace, the British Parliament, Trafalgar Square, Big Ben, Westminster Abbey, and the London Bridge; writing in my journal about my experiences; and just resting.

My three days passed faster than I had expected. Finally, the memorable moment arrived when I could board a plane bound for the US, the country I had been dreaming about for so long. I was 27 years old and had never been on a domestic plane before, let alone on an international flight crossing the ocean. The excitement of flying on a Pan Am Boeing 707—the largest and fastest plane then in existence—was overwhelming.

I was so eager not to miss my flight that I left the YMCA in central London for Heathrow Airport in the morning, even though my flight was not scheduled to take off until 5 pm. London's excellent public transportation system delivered me to the airport quickly. After checking in my suitcase and passing through immigration, I waited in the departure lounge for several hours before boarding the plane. I spent some of that time worrying about my baggage and kept asking myself, "What if someone forgets to load my suitcase on the plane?" But my fears were replaced by excitement when I was assigned a window seat. I would be able to capture every thrill of takeoff—from taxiing down the runway to viewing London from above.

I was indeed mesmerized by the sight of the whole city glittering with lights. Buildings, monuments, and cars shrank as the plane continued to climb higher and higher. And when the pilot announced that we had reached the cruising altitude of 37,000 feet and should expect a smooth ride, I had to ask myself, "What did I do to deserve this rare privilege at such a young age?"

I suppose my euphoria went to my head. When the hostess came around to take orders for drinks, I decided to have one. I had grown up believing that only the British and Indian people of bad character drank alcoholic beverages. I did not have the slightest idea how alcohol tasted or what it did to a person physically. But I had left India and I was flying to the US. The thought of being able to order a drink like a Britisher thrilled me.

My first hurdle in this novel undertaking was to decide what to order. I did not know the names of any drinks. So when the hostess asked what I would like, I was stumped. I asked what she would recommend. She suggested since dinner would be served shortly, a Martini on the rocks or a Bloody Mary might be appropriate. I did not like the sound of the second choice, so I told her I would have the martini. When the hostess brought my drink, I took a deep breath, held it, and took a big swallow. That first gulp—which was thankfully also the last—convinced me that a martini on the rocks could be employed to put convicts to death. My esophagus burned for hours.

My failed attempt to be urbane was further underscored when the hostess returned to collect $3 for my drink. I had not paid attention when the cost of the drink was announced, so not only had I nearly poisoned myself, but I had also inadvertently spent a whopping $3 to do it. I couldn't help but recall that the same amount of money could have bought four cans of sardines and four loaves of bread in France, sufficient to cover all my meals for two days!

The same hostess soon returned to serve a full dinner—roasted chicken, salad, boiled cabbage, peas, mashed potatoes, a dinner roll, chocolate cake, and a soft drink. The sight of the dinner made me shudder, and too afraid to ask, I wondered to myself, "If a single drink costs $3, how much is this elaborate dinner going to cost?" To my delight, I learned that my meal was free and that airlines charged only for the poisonous drinks. Although this dinner was no match for the superb Indian meal I had in London, it tasted far better than the sardines and dry bread I had in Europe.

And then the moment I had been waiting for—we landed in New York City! I was finally in the US, although before I could be formally admitted into the country, I had to pass immigration. Like all students arriving in the US to pursue higher studies, I was carrying with me a large sealed envelope containing my chest X-ray from India and a report on my physical condition produced by a US-appointed physician in Bombay.

I had been informed that an immigration officer would open the envelope behind closed doors and examine the reports. My chest X-ray must not show signs of tuberculosis or another contagious disease. The medical report had to certify that I was physically capable of carrying out higher studies in an American university. If the immigration officer decided that I was a potential health risk, he could pack me right back to India. I could do or say nothing to stop him.

I had traveled all this way not knowing what the doctor in Bombay had diagnosed. While I was waiting for the officer to approve or deny my entry, I suddenly remembered that years ago I had exposed myself to tuberculosis when I visited my sick friend Hari. "Could my medical report somehow show evidence of such exposure?" I wondered. I started sweating.

Fortunately, my medical report did pass muster. I was officially granted entry. Just to make sure that I was not dreaming, after I passed through immigration, I opened my passport and noted with great delight and relief the bold US Immigration stamp, which read, "Admitted, United States of America: August 29, 1957." I paused for a moment to look at my watch, which read 7:33 pm. I took a deep breath. I had arrived in America, the land of opportunity. Surely, now my problems were finally over.

Well, not exactly.

After clearing customs, my next step was to find my way from the airport to the small university town of State College, Pennsylvania, where Raj lived. The airport, as seen through my jetlagged eyes, was just a large room with lots of booths and confusing signs. I could see nothing that would have suggested where I could find a bus. I decided to approach a uniformed officer for help. I told him that I had to catch a bus to State College, and that I did not have much money. The man turned out to be an airport porter instead of a policeman. He tried to explain to me that his job was to follow the orders of passengers about where to deliver their bags, not to direct them through New York City's transit system. I barely understood what he said.

Exasperated, he finally quit trying to convince me. Giving me a look of hopelessness, he picked up my bag and carried it to the city bus that would take me to the Greyhound bus station. He did not even charge me for providing that service. And, to top it all off, he talked the bus driver into allowing me to carry my suitcase on the bus by pleading my case that I had no money to hire a cab. Unfortunately, I did not even tip him because I had no knowledge of the tipping customs in America. But I thanked him for his generosity. I learned that apparently there are many angels waiting to aid lost souls like me.

The city bus took me to the Greyhound station, where I boarded another bus for a 250-mile journey to State College. Although I looked forward to enjoying every moment of the ride, my exhaustion from the international flight followed by the hassle in the airport overcame me, and I soon dozed off without waking until we were practically there.

My three-day stay with Raj was bliss. I enjoyed a separate guest room with all the modern comforts. I ate whenever and whatever I wanted. I spent hours in shopping malls, looking at spectacular exhibits of clothing, electronic equipment, and other consumer goods, and beautiful girls in various states of undress. And I watched many programs on TV, all of which I found intriguing. I especially enjoyed watching the wrestling matches. They reminded me of the neighborhood matches I used to attend when I lived in Agra. I looked for soccer matches but was disappointed when I couldn't find anything that even remotely looked like soccer.

One evening during my stay, Raj and I were invited to dinner at the home of his colleague, Professor Bill O'Conner, and his charming wife Dorothy. Taking great interest in my travel experiences, the O'Conners were surprised to hear that I had managed to travel such a long distance with only $58 in my pocket and no prior experience as a foreign traveler.

During the course of the conversation, Dorothy remarked that I had good command of English and that she found my British accent *cute*. Then, as if to test my understanding of the language, she said, "Sid, don't you think Bill should buy me a girdle for Christmas?" Clearly, it was meant to be a joke, and I am sure she expected me to say, "Of course, not." But I had no idea what a girdle was, and I was too embarrassed to ask. However, since Dorothy spoke of it as a Christmas gift, I assumed that a girdle was some kind of ornament that would look good on an attractive lady like Dorothy.

"Dorothy is absolutely right," I told Bill. "Why don't you buy a girdle for her as a Christmas gift?" A stunned silence followed, which conveyed more than I cared to know. I recognized instantly that I had failed the test and decided to keep my mouth shut in the future whenever someone asked me a question I did not understand.

On my final day with Raj, he took me to the Greyhound bus station and gave me some money to supplement my nearly exhausted personal funds. I boarded the bus for what I assumed would be a relatively quick ride. When in India, I had heard that the US was such a technically advanced and efficient country that everything there worked with lightning speed. I figured that after we left State College, it would take our high-speed bus no more than a few hours to reach Florida. So when I did not see any signs of Gainesville even after six hours, I began to worry about missing my destination.

I finally asked the driver what time we would reach Gainesville. He did a double take. "Mister, take a good look at me," he said. "I am the fastest driver you will meet on this trip. I will be driving this bus all day and all night. I will get off sometime tomorrow morning, and a gorgeous blonde will replace me. She will do the same thing I am doing—drive all day and all night. In the morning after that, a skinny guy will replace her. After driving for several hours, that driver will begin to look tired. That would be the perfect time to ask him how far you are from Gainesville. Think you can do that?" he added sarcastically. Red with embarrassment, I told him I could.

Thanks to Raj's generosity, I had plenty of money with me and could eat anything I wanted when the bus stopped for meal breaks. At the first such stop, determined to carefully avoid sardines and bread, I went to a restaurant I'd never heard of before named McDonald's. The menu was written in a strange way: #1 hamburger; #2 double hamburger; #3 cheeseburger; and so on. I was not familiar with any of these food items, so not knowing what else to do, I ordered a #1 hamburger—without realizing that it contained beef, which Hindus don't touch. I had never in my life had beef in India, but I must say I definitely liked the taste of it.

After that, I found the same restaurant near every bus station, and I ordered the same #1 hamburger over and over again. Finally, somewhere in Georgia, I felt I needed to change my order because I was getting tired of hamburgers. After much forethought, I ordered a #3 cheeseburger. To my great surprise, it turned out to be the same hamburger with a piece of cheese added, which I enjoyed even more.

Three days after I boarded the bus, I arrived in Gainesville to find that my suitcase, which I shipped from State College, had not arrived yet. I had to concede that the US still had a few bugs to work out in the long-distance bus department. I was agitated because the bag contained all my clothes and toiletries. Fortunately, Ivan Putman, the University's foreign student advisor, had sent an Indian graduate student named Partha Sarathi to receive me at the bus station. He promised to take care of my immediate needs as well as the baggage, whenever it arrived. I also stayed with him that first night.

After I'd had a good night's sleep, Partha dropped me off at the Student Center to attend to the administrative details of getting settled in my new home. I received my post office box key but wasn't expecting to find anything in my box quite this early. I tried unlocking the box just to see how it worked, and my spirits soared when I found an aerogram waiting for me from Bani. I recalled that in bidding her goodbye in Bombay, I promised to acknowledge my arrival in Gainesville only if I found a letter from her waiting for me when I got here. I meant that as a joke, of course, and I never expected her to take me seriously. But after I picked up Bani's letter, I stood there, holding the unsealed letter in my hand. I wondered not so much about what she might have written in that letter, but rather what she *really* meant by sending it to me.

Epilogue: Life's Lessons

I discover that flying from Bombay to Gainesville is prohibitively expensive, and ultimately settle on a patchwork plan that requires traveling fourth class (with prisoners) by ship to Marseille, by train to Amsterdam, by ferry boat to London, by plane to New York, and finally by Greyhound bus to Gainesville. Next, I learn that due to various regulations, I can carry only $8 with me but manage to get permission to take an additional $50. Before leaving India, I get a chance to visit Bani, an enchanting girl I met in Bombay several years ago and can't forget. Because of Bani's shyness, I hardly get to know her before leaving for America, but we agree to stay in touch.

I set sail and am chastised for atrocious table manners by a fellow cruise passenger, befriend an Indian man who becomes a logistical guardian angel, fight the language barrier, live on sardines and bread, and bumble through learning how to travel in a foreign land while being constantly reminded of my fast-dwindling dollar reserves. Eventually, I arrive in Gainesville, feeling every bit as disoriented as Alice when she went through the looking glass. And there waiting for me is a letter from Bani.

The following Four Ps list identifies the P(s) that I have covered in this chapter:

[X]   Persevere with passion.
[X]   Pursue professional, family-oriented, social, and spiritual goals.
[X]   Persuade family and friends to help.
[   ]   Promote a culture of giving back.

9

HAVE GUN, WILL TRAVEL

Nothing is impossible, the word itself says "I'm possible!"
—AUDREY HEPBURN

In addition to my post office-box key, I also picked up my student ID, my dorm room key, and a campus map. The staff at the Student Center gave me a briefing on how to find my way around, and then I headed for my dorm. The map and the personal briefing helped some, but I still kept getting lost in this huge campus. The buildings weren't numbered and I found their names confusing. After running around for 30 minutes or so and asking scores of people for help, with great relief, I found Murphree Hall.

Exhausted, I climbed the stairs to the second floor and headed for room number 13. I found the door wide open, with loud music, which I later learnt was called rock 'n' roll, blaring. In the middle of the room, a tall, skinny, bare-chested American boy in shorts was wildly dancing to a song called "That'll Be the Day" by the Crickets. He was having a fabulous time. I assumed this was my new roommate, Marshall Jackson.

I had barely entered the room when Marshall glanced at me and called out, "How the f—are you?"

I froze in my tracks, stupefied. I had never heard such foul language before, and from a total stranger no less. Struggling to

recover from the shock, I answered meekly, "I am Sid Mittra."
Marshall laughed hysterically.

"I know who the f— you are," he yelled in response. "Now tell
me how the hell are you?" I soon learned that Marshall (a fresh-
man from Palm Beach) had never been exposed to a foreign
student—either from India or from anywhere else. So it wasn't
surprising that he assumed I was from an Indian reservation in
New Mexico or Arizona. Our unlikely pairing was the result of a
university policy that placed all foreign students with American
roommates to expose us to the American culture.

My relationship with Marshall progressively soured. I was
bothered by his constant use of foul language as well as his habit
of continuously playing loud music. Since he refused to change
his habits, I tolerated them but I never got used to them.

I wasn't exactly crazy about my other dorm mates either. They
were known for playing tricks on the foreign students just for
kicks. Although these tricks may have amused the Americans,
they sometimes seemed outlandishly cruel. The most distasteful
incident occurred when an American student had learned that
after taking a shower, if a Muslim man came across a naked man,
then his religious beliefs compelled him to take another.

We had a Muslim student from Pakistan named Amir Khan
living in our dorm. A group of American students made it a practice to stand naked in front of Amir's room when he was in the
shower. As soon as Amir returned to his room, he would see naked
students standing there and would feel compelled to march right
back to the bathroom.

I privately sympathized with Amir and felt that either he or I
should report this incident to the authorities. However, since we
were new to this country and could not predict the consequences,
neither of us felt comfortable doing anything about it. Fortunately,
after a while, the American jokesters decided the prank had
become boring and so quit it.

My academic life held challenges as well. Prior to attending my
first graduate class, I met Dr Clem Donovan, chairman of the
Economics Department. Dr Donovan was a full 6'4" with a towering

personality. A New Yorker who had settled in Florida, he spoke so fast and with such an unfamiliar accent that I could understand only every other word he said (not counting the strange sounds he made, such as *um*, *er*, and *wull*). After some time, I finally deciphered his speech and understood his point—that the continuation of my graduate fellowship would depend on getting high grades.

That the school paying my way should expect me to earn high grades was logical, but I wondered, "Could I deliver?" After all, my master's degree was in business administration, and I was now in a PhD program in economics. In India, I had taken only one course in economics. That course was merely a review of the outdated Indian economic system. It did not deal with modern economic theory or policy. My business administration degree had not required or expected me to take any math courses. And the statistics course I took was too rudimentary to be of much value. In contrast, all the American graduate students had as undergrads completed courses in economic theory, marketing, theory of finance, advanced statistics, calculus, business management, quantitative analysis, business psychology, decision sciences, and business development.

It got worse. Under the Indian system I was used to, each course had only one exam, a final exam made up of only essay questions. To my dismay, I had learned that in the US, professors often gave quizzes, a mid-term, and a final exam (which usually consisted of multiple-choice questions), and that grades also depended on our class participation, term papers, special make-ups, and oral exams. Had I realized how daunting the task would be, I would have quit then and returned home. However, here was a case when ignorance was bliss.

Considering the make-up studies I needed, I thought I would be lucky to get a C in any of my graduate courses, at least during the first semester. But as Dr Donovan made it clear, that was not an option. And by resigning from the Reserve Bank, I burned my bridges.

My first testing hurdle was passing the Graduate Record Exam (GRE): it was a prerequisite to enter the University's graduate program. But as I was from a country that did not administer the exam, the University had permitted me to take it after my arrival.

The experience was a total disaster. When the professor conducting the exam handed me the test, I failed to recognize that all the questions were multiple-choice—a system I had never even heard of. In my naïveté, I assumed that the professor would also provide me with a notebook for answering the questions in essay form as I expected, but I was nervous and did not bother to ask the proctor why I was not getting the notebook. Not surprisingly, it never arrived. When time was up, I had little choice but to turn in a blank multiple-choice answer sheet with predictable results.

I had no one to blame but myself, since I should have become familiar with the American educational system *before* coming to this country. Luckily, recognizing what happened, the dean of the graduate school graciously allowed me to retake the exam at the end of my first semester. So in January 1958, I received an 85 percent in my GRE, not quite *first division*, but a good grade.

During my first semester, I took four courses. I selected Accounting Theory, and Money and Banking. I thought they would be the most familiar, considering my background and training. I also selected Economic History and Development of Economic Thought.

I knew I would have to get up to speed in economics and math, the two areas in which I had no background. I did so by studying an introductory economics text on my own and auditing a basic algebra course. I had no idea how I would do with such a study load. Still I knew that I would have to get by on no more than five hours of sleep a night. That was a practice I had perfected in Kanpur when I was working toward my master's degree, riding my triangular bicycle route every day.

The professor of my Development of Economic Thought course, Dr Webb, was a gentle, soft-spoken old man. He began the first day by saying, "In this class we are going to have intense discussions on advanced macroeconomic theory. So I need to ask if everyone in this course has a good knowledge of John Maynard Keynes' General Theory of Employment, Interest and Money."

John Maynard Keynes? I had never heard of either him or his book but because all the other students raised their hands, I did too. I justified this white lie with a secret pledge to acquire a copy of Keynes' book the same day. I figured I could breeze through the book's highlights in time for our next class.

I did start on Keynes' General Theory that evening. But after toiling for five hours, I had merely finished the preface and two pages of the first chapter. So I started studying a simplified book on Keynes by Professor Alvin Hanson. I kept studying the subject throughout the semester, and eventually I developed a passable knowledge in advanced macroeconomic theory. When I ended up with an A in the class, I assumed my professor had given me a break by grading my exam generously. Long live beginner's luck!

Unfortunately, I was not as successful in the Money and Banking course, even though I chose it believing it would be easier than other courses. My confidence was misplaced because my experience at the Reserve Bank of India did not help much. For one thing, the Reserve Bank operated as a branch of the Indian government, while the US had 12 Federal Reserve Banks, all of which operated as independent institutions. Patterned after the British banking system, India's Reserve Bank controlled a small number of very large banks, while the US had thousands of national banks. The two systems shared little in common.

My greatest difficulty in handling the course had to do with currency. I was familiar only with Indian measures of *lakhs* (100,000) and *crores* (10 million) of rupees, and it took me a long time to become comfortable referring to hundred thousands, millions, and billions of dollars. (It was a good thing that in those days, no one talked about trillions!)

Despite these differences, I thought I was doing well in my Money and Banking course until I received a B in my mid-term exam. I was disappointed. I complained to my professor that he misled me. Professor Charles Matthews was a Korean War veteran who still wore his hair in an army-style crew cut. He was proud of his honesty, integrity, and fairness. Upon hearing my complaint, he balked.

"Mr Mittra, that is a serious allegation. What makes you complain that *I* misled you?"

"The mid-term exam was very hard," I replied, "but you promised it would be easy."

"Why would I make such a preposterous promise?" he demanded, thunderstruck.

"Last week I came to your office to get advice on how to prepare for the mid-term exam. At the end of our conversation you said to me, 'Take it easy.' Didn't you mean to say that the exam was going to be easy?" I asked more than half-defensively.

Professor Matthews burst out laughing. After he had regained his composure, he apologized for the misunderstanding and offered to help me. He did. But I still wound up getting a B in that course.

I found the B that I received in my Accounting Theory class much harder to swallow, however. I deliberately selected that course because I had a solid background in accounting and was convinced that I would get an A. And after comparing my work with that of other students who received As, I concluded that I, too, should have received the same grade. But I did not dispute the grade with my professor, a New Yorker named Scott Lanham, who had an air of arrogance about him.

Among my challenges with that course was that Dr Lanham required us to submit a typewritten term paper, although I had never used a typewriter before. I'd hired a professional typist to type my master's thesis in India. That was a luxury I could not afford now. So during the Christmas holidays, I spent $10 on a used typewriter (the keys of which constantly got stuck) and bought a book called *Typing Made Easy* for 50 cents. I did not enjoy spending the holiday break learning how to type, and I consoled myself that I did not celebrate Christmas.

When Dr Donovan first told me that I was expected to receive high grades in all of my courses, I assumed that I had to earn all As, and that an occasional B would merely be tolerated. So when I received two Bs in the first semester, I got worried. Fearing that I might lose my fellowship, I went to see him. Dr Donovan was sympathetic and assured me that the fellowship would continue through the winter semester. But he also encouraged me to work harder so that I could earn all As in the winter semester.

I took his advice seriously. After that first semester, I managed to get As in all of the rest of my courses but one—a course in which the professor joked that only God and his mother got As. In time, I was even inducted into the prestigious *Phi Kappa Phi* honors society.

〰

For the most part, during my first year of graduate school I studied hard, slept little, socialized even less, and tolerated Marshall's annoying behavior. What made this strange lifestyle bearable was a steady flow of letters from Bani. In those days, the world had not yet been blessed with laptops and e-mail. Prohibitively expensive overseas phone calls were reserved mostly for the superrich and official use. Besides, Bani's house did not have a phone, so the only method of communication between us was aerogram which took three weeks each way. Because of the time lag, we religiously replied to each other's letters on the day received.

But an established Indian tradition put a damper on how comfortable we felt expressing our true feelings in these letters. Since I hardly knew Bani when I left for the US, we were surprised (and very thankful) that her parents even permitted us to correspond. But her parents still retained the privilege of opening her mail anytime they wished. Mindful of that, we limited our communication to mundane matters. In one of my letters, for instance, I spelled out in gory detail how miserable I felt in my first class in economic history when the professor extensively discussed the work of a nut named John Maynard Keynes, a man whom I had never heard of before but who had achieved international fame.

In response, Bani laid on me an equally depressing episode. "As the time for my graduate Indian music exam approaches," she wrote, "I get the sinking feeling that I may not be able to do well in it. And if I fare poorly, I'm afraid my parents won't allow me to correspond with you anymore."

Our relationship continued to grow in very slow motion. We shared our frustrations and disappointments, occasionally interspersed with good news. Yet strangely enough, despite our exchanges being routine and devoid of any romantic overtones, they helped me pull through

But one day I had a strange conversation with Marshall that really shook me up. Upon finding me engrossed in Bani's latest aerogram, Marshall asked me what I was reading with such intensity. I told him it was from the girl I had left behind in Bombay. That I had a girl back in India was a surprise to him in itself. But when I told him that I could not ask her to marry me until I received my PhD and secured permanent employment in the US, he decided I needed serious, straightforward romantic advice. He then delivered a stern lecture about his ideas on love in the US.

One of Marshall's cardinal rules was that a man in love should never leave his girlfriend out of sight. Anyone foolish enough to do so risked allowing the girl to become attracted to someone else, thus losing her forever. I had obviously broken that rule.

He then showed me a picture of his girlfriend, Glee, an attractive blonde who lived in Palm Beach. Marshall said he was deeply in love with her and wrote to her every day. He showed me how he deliberately put the stamp on the envelope upside down to demonstrate to Glee that he was head-over-heels in love with her. Unfortunately, I couldn't follow that rule either because the aerograms I used to write to Bani already had the stamp printed on them—right side up.

Each night, Glee would phone Marshall to make sure that he was in his dormitory and not out, gallivanting. The dorm had only one phone on each floor, so Marshall would stand in the hallway, waiting so that he could answer it as soon as Glee called. Waiting by the phone was absolutely necessary, he explained next, because that demonstrated to Glee that he could not wait to hear her voice. Once again, according to Marshall's rules, my relationship was doomed because Bani not only did not have a phone, but I also could not afford to make overseas calls to her even if she did.

Having broken all three of Marshall's rules for a successful romance, I became convinced that in order to succeed in my romantic life, I definitely needed to make amends. So despite the perceived risks, I became progressively bolder in expressing my feelings toward

Bani in my letters, although I carefully avoided trespassing on good manners. In return, she opened up *somewhat*, but never sufficiently.

I did, however, manage to convince her to do something that made a huge difference in our relationship. At my request, she had her songs professionally recorded on a reel-to-reel tape (because cassettes were not yet available in India) and mailed it to me—despite the numerous administrative difficulties and enormous financial costs involved. The process took a while, but as soon as the tape arrived, I began listening to Bani's songs every day. This experience truly energized me and brought me much closer to her than would have otherwise been possible.

Toward the end of my first year, Dr Donovan called me to suggest that I come to his office so that he could give me some good news. When I did, he informed me that my fellowship grant had been extended for another year. Then he asked me what my plans were for the summer. Assuming that I was covered by my fellowship, I replied with confidence that I was planning to attend the summer session. That's when he dropped a bombshell.

"Sid, you know your fellowship grant covers only the fall and winter semesters and *not* the summer term," he said. "I'm sure you also know that your student visa does *not* allow you to work outside the campus, and I suspect by now most campus jobs have been filled. So how are you going to pay for the courses and support yourself for the summer?" "What? I don't know anything about that," I blurted out frantically.

"What I am telling you," Donovan said, "is that you might have a serious financial problem this summer. I suggest you immediately contact Dr Putman [the foreign student advisor] to find out if there is anything he can do for you." I left crestfallen, wondering how I would survive. What little savings I had would support me for only about a week. If I could not pay for my dorm and meals, I feared, I would become homeless, revert to eating sardines and dry bread, steal, go begging, or die on the streets.

The next day, I went to see Dr Putman, who said he would do what he could and promised to call in a couple of days—two of the longest days I ever spent. "With great difficulty," he said when he finally called, "I've been able to line up a job for you on campus. But I warn you that it is a terrible job, and you might not find it acceptable."

"Beggars can't be choosers," I responded emphatically. "I have no other choice. I will accept anything, and I mean *absolutely anything*."

"Well then," he said, "the Agricultural Experimentation Station has a job opening. Go and see Director Joseph Beckenbach right away. He has agreed to hire you." I sprinted over to the Agricultural Station and introduced myself to the director. Dr Beckenbach had a stern appearance and a well-pressed suit that made him look more like a company president than a university professor. As soon as I entered his office, he got directly to the point.

"Sid, I am assuming Dr Putman has already explained to you the nature of this job," he said. "So let me dispense with the preliminaries and outline what I expect. You will work seven days a week. Every day, you will report for duty at 5 am. Your day will end at 10 pm, and for obvious reasons, you will not have any meaningful breaks—not even the usual lunch or dinner breaks. We will pay you 50 cents an hour."

I had no idea what the obvious reasons were that would prevent me from getting lunch and dinner breaks, or what this job really entailed. But afraid to sound stupid, I remained silent. No breaks, I thought, would at least save money on food.

"Well then," Dr Beckenbach said. "That just about covers it. If you agree to these conditions, then go to the back room and pick up your gun."

"My gun?" I screamed in my head. "What have I got myself into? What sort of job is this that requires the use of a gun? There is no way I am going to shoot someone with a gun, even if my life depends on it."

Not able to keep silent any longer, I took a deep breath and asked, "Dr Beckenbach, what do you want me do with a gun?" He was almost as surprised by my question as I was, having assumed that Dr Putman had already told me that my job was rodent

control. As it turned out, the Agricultural Station was experimenting with different techniques for growing citrus fruits, but squirrels were eating the fruit, thus ruining their experiments. My job
was to arrive at the station at daybreak and stay until it got dark,
shooting any squirrels that dared to venture in.

However, I had never used a gun and could not imagine even
holding one in my hand. Perhaps, I rationalized, I could coax
myself into just pointing the gun at the squirrels, as long as it
wasn't loaded. With profound reluctance, I accepted.

The job began at the crack of dawn the next morning. Because
I had no breaks, I was cut off from all meals at the university cafeteria. So I decided to bring a generous supply of boiled eggs,
rolls, and butter. The way I saw it, this job would be easy because
I would not have to do much to earn my 50 cents an hour. A week
went by without any bloodshed. At the beginning of the second
week, Dr Beckenbach called me in. I expected accolades because I
diligently reported for duty on time and stayed until 10 pm,
despite missing all the cafeteria meals.

"Sid," he said, looking grim, "I am sorry to say that I have to
replace you." I was petrified.

"Dr Beckenbach," I said, panic-stricken, "I have been here
every day as you had asked me. I don't understand."

"You have not used the gun even once, and the squirrels continue to ruin the citrus fruits. Your job was to scare them away,
and you haven't. I'm sorry, but I have to let you go." It was true
that I had not used the gun, but I *had* tried to scare the squirrels
away by shouting and throwing stones at them. I mistakenly
thought that I had succeeded. But now, I realized that was merely
wishful thinking.

I returned to my dormitory room and burst into tears. "How
was I going to survive now?" I lamented. Right about that time,
Marshall walked in the door.

"That's what I don't like about these goddamn Indians," he
shouted. "They are always crying!" Then he stood directly in front
of me and demanded, "What the hell is your goddamn problem
now?" I explained the entire story, and he burst out laughing.

"S—," he said, grinning. "I can solve your problem in a jiffy. Go
back to the station and tell that jerk that you have just learned

how to shoot a gun and kill those goddamn squirrels. You want your goddamn job back!"

I followed Marshall's advice to the letter, but carefully deleted all of his expletives. His instructions worked, even without the swearing.

After that, every day about 11 am, Marshall would show up at the station, pick up the gun, and in a matter of 15–20 minutes kill a dozen squirrels. He would then line up the dead bodies for Dr Beckenbach to inspect and leave for the day. The gunfire and dead bodies convinced the squirrels' siblings and cousins—as well as the honored director—never to mess with me (or, to be more precise, with my surrogate gunman) again.

At the end of my last day of work at the Agricultural Experiment Station, I returned to the dorm to find a big sign on my desk that Marshall had made just for me. The sign read:

HAVE GUN, WILL TRAVEL
Sid Mittra
The Indian Chief

Despite all his loud music and swearing, Marshall had ended up being a miraculous roommate after all.

Epilogue: Life's Lessons

My immersion in the US culture is both frustrating and comical. I wonder what I've gotten myself into when I meet my roommate, Marshall Jackson, a tall, skinny, crazy-looking, bare-chested, boy dancing wildly to loud music who greets me with a hearty, "How the f— are you?" At the end of my first academic year, however, I am forced to take a job shooting squirrels at the school's Agricultural Station to survive when I discover my fellowship doesn't cover the summer term. I am fired when I can't bring myself to pull the trigger, but Zany Marshall steps in to save my job.

I recall the story of my father, the son of a land baron, who began his professional career as a street hawker and a rickshaw puller. Despite having only a sixth-grade education, he miraculously succeeded in becoming the first Indian president of a world-renowned bank. I realize that I am more like my father than I ever imagined—determined to succeed in the face of insurmountable odds.

The following Four Ps' list identifies the P(s) covered in this chapter:

[X]   Persevere with passion.
[X]   Pursue professional, family-oriented, social, and spiritual goals.
[X]   Persuade family and friends to help.
[   ]   Promote a culture of giving back.

10

ANGEL IN A DEVIL'S NIGHT

One who is injured ought not to return the injury, for on no account can it be right to do an injustice.
—SOCRATES

After barely surviving my ordeal of the summer of 1958 as a pseudo shooter of squirrels, I continued my studies in full force and completed all my coursework. During the next year, I also got through the two prerequisites for the PhD program: proficiency in French and German. I was so proud of my command of the foreign languages that during my next social visit, I got carried away and asked our hostess where she had placed the hors d'oeuvres, mispronouncing it as *horse-do-overs*.

I was even more pleased about getting through the required math courses, since I had no background in that subject when I entered the graduate school. So when I aced my last class in differential and integral calculus and mathematical statistics, I couldn't wait to share the good news with Bani. Trying to appear smart, I whipped out an aerogram and scribbled:

Dear,

Remember I told you I had no background in math when I left India? Well, guess what? I have now aced all of the high-level math courses I took at Florida. Aren't you proud of me?

Signed,

Y=ff(X) Elimit → n∞.

Although I used that mathematical equation in place of my signature to impress Bani with my newfound knowledge in mathematics, it backfired. Six weeks later, I received a reply in which she politely enquired if I had finally gone off the deep end.

I was relieved when I passed the qualifying exam for my PhD in November 1959. I then began directing all my energies toward completing my dissertation—easier said than done. My dissertation topic was based on a study of the Reserve Bank of India's role in economic development. I chose that topic because I wanted to become a specialist in devising novel ways for central banks to accelerate the development of emerging nations. But the UF's library did not house any of the Reserve Bank publications I needed for my research. The closest place that had these publications was the International Monetary Fund in Washington, D.C. I figured it would take me about three weeks, working hard and fast, to complete my needed research there. Unfortunately, I did not have enough money to travel to Washington, D.C., stay in a hotel, and eat in restaurants for three weeks.

I did some research and was overjoyed to discover that the Washington, D.C., YMCA offered rooms to bona fide students for only $5 a day. I never dreamed I would be able to find a room in the nation's capital that cheap. But still, the $100 round-trip Greyhound bus fare from Gainesville to Washington was too steep for me.

Then a friend directed me to the cafeteria bulletin board, where people posted notes about all sorts of bargains—including ride shares. My eyes fell on one in particular: "Need a student to share a ride to Washington, D.C. For further details, call ...." The note did not specify how much it would cost to share the ride, but I was desperate to find out.

When I phoned to ask about the ad, the woman who answered introduced herself as Ann Fletcher. "I work at the university library and plan to drive to Washington," she told me. "I will drive my car and pay for the gas. All I'm looking for is someone who will ride with me as a male companion." I wondered about the *male companion* part but didn't ask.

Ann was pleased to hear that I needed a ride to Washington, but she hesitated momentarily when I told her I was a graduate student from India. Quite as a matter of fact, she collected some basic information and promised to give me her decision soon. After I hung up, I wondered that she might not want to share a ride with a male companion from India.

I was pleasantly surprised when Ann called back the next day to say she would be happy to offer me a ride. At the very least, I expected that she would insist on meeting with me personally before making her decision, especially because I was dark-skinned. Those were the most controversial days of the Civil Rights Movement, days in which the Blacks and those who supported them were being beaten and sometimes killed. (There were several civil rights laws on the books, of course, but they were not enforced.) I was aware that people outside the university community might not react well to our traveling together. I considered raising that issue with her, but I quickly decided against it for fear of losing my ride. Instead, I thanked Ann profusely.

Then she asked me whether I would mind if she drove through the night to save on hotel costs. Her suggestion threw me off guard. While it was a good idea to save the cost of one night's hotel room, I asked, "Isn't it risky to drive more than 700 miles without resting for the night?"

"I am used to nonstop driving over long distances, so there is no reason for concern," she said dismissively. "Not only am I a good driver, but I'm also a safe driver." She offered me no return trip, so I guessed I would have to take a Greyhound bus back. Even so, I was most grateful.

I hung up the phone satisfied that I had gotten a free ride and a cheap place to stay. Not sharing the cost of the gas, however, seemed unfair. By accepting this free ride, I felt I would be exploiting her generosity. I agonized over this for a little while, finally concluding that the offer was too good to pass up. I promised myself to return her favor in some way in the foreseeable future.

ᔕᕫ

On a beautiful June evening, Ann Fletcher pulled up in front of my apartment at 7 pm, driving a huge red and white Oldsmobile convertible. I had never been in a convertible, and the thought of riding in such a fancy car all the way to Washington added to my excitement about seeing more of the US. Ann put the top down, turned on the radio, and off we went. I still remember the pulsating thrill I had as we drove away.

I was slightly edgy about the risks of riding through the Deep South in a convertible with a beautiful young woman. But our foreign student advisor had assured me that because I was a dark-skinned foreign student and not an American Black, I would not be subjected to racial profiling. I said not a word of my concerns to Ann, hoping that she, too, was aware of the special dispensation accorded to students from third-world countries.

After driving north for about two hours, we crossed the border into Georgia. Arriving at a small town named Valdosta just as it was getting dark, Ann stopped at a gas station. The attendant filled up the tank and checked the oil. Ann paid him, said good night, and pulled out, the top still down. But as soon as we left the gas station, we saw a flashing red light behind us. Since Ann had just pulled out of the station, she could not possibly have been speeding, so neither of us had any clue as to why a police car would be signaling for Ann to pull over.

Ann pulled the Oldsmobile to the curb and rolled down her window. The flashing light sent an ominous signal. Even before I could see the officer, I smelled trouble. I started trembling. The policeman stopped behind us and got out of his cruiser, walking toward Ann's side of the car. He looked sober in his uniform and hat, a pistol tucked on his side, and his big belly bulging out over his belt. His expression had a ferocious quality, the kind I had seen in news clips in which white police officers beat up terribly frightened black men. I kept silent but was ready to whip out my UF student ID to impress the officer that I was a foreign student.

"Your drivah's license and registration, please," the officer ordered gruffly. Ann dutifully handed them over. After glancing at them, the officer started grilling her.

"Wheh you headed?"

"Washington, D.C."

"Who you goin' to see theh?"

"I am going to visit a relative."

"And how long you stayin' theh?"

"About a week."

"Wheh you comin' from?"

"Gainesville, Florida."

Ann began wondering what was going on. I sat there dumbfounded but got a strong feeling that trouble was coming. Fast.

The officer finally came to the point of his interrogation. "Why you ridin' with this nigah?" he asked, glancing at me.

"Officer, he is not a black person," Ann replied almost defiantly. "Mr Mittra is a graduate student from India at the UF. He's going to Washington, D.C.. to do research, and I am providing him a ride. Is there anything wrong with that?"

"Plenty," barked the officer. "I don't care if he is from India or Timbuktu or wherever the hell these foreignahs come from. All people can see is that he's black, and by ridin' in the same car with him, you are riskin' your life, miss."

We were stunned. But the officer wasn't through with us.

"I could put both of you in jail for breakin' Georgia law. But since it looks like you don't know what you doin', ah'll give you a break. Get this guy out of yohr car and git lost, *now*!"

"I can't leave him alone in the middle of the road!" Ann protested. "I promised him a ride and I am responsible for driving him to Washington, D.C. He is a foreign student, so I should be allowed to take him with me."

"You get out of heah, young lady," yelled the officer, "or you'll be in deep trouble. Ah'll take this guy with me and put 'im in jail. Tomorrow mornin' the judge'll decide what to do with him." That made Ann extremely upset, but she realized that she had no choice but to obey the officer or we'd both be arrested. She reluctantly let me out of the car and slowly drove off.

There I was, as night was falling, alone with a Georgian state policeman. Almost half a century later, I can still feel the chill run down my spine. I had heard horror stories about Southern police brutality, and I was sure I would soon get a bullet in my head and no one would ever hear from me again. My life, just beginning to show signs of progress, was about to end by the side of a road somewhere in rural Georgia, where I would silently pass into oblivion.

Without a word, the officer led me to his black-and-white cruiser. To my great surprise, instead of shooting me, he took me to the county jail. I was neither fingerprinted nor photographed. In fact, no one even asked me my name or ordered me to sign anything. A jailor simply took me to a jail cell, opened the door, and then locked me behind it.

The cell was a 10-by-12-feet cage. The floor was filthy. A bed and a small table stood in the corner. A sink and a toilet, both putrid, were near the bed. In the opposite corner on the floor sat a sullen, bedraggled, middle-aged black man. Badly shaken, I had no idea what to do with myself and was not at all sure how to treat my cellmate, who started staring at me. Sitting down on the floor beside him, I managed a tentative "Hello."

"What the f— you in fo', man?" the man asked as he looked up at me with an intent expression. He spoke with such a strange accent that I did not fully understand what he was asking, so I didn't answer.

"S—! Who the f— are you anyways?" he retorted. "Did'ja shoot a cop, or scare the s— out of some nigger-hater?" I understood these questions. I composed myself and told him I had not shot anyone, and I did not know why the officer had brought me there. But I was not at all sure that the man understood my accent any better than I had understood his. Finding that I was neither a threat nor of any particular interest, my cellmate waved me off.

"F— you," he said. "Theh's no talkin' to you. So just get lost, busta, and let me catch up on mah sleep." He left me steeping in my own fears, locked up in a rank jail cell, with no idea what was going to happen to me next.

I agonized over my plight for a while, clearly recalling with great irony that the University had repeatedly assured the foreign students that there was no federal or state law that prohibited us from mixing freely with whites. In fact, we were encouraged to socialize with them, but we were also told that if there was any confusion or trouble with the law, we should merely let the police officer know that we were foreign students. We were promised that would solve the problem. So much for the power of the Ivory Tower. As I discovered that night, they had their own rules in Georgia. After spending a long time, while feeling sorry for myself, sitting uncomfortably in this cell in my *new democratic country*, I glanced over at my sleeping cellmate, shut my eyes, and passed out.

Five hours later, at about 3 am, a jailor kicked me awake and told me to get up. With no explanation, he led me to the front gate of the jailhouse. There, a white, middle-aged man in a black turtleneck shirt and a tweed jacket stood by a blue Chevrolet, waiting to receive me. Looking relaxed and smiling, the man extended his hand.

"Hello, Mr Mittra. I am Sidney Jones, pastor of the local Baptist Church," he said in English I could actually understand. "I am here to take you home."

I was stunned. After all that had happened to me that night, I found it hard to believe that a total stranger standing outside a jail would greet me by name and with such kindness. "How did he know who I was?" I wondered. From the time I got out of Ann's car until now, no one had ever asked me for my name, nor did I volunteer it to anyone. And why, I also wondered, was this man interested in taking me *home*? I just stood there, baffled, and still a bit frightened.

"Mr Mittra," the man offered in a decided but clear Southern accent, aware of my hesitation, "Ann Fletcher called me and explained what happened to you. I understand your confusion. Please be assured that you will be perfectly safe with me. As I said, I am the pastor of our local Baptist Church, and I am mighty pleased to welcome you to my home here in Valdosta. In fact, my family is anxious to meet you." Only the words *Ann Fletcher* relieved me.

Pastor Jones told me later that while Ann had driven off as ordered by the officer, she had not abandoned me. She drove straight to a phone booth and, as a Baptist herself, phoned the local Baptist church and explained to Pastor Jones what had happened. He negotiated my release and made sure there would be no charges against me so that I would not be blacklisted for life. All this had taken half the night, while I, completely unaware, had been sitting miserably in my jail cell with my unfriendly cellmate.

Pastor Jones drove me to his home, a neat and tidy house in a posh neighborhood. I walked through his front door exhausted but truly relieved, feeling the concern of both Pastor Jones and his sweet and caring wife. In their cozy kitchen, at 4 am, Mrs Jones lovingly served us sandwiches, potato chips, and Coca-Cola. I wasted no time digging in. Pastor Jones waited patiently for me to finish, and then he spoke, addressing me with great compassion and respect.

"Mr Mittra—well, I hope you don't mind if I call you Sid. What happened this evening is a sad commentary on all of us as a nation, and I hope that someday you will get over the pain we here in Georgia have caused you." He paused for a moment to collect his thoughts before continuing. "When you've had time to think it over, I'm sure you will realize that *you* had nothing to do with the way these people treated you. Tonight, they expressed their stark fear, their insecurity, and their inability to understand who they really are. We are all equal in the face of God. That is what our religion teaches us, and that is the truth that will ultimately triumph." His words sounded like something right out of the Sermon on the Mount, and they were reassuring to hear from a fundamentalist Christian.

After my late-night dinner and his informal sermon, Pastor Jones put me to bed, where I fell fast asleep thinking of God-like Baptists. A few hours later, he awakened me with a hearty greeting.

"Good morning, Sid! I hope you enjoyed at least a few hours of rest. Now get dressed, come down to the kitchen, and have a quick breakfast. A police officer—this time a *polite* one—is here to take you to the Greyhound bus station. Don't be afraid of him."

When I came downstairs toting my suitcase, I indeed found a police officer standing near the front door. He stared at me silently and did not shake my hand. When I finished my breakfast, he asked me to get into the police car. I expressed my sincere thanks to the pastor and Mrs Jones, and told them I would love to see them again under better circumstances. The pastor wrote down my address and assured me that he would get in touch with me when he and his family next attended a Southern Baptists' meeting in Gainesville.

Tentatively, I got into the back seat of the patrol car, and the policeman and I drove off without speaking. I had an eerie feeling that I was going to end up locked in jail again, this time with no one to save me. I felt helpless and started shaking with fear. But soon, the officer pulled up outside the Greyhound bus station, handed me a one-way ticket to Washington, D.C., and made sure I boarded the bus. Pastor Jones must have paid for the ticket, because I am certain that the steely-eyed officer would never have done so. In my heart, I was deeply grateful to Pastor Jones for his generosity and promised myself to thank him yet again when I saw him next, hopefully in Gainesville.

After traveling on the bus for 24 hours, I arrived at the Washington, D.C., Greyhound station, hired a cab, and went straight to the YMCA. I checked in, settled down in my clean Christian room, and quickly fell asleep. I would have slept straight through the night, but a sharp knocking on my door startled me awake. It turned out to be the desk clerk, who had come to tell me that a lady had called for me and he had told her to call back using the number for the phone on our floor.

When I answered the phone down the hall a few minutes later, I was delighted and relieved to hear Ann's voice on the other end. She had arrived safely in Washington, D.C., and was anxious to make sure that all was well with me. She agreed to pick me up the next morning, convertible top up this time, so we could share our experiences during breakfast at Howard Johnson's.

Over a cheese omelet and fresh-brewed coffee the following day, Ann recounted the *real* story of that fateful night—the story she had heard from Pastor Jones. Apparently, the police officer had been following us for some time before Ann had stopped at the gas station. It had been getting dark, but the officer thought he saw a black man riding in a car with a white woman. In 1959, with the Civil Rights Act still a few years away, it was illegal in Georgia for a white woman to be associated in any capacity with a black man. The officer told Pastor Jones that he had stopped Ann because she had clearly broken the law.

However, when Ann told him that I was a foreign student from India, the officer said he became concerned for my safety. In fact, according to the officer, if he had allowed us to leave together and drive through Georgia at night, there was a very good possibility that Anne's car would have been mobbed—and one or both of us would have been killed. He ordered me to get out of the car and told Ann to drive on without me *to save us both*. The only way he could fully guarantee my safety, he had told the pastor, would be to jail me and let the judge decide how and when to release me the next day.

There may have been some truth in his account. Maybe he did save our lives. I would never know how much of what Pastor Jones told Ann was actually true, and what role the officer played in making sure that I was treated humanely and with dignity. Regardless, the experience continues to upset me decades later. I still feel cold chills at the sound of an errant siren in the night, remembering that it was in fact a law enforcement officer who actually broke the law by jailing a foreign student for riding with a white girl—this in the land of the free and the home of the brave.

Epilogue: Life's Lessons

Needing to go to Washington, D.C., to conduct research for my dissertation, I decide to save money by accepting a ride with Ann, a young blonde woman working at the university library. We take off of what at first seems like a fun drive, motoring through the night with the convertible top down. When a policeman stops us in Georgia and jails me for violating the then-prevailing civil rights law, I spend tense several hours behind bars with seedy cellmates. A Baptist minister gets me released and helps him get on a bus to Washington, D.C. I later meet up with Ann, who explains how she found the preacher in the Yellow Pages and called him in middle of the night for help. I learn that had the policeman not stopped the travelers and put me in jail, it was very possible that I might have been killed by racist ruffians.

The following Four Ps' list identifies the P(s) covered in this chapter:

- [X]   Persevere with passion.
- [X]   Pursue professional, family-oriented, social, and spiritual goals.
- [X]   Persuade family and friends to help.
- [   ]   Promote a culture of giving back.

11

A MODEST PROPOSAL

Family is the longest surviving institution of India irrespective of the ages, transformations, religious and political views. Loyalty, integrity and unity are the three pillars upon which Indian families and Indian Culture stand.
—INDIAN CULTURE AND FAMILY VALUES, DECEMBER 16, 2010

After returning to Gainesville with my hard-won dissertation research, I set to work finishing my thesis. I also returned to what had by this time become an active social life. One day, my friend Alan Keys invited me to attend a special dance organized by his fraternity, Phi Kappa Alpha. I had heard about fraternity and sorority houses soon after I arrived on campus, but I had little interest until Alan's invitation.

Although fraternity parties at Florida had always been strictly limited to members only, Dr Putman, the foreign student advisor, had made a special request that the fraternities consider exposing foreign students to the American culture. Alan's fraternity had decided to invite a select number of foreign students, including me, to its party. However, I had to bring a girlfriend. That created a problem. I felt uncomfortable asking Ann, who was not my girlfriend. I could not think of anyone else who would go with me. So I declined.

But when I casually mentioned the invitation to Sylvia Booma, a girl I was working with on a couple of projects involving foreign students, she said she thought going to the party would be a great experience for me. She happily offered to be my *girlfriend* for the evening. At first, I hesitated because Sylvia was extremely popular. Boys were constantly chasing her. I didn't want to appear to be competing with them. However, I decided to accept her generous offer simply because I didn't want to miss such a unique opportunity.

Taking an American girl out was new for me. I was very uncomfortable walking with Sylvia into a party filled with strangers. I noticed that the room was beautifully decorated with colorful balloons and innovative trappings that made the whole place look like a massive Greek courtyard. On one side of the hall, a large band played loud music while at the opposite end of the room, people crowded around a cash bar selling beer and wine. In the center, fraternity brothers danced with beautiful girls wearing dresses that were much too revealing. A few young men and women were passionately kissing in the corners.

I was thunderstruck. Even though I was 29 years old, I was still completely naïve about the American party scene and had never seen anything like that. I was so overwhelmed that I just sat on a bench, speechless. Suddenly Sylvia, whom I had virtually forgotten, broke the silence by asking me if I would like to dance with her. I was too embarrassed to tell her that I had never danced before; so I kept quiet. Sylvia instantly guessed my predicament. She offered to teach me a few simple steps.

I trembled with fear and nervousness like a pre-teen on his first date. My hands started to sweat as we walked to the middle of the dance floor. Sylvia placed my right hand around her waist, took my left hand in hers and held it high. She showed me three simple waltz-like steps. I moved very awkwardly, often stepping on her toes, and I made a total fool of myself. I had never held a girl that close in my life. The challenge of dancing with her with so many other people all around me was simply too much. I nearly fainted.

Cutting our dance short, I staggered back to my bench, babbling, while Sylvia was whisked away by a young man who invited her to dance with him. After composing myself, I noticed many things I had missed earlier. Not too far from me, three men and one girl were sitting around a table, gulping beer, and stacking their empty cans one on top of another. They seemed to be competing to see who could stack the highest number of cans in the shortest possible time. In a corner, a man and a girl, all but naked, were falling on top of each other, oblivious to the people watching them. Someone with a microphone was singing: "Sugar in the morning, sugar in the evening, sugar at suppertime." Not being familiar with American music, I didn't recognize the hit tune by the McGuire Sisters but at the same time, the odd song seemed rather fitting for such a completely bizarre environment.

Sylvia was gone for a long time. That was fine with me since I had been humiliated by our disastrous dance. I did not want to face her. Eventually, she returned and asked with a smile if I wanted to leave the party. I nodded, scurrying out with immense relief.

After we walked to her dorm, I thanked her for being my friend for the night and wondered out loud if I had spoiled the evening for her.

"Did you have a good time at the party?" she asked in response, choosing not to answer my question directly.

Since she had been so nice to me, I didn't want to disappoint her. So with a sheepish smile, I answered with a loud, "*Yessss!*" and then slunk away into the night.

Such forays into the American culture notwithstanding, I was very interested in sharing foreign culture with the university community. In fact, not long after I arrived on campus, Dr Putman surprised me by saying, "Sid, from this day on you are an unofficial

The Mittra family (1949). I am standing second from left, age 19

My mother, Taru B. Mittra, after marriage

My father Kashi N. Mittra, President, Imperial Bank

Home in Banaras where I was born in 1930

Our bungalow at 14 Lukergunj in Allahabad, where Father passed away

Our apartment in midtown, Calcutta

Replica of our home, Banpur

Elephant ride, Banpur. *Courtesy:* Pixabay

My outdoor school, Banpur

Pond near our suburban home in Calcutta where I nearly drowned

View of Phulatti Bazaar in Agra where we rented our house

Example of how we studied at night around a hurricane lamp
(no electricity in the house)

Our home in Chili Int Road: Part of the large building structure on the right

Brother Sailo as superintendent of Hallet Hospital, Kanpur

Mrs Minati Mittra, who acted as my surrogate mother
after Mother had passed away

DAV College, Kanpur, from where I earned my master's degree

Local train ride, Bombay

Monsoon at Victoria Railway Station, Bombay

Bani Mittra's (then Rani Sarkar) home in Parsi Colony, Bombay

Brother Raj Mittra, assisting in my trip to the US

Air letter application to the University of Florida for a fellowship grant

Marshall Jackson and his girlfriend in Gainesville, Florida

Shooting squirrels in Agricultural Experimentation Station in campus to survive during summer term, 1958

Voldosta jail where I spent the night for violating racial laws

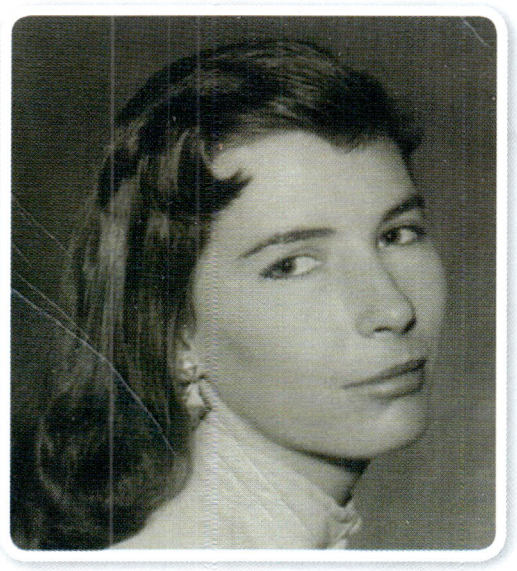

Ann Fletcher who gave me a ride to Washington, D.C.

Sylvia Booma, student at University of Florida and an active
participant in foreign students' programs

Photograph of Bani Mittra (then Rani Sarkar) received upon
arrival at Florida campus

In my Gainesville dorm, proposing to Rani Sarkar

Marriage with Rani Sarkar (January 31, 1961)

Receiving PhD degree from Dr Alan Sievers, January 1962

Parole visa issued by US Immigration for traveling to Venezuala

United Nations identification badge, 1965

Our family in Rochester, Michigan, 1973

Meadowbrook Montessori School in Rochester, Michigan, owned and operated by Bani Mittra

Bani Mittra's performance on national television, 1974

Publication of the first edition of *Practicing Financial Planning*. It has gone through 11 editions, and the Indian edition is being published by SAGE

Our home in Rochester, Michigan, 2015

Our daughter, Rita Sherman

Our son, Robert A. Mittra

Posing with the entire family (children and grandchildren)

Indian cultural ambassador to America. You will carry the responsibility of enlightening us about your culture, religion, and social beliefs."

I felt honored that he would place so much confidence in me and decided to take my responsibility seriously, although I was way too overwhelmed to do much about it back then. But now that I was working on my dissertation, I felt it was important to do more than represent just my own country. So I decided to join the International Student Organization (ISO). It focused on social and cultural activities of students from many countries.

Joining the ISO was easy but helping it become a truly representative international organization was not. I soon discovered that the administrative structure was cumbersome and its scope was extremely limited. For instance, all the activities had to be cleared by the foreign student advisor, which typically took weeks. Also, all the programs had to be *international* in scope, which precluded programs focusing on individual countries. I disagreed. But busy with my dissertation, I remained on the sidelines and hesitated to change things.

But eventually I decided to take action. As a start, I put forth the argument that the primary objective of the ISO should be to help promote friendship and understanding between all foreign students and the American students. Therefore, we should be free to design our programs without outside interference as long as we operated within the broad guidelines established by the Foreign Students Office (FSO). Both the ISO Board and the FSO agreed. All restrictions were removed, and the new and improved ISO was hailed as the perfect organization to promote international friendship and harmony between the American and foreign students.

The ISO Board went ahead with grandiose plans, although it was rough going at first. I spearheaded many activities involving foreign cultures and encouraging American students to participate. Finally, when foreign students began presenting colorful programs that attracted all types of students and American students began playing an active role in the operation of the ISO, it was transformed into a bona fide international organization whose status exceeded Dr Putman's hopes. Indeed, by the time I left, Dr Putman awarded me a plaque.

The citation he wrote at the time read in part, "[Sid] Mittra … has made a varied contribution to cultural life and student activities on the campus [through the ISO], perhaps the greatest such contribution made in the past ten years by any foreign student."

Once I completed my dissertation in June 1960, I went to see Dr Donovan, the department chairman, to set a date for defending my thesis. "It won't be long now," I thought. "I'm almost there." But instead of agreeing on a date, Dr Donovan dropped a bombshell.

"Sid," he said, "Dr Sievers [my thesis advisor] is going to be on sabbatical next academic year, so you'll have to wait until the fall of 1961 to defend your thesis." Dr Donovan paused for a moment, as if to gauge my stunned reaction, and then continued, "I am sorry that I can't do anything to change the situation. But I suggest you take this opportunity to find a one-year teaching position to gain some valuable classroom experience. I will help you find such a position, if you want me to."

"Fall of 1961?" I thought, incredulously. "That's more than a year away!" After thanking Dr Donovan for his generous offer, I returned to my dormitory totally heartbroken. My angst wasn't just about putting off earning the degree. For some time, I had been dreaming of proposing to Bani as soon as I completed my PhD. But with this unexpected delay, I would have to wait for at least a year before I could propose.

I briefly considered requesting a replacement thesis advisor, but quickly abandoned that idea for fear of reprisal. That night, restless and somewhat disoriented, I poured my heart out to Bani in a long letter, accusing everyone at the University of spoiling my well-laid plans. While I didn't mention any specifics, I did emphasize that because of this sudden change, my future plans had become uncertain.

Making good on his word, Dr Donovan did manage to find me a temporary teaching assignment at Stetson University, a small Baptist College in DeLand, 20 miles west of Daytona Beach. Initially, I wasn't too thrilled about this opportunity. Stetson was a relatively unknown college at that time, located in a sleepy southern town unknown to most Americans. But since I had little choice, I grudgingly accepted Stetson's offer for the 1960–1961 academic year at an annual salary of $5,500.

In the morning of August 10, 1960, three years after I left Bombay, I packed up my bags and textbooks and loaded them into a beat-up green Renault that I managed to buy at a throwaway price. Then I headed for the university post office, hoping to receive a sympathetic letter from Bani in response to the disoriented letter I had mailed her six weeks before. I did find something from Bani, but it was not exactly what I expected.

Instead of an aerogram, a large 5-by-8-inch envelope with Bani's return address was waiting for me. I naively concluded that after receiving the news of the delay in earning my degree, Bani's parents had decided to fix her marriage with someone else in India, and this formal envelope contained a confirmation of that decision.

I returned to my car with the envelope, still sealed, and could not muster sufficient courage to open it. I sat there for a while, my anxiety mounting, blaming everyone on earth for my misfortune. Expecting the worst, and with enormous trepidation, I finally opened the envelope.

Inside was only one thing—a 4-by-6-inch glossy color photograph of Bani. Dressed in a peach-colored *sari*, her hair in a bun, Bani looked charming, serene, and supremely confident. I got lost in the photograph, feeling as if I had gone back in time to when we first met at the musical program in Bombay. I recovered sufficiently to turn the picture over, only to find that on the back, Bani had scribbled, "Dear, For You.... Yours, Dearest."

Still lost in my romantic reverie, I must have laid the photograph on the seat beside me and started the car. I don't quite recall driving away, but I distinctly remember that soon after hitting the highway, I heard a police siren and saw a flashing light behind me. When I stopped and rolled down my window, a police officer came over and asked me for my registration and driver's license. I quickly handed them over, along with my UF student ID.

"Where are you rushin' to, young fella?" the officer asked, examining my papers.

"I just received a photograph from my girlfriend in India, whom I have not seen or talked to for three years," I answered without hesitation. "I got carried away and forgot to watch the speed limit. I am sorry, officer." Then I handed over Bani's picture to him.

The policeman glanced at the photograph and smiled.

"Please watch your speed, will you?" he warned in a soft voice. He paused for a moment, and then handed back my papers and the photograph, adding, "Good luck with your girlfriend."

Returning to his cruiser, he drove off without issuing me a ticket. I watched him disappear down the highway and whispered to myself, "If I ever have to choose between a Georgian and a Floridian police officer, I would definitely choose the latter."

I drove back onto the road, more mindful of my speed this time, but I soon got distracted trying to figure out what was really on Bani's mind when she mailed the photograph, and more importantly, how I should respond to this gesture.

Until now, I had stood firm on my decision not to propose to Bani until I had earned my PhD and had a steady job. But the photograph had considerably weakened my resolve. "Should I still keep to my original promise to myself to propose only after having earned my PhD and gotten a permanent job? I wondered. Or should I say to heck with such a baseless promise and give in?"

By the time I reached DeLand two hours later, I had made up my mind.

I drove straight to the home of Ed and Peggy Cox, where Dr Donovan had arranged for me to stay as a paying guest. The Coxes lived in an old four-bedroom home with no basement and no central air conditioning. Ed, who stood 6'4", was the city's chief of police and was mighty proud of his exalted social status. His friendly wife Peggy went out of her way to impress everyone that she was a liberal in this otherwise super-conservative southern town. The couple had no children.

I felt embraced by warmth as they invited me into their lovely home. After supper, I said good night and retired for the evening. Without even unpacking my suitcase and books, I went straight to the desk in my room. Whipping out an aerogram I had been carrying with me, I sat down to write the most important letter of my life. Although my mind was firmly made up, I suddenly felt nervous and started to perspire profusely. I wiped my sweaty palms a few times and then started to scribble. I wrote:

August 10, 1960
Dearest,
I was determined to earn my Ph.D. and have a permanent job before asking you to marry me. Today I have neither. But I do believe I will have my degree as soon as my advisor returns from sabbatical. I also have a temporary teaching job at Stetson now, and I'm sure it will become permanent if I ask for it.
So considering all that, will you marry me
   Now?
Yours,
Dear

The next morning, I rushed to the post office and sent my proposal by certified airmail. I had no idea how I would find the patience to wait the six weeks it would take for Bani's response. Indeed, for the next month and a half, I moved about like a zombie, unenthusiastically preparing for my lectures and going through the motion of teaching classes. Because I didn't know anyone in town who would sympathize with what I was going through, I drove to Daytona Beach every evening and watched the restless waves crash upon the sugary white sand, depositing bits of mostly broken seashells on the shore.

Peggy noticed my perpetually depressed mood and politely enquired if her cooking did not agree with me or if somehow I felt I was not being treated well. I assured her that she was an excellent cook and that no one had ever treated me better. To put her mind at ease, I told her that my discomfort came from my being a teacher in the classroom for the first time. She bought my excuse.

∽

After six weeks, I still had not received any response from Bani and my hopes were as shattered as the shells on the beach. Naturally, I was devastated, fearing that due to my unsettled future, either Bani or her parents had decided against our marriage. Equally frustrating was the fact that I had no way of calling her to discuss it.

But eight weeks after I mailed the proposal, I did indeed receive an aerogram from Bani. Convinced that this was merely a rejection letter, I wasn't too keen on opening it right away. When I eventually unfolded the missive, I was surprised to discover that it contained only one line—the shortest letter I ever received from her.

"Would you please directly ask my father to give us his blessings?" she'd written.

Initially, I was put off by her lackadaisical response. But I suddenly realized that, as per our established Indian tradition, I had breached good manners by neglecting to ask for her father's blessings *before* proposing to her.

I quickly obliged her request, although the issue of her two-week delay in responding to my proposal continued to be a sore point with me until I discovered the real reason for the holdup. As Bani would later explain, when she had informed her parents about my marriage proposal, they became apprehensive about the thought of her taking such an enormous risk, marrying a man who did not yet have either a PhD or a steady job. They had read horrific newspaper stories concerning Indian boys living in America and betraying their Indian fiancés. Trusting their boyfriends, these girls came to America to get married; but they were quickly dumped and had no choice but to return to their homeland empty-handed.

Although no one kept track of how frequently these incidents actually occurred, it was generally believed that the practice was rampant, and Indian parents were understandably hesitant to permit their daughters to assume such risk. Despite these legitimate concerns, Bani's parents eventually recognized that she had quietly made up her mind about accepting me as her life partner, and so they finally acquiesced. The turnaround had taken about two weeks.

After receiving my letter requesting his blessings, Bani's father quickly obliged. And with that, Bani Sarkar, who had never before left home alone nor made any major decision without the guidance of her family, made a vow to travel all by herself halfway around the world in order to become my wife. Her reason for taking this enormously risky step, as best as I could tell, was extraordinary: She had complete trust in me.

I was a different person from the time I received blessings from Bani's parents. She and I were now free to express our true feelings for each other in our letters, and we did so without reservation. Shortly after our engagement, I received an emotionally charged letter in which Bani noted that she was dreaming of having a gala wedding ceremony in Bombay.

Traditional Indian weddings are normally quite majestic and include elaborate rituals before, during, and after the actual marriage ceremony. The event begins under a *mandapa* or canopy decorated with flowers as a sacred fire burns nearby. The bride's family welcomes the groom, and then the priest asks Lord Ganesha for peace and wisdom. The bride and groom exchange garlands before the bride's father gives his daughter away to the groom amidst chanting of sacred verses. The groom applies a powdery red pigment called vermillion to the bride's forehead, and the priest ties a marriage knot between a scarf the groom wears around his neck and the bride's sari. Finally, the bride and groom take seven steps around the sacred fire together, one step each representing nourishment, strength, prosperity, happiness, progeny, long life, and harmony. The entire ceremony lasts *four or five days*, with every part rooted in ancient Vedic tradition.

I did not have the courage to break Bani's heart by informing her that I could not afford to travel to India to get married; so I cowardly said nothing at first. When I finally told her we'd have to settle for a civil marriage in a Florida court, she must have been devastated. I truly dreaded a sharply critical response from her. To her credit, she did not once express her disapproval of my unilateral decision.

She did, however, keep me apprised of all the preparations her family was making to get her ready for the big day. And I, in turn, let her know in great detail my plans to take off from teaching for a week and receive her at the Orlando International Airport. In my excitement, however, I totally forgot that after she arrived in New York following the 28-hour flight from Bombay, she would still have to clear customs, carry her luggage from the international terminal to the domestic terminal, and check her bags again before catching a plane to Orlando—a daunting proposition.

Fortunately, Raj (who by that time had left Penn State and was an engineering professor at the University of Illinois in Urbana) offered to meet Bani at the JFK airport in New York and then fly with her back to Chicago. He also graciously decided to arrange a short but dignified Hindu marriage ceremony in Urbana. I could never adequately express my gratitude to him for his generosity.

On January 29, 1961, Bani safely arrived in New York in the middle of a heavy snowstorm that blanketed the city. She was tired, confused, and a little frightened about what would happen if no one came to meet her at the airport. But her fears were allayed when she spotted Raj holding a large sheet of paper on which he had printed her name.

The next day, I flew to Chicago from Daytona Beach, arriving in time to receive Bani when she flew in from New York. Then Raj took another flight to Champaign-Urbana, while Bani and I went to the train station and boarded a nearly empty train bound for the same town, about 150 miles away.

This was the first time we had seen each other in almost four years, and I wanted to say a million different things that I had been mulling over for a long time. But to my great surprise, something totally shut me off, and I couldn't utter a single word. Being an Indian girl (and shy, besides), Bani also remained completely silent. We sat facing each other, as I lightly held her hand, travelling for three hours without sharing so much as a single word.

We were married in Champaign on January 31, 1961. It was a typical wintry day in Illinois, with piles of snow already on the ground and an additional foot expected that afternoon. I had initially anticipated nothing more than a simple civil ceremony in a Florida court, so when Raj, his wife Mira, and their close friends made a heroic effort to create the ambiance and the atmosphere of a typical Indian wedding. I was deeply moved. With an Indian priest presiding, Bani and I took our vows by exchanging garlands and circling seven times around the purifying fire. To me, it seemed like nothing short of an extravaganza.

Bani, no doubt, must have felt quite differently about the relatively succinct event, which lasted only a couple of hours. But she never once made a critical comment about the brevity of our wedding ceremony, nor did she express any dissatisfaction over the inadequacy of our abbreviated rituals. On the contrary, everyone felt that she was grateful for the *elaborate* arrangements that had been made, and despite major inconveniences and the lack of accompaniments, Bani graciously entertained the guests with her singing—something a bride in India would never have had the courage to do on her wedding night.

A couple of days later we bade Raj and Mira goodbye and headed for Florida. Little did I realize at the time that our ceremony, as beautiful and meaningful as it had been for both of us, lacked one essential element: legality. I had neglected to obtain a marriage license. Appeasement of Hindu Gods aside, as far as the US government was concerned, we were not yet man and wife.

I would like to say that I realized my error once I had returned to Florida and arranged for a civil ceremony, complete with license.

However, that was not the case. The truth is that it was almost two years later, while I was teaching at the University of Detroit (UD) and Bani and I were expecting our first baby, that I realized my blunder.

Fearing that our child would be born out of legal wedlock, I made some inquiries and soon learned that the city of Detroit had a plan already in place for solving such problems. Bani and I rushed downtown to see a clerk in the bureau that issued marriage licenses. There, we were directed to a small office where a fat woman with unruly hair asked Bani, "How many months?"

"What?" I responded without thinking.

"Honey, I don't have all day," she said, looking straight at Bani. "Do you understand English? How many months are you pregnant? The judge needs to know before he signs the papers." Bani was speechless.

"Seven months," I blurted out.

"What date do you wish to be put on the marriage certificate?" she continued matter-of-factly.

"We were married on January 31, 1961," I said meekly.

"Yeah, yeah, everybody says they were legally married when they come to see me, so let's skip the crap," she said with more than a hint of irritation. "Give me 20 bucks and go in there."

Waiting in the next room was a grim-looking, middle-aged man who I guessed was the judge. He signed the marriage certificate in front of us, and then two other women who worked for the court indifferently added their signatures as witnesses to the *ceremony*.

The judge handed me the marriage certificate and shook my hand. "Good luck," he muttered, looking away.

That day, in January 1963, we were legally pronounced man and wife, effective January 31, 1961. I now had an official license to fall in love with my *new* bride.

Epilogue: Life's Lessons

I continue to explore American college life when I am invited to a wild fraternity party where, at the age of 29, I dance with a girl for the first time. The result is a cultural disaster. Unfazed, I plan to ask Bani to marry me as soon as I get my PhD.

While scheduling my thesis defense, I discover that my advisor will be on sabbatical and I'll have to wait a whole year. Heartbroken, I take a one-year teaching job at a nearby college, but I decide I can't wait for the PhD to ask Bani to marry me. With sweaty palms, I pen a quick proposal on an aerogram, knowing it will be six weeks before I will know Bani's answer. The reply is eight weeks in coming and contains a single line—a request that I ask Bani's father for his blessing before proposing. I do so, and the blessing is granted. Bani, who has never before left home on her own, agrees to travel 10,000 miles by herself to move to the US to marry me.

My brother Raj, who lived in Illinois, arranges a Hindu marriage ceremony for the couple in Urbana. While overjoyed, I neglect an important detail—a marriage license. (I don't realize this until two years later, when Bani is about to give birth to our first child.) We quickly rectify the situation, despite needing the help of a clerk with an attitude.

The following Four Ps' list identifies the P(s) that I have covered in this chapter:

[X] Persevere with passion.

[X] Pursue professional, family-oriented, social, and spiritual goals.

[X] Persuade family and friends to help.

[   ] Promote a culture of giving back.

12

THE LONG WAY HOME, SWEET HOME

Accept responsibility for your life. Know that it is you who will get you where you want to go, no one else.
—LES BROWN

Bani and I left Champaign one wintery morning and drove all the way to Florida, arriving in DeLand the evening of the following day, exhausted and somewhat grumpy. We got a ride back from my friend Dick Shapiro, a dorm mate from my days at the UF. Dick had earlier planned to drive from Florida to Chicago to visit his girlfriend, and when he heard that I was going to get married in Champaign about the same time he'd be in Chicago, he generously offered to give Bani and me a ride back to DeLand when he made the return trip. Thinking only of saving money, I readily accepted his offer without considering that Bani was not used to long-distance driving (and without knowing that she was prone to getting car sick). I also didn't think about the fact that my new bride and I would be totally unable to have a private conversation during the entire trip. Too late, I realized I should have known better and hoped she would forgive me once we arrived at our new home.

Before leaving DeLand for the wedding, I rented a semi-furnished apartment on top of a garage and decorated it in a haphazard manner. I had also filled the refrigerator with two weeks' worth of groceries. To make it easy for Bani, I bought toiletries, pots and pans, and other essentials. I was sure our new home was ready for the lady of the house.

Bani was thrilled to enter her own home for the first time. At first, she just wanted to sit on the sofa and savor the moment. But I pleaded with her to cook something simple so we could finish our dinner early and retire for the evening. After she agreed and headed for the kitchen, I went to take a quick shower and get ready for dinner.

I still remember seeing Bani standing near the kitchen counter, her face reflecting shock and disbelief, when I walked into the kitchen after my shower. It didn't take long for me to realize that the staples I had purchased in advance were only appropriate for making a quick American dinner—tuna helper, rolls, and salad. But Bani was not familiar with any of that. To her, a simple dinner consisted of rice, *daal* (lentils), a vegetable dish, such as cauliflower with potatoes, and fish or chicken cooked with Indian spices. She could not find any of the items she needed to prepare such a meal. I was embarrassed when I realized that. I should have known better.

But thanks to this little fiasco, on the first day of our married life, in Florida, I introduced Bani to the world-famous McDonald's. The whole mess turned out to be a boon in disguise because I was never again permitted to go grocery shopping.

The next day I began teaching my classes back at Stetson. When I returned home in the evening, I was elated to find that Bani had prepared a succulent Indian dinner which she served on a beautifully decorated dining table. I could not help remembering the days when my dinner in Gainesville consisted of half-boiled eggs and butter spread on a roll. "What a difference a devoted and loving Indian wife can make," I thought. After the meal, I complimented Bani profusely on her culinary skills.

"My mother is an excellent cook, so I never got to learn cooking at home," she responded in a soft voice. "I am sorry I am not a good cook." Her response did not surprise me since I was familiar with the Indian tradition of female humility. But when I started to pick up the dirty dishes, preparing to wash them, Bani panicked.

"Oh no," she yelped, "Please don't do that! You are married now, and it is *my* job to cook, clean the dishes, and take care of all the other household chores. If my parents ever found out that I let you do the dishes, they would never stop scolding me, and I would never be able to live it down." Not surprisingly, along with her luggage, Bani had brought a bit of cultural baggage with her to America.

Soon thereafter, I invited my dean, Hugh McEnry, and his wife Lisa for dinner to meet Bani. This was their first exposure to an authentic Indian dinner. Both Hugh and Lisa were profuse in their praise of the feast Bani had prepared. Still, not surprisingly, she apologized that her cooking did not turn out well. They were puzzled by her response, but repeated the compliment and left smiling.

The next day, I explained to Dean McEnry that because the words *thank you* are rarely used in the Indian culture, a hostess who has been complimented on a meal as a matter of form merely says, "My cooking turned out to be really bad."

"I'll be damned," he said in amazement.

Several months later, we again invited the McEnrys for a gourmet Indian dinner. This time, following a sumptuous meal, Lisa smiled and complimented Bani the *Indian* way by saying with confidence, "Thank you, Bani, for your *not so good* dinner."

The McEnrys were not the only DeLand residents who weren't familiar with Indian customs. We soon discovered that unlike in cosmopolitan Gainesville, people in DeLand had not received much exposure to the world outside. No one there had ever seen anyone from India, and most people assumed that all Indians were American Indians. So when Bani was first seen in public, walking down the street wearing her beautifully embroidered, multicolored silk sari and Indian gold jewelry, traffic virtually stopped. Everyone stared at her as if she were from fairyland. Although it took months for most people not to do a double take when they saw Bani, they eventually greeted her graciously instead of gaping when they met her on the street.

Still, we were hardly ordinary residents. Once, I took a sari in for dry cleaning. Taking a look at the long piece of cloth, the manager asked what sort of garment this was so he could check the appropriate box on the dry cleaning form. When I explained that it was a six-yard-long lady's dress, he shook his head in disbelief. Then he checked *other* on the dry cleaning form, adding a special note: "Extra-long bed sheet."

For Bani's part, she soaked up American culture by socializing with American friends. She also attended classes in Art and Spanish. She gave live musical performances on stage. She loved her new life, and everybody we came in contact with loved her, too. Since everything was going so well for us, I thought it would be best if we made a few small, but significant, changes in our respective domestic roles. To that end, I began performing small household chores, such as vacuuming. That constituted step one in de-programming.

Bani was comfortable with this arrangement at first, but one day when I began doing the dishes in the presence of invited guests, she felt so self-conscious that she blurted out, "Yesterday during an argument, my husband raised his voice, apologized for it, and by way of punishment, volunteered to do the dishes for one week." Everybody laughed, I the loudest—and Bani felt better.

At the same time, Bani started making a few simple financial decisions. I would occasionally give her *blow off* money that she was free to spend anyway she liked without consulting me. She was excited about receiving it, but for a long time she could not get over the habit of asking for my permission to spend it.

Notwithstanding these marginal gains, I thought that, until we settled down permanently, it would be prudent to let Bani mainly play her comfortable and convenient role of homemaker. Even so, I also encouraged her to pursue music and painting, two areas she loved.

Despite the various failures and disappointments I had experienced along the way, I still yearned to make America my permanent home. This country had offered me the complete freedom to choose what I wanted to do and the opportunity to take the necessary risks to get there. And I knew that if I failed, I'd have more opportunities to move on and take even more risks to try to succeed again. All the people I had met there had also encouraged and supported me in becoming the best that I could. This seemed an ideal environment in which to settle down and raise a family. I hoped I'd have a chance to repay this country and its people by encouraging and supporting others to succeed.

I was, of course, being naive in assuming that once I was in the US, the American government would welcome me with open arms. In fact, I should have expected only the opposite. That's because for students from third-world countries entering America on student visas in the 1950s, becoming *permanent* US residents was well-nigh impossible.

When foreign students were admitted to American universities, they were granted student visas solely for the purpose of studying in a US college or university. After earning a degree, these students were permitted to work in the US for a period of up to 18 months to gain work experience. Once that period ended, they were required to return home.

One exception to this rigid rule remained on the books. If a US company succeeded in convincing the US Labor Department that the company *had* to hire a foreign graduate because no American possessed the skills it urgently needed, then immigration would allow the American company to apply for a permanent resident visa (the all-mighty *green card*) on behalf of the newly hired graduate. The waiting period for obtaining permanent visas varied widely. It depended on the quotas allotted to the respective countries.

For Indian citizens in the 1960s, the quota was overfull. That meant that even if an Indian citizen was fortunate enough to find a legitimate sponsor, he or she might have to wait for a decade or more before obtaining a permanent resident visa. During this waiting period, foreign graduates were legally authorized to work in the US, but if they left the country *for any reason* without first obtaining a valid return permit, which was virtually impossible, they would not be allowed to reenter the US. Foreign graduates who were waiting to receive their permanent resident visas were virtual prisoners confined to this country.

In January 1962, I marched onto a podium at the UF and received my PhD degree in economics. Soon enough, I became painfully aware of the difficulties involved in obtaining the much-revered green card. Officially, of course, I could still stay in the US for an additional 18 months, but thereafter my future looked bleak. I had trouble landing a teaching job following my graduation. I felt certain that immigration would expel me after my 18-month training period expired.

My temporary teaching position at Stetson University expired in April 1962. Fortunately, after a series of interviews, I landed at another teaching position at the University of Detroit (UD), starting in the fall of 1962. Luckily, the University also agreed to sponsor me for a green card. Yet I was worried because the Indian quota for permanent visas was overfull. I was afraid that the UD officials might withdraw the University's sponsorship once they discovered that it might be a decade or more before I could become a permanent resident.

Even though I felt uneasy about that, the fall semester at UD started smoothly as I bravely faced the challenge of a four-course teaching load and very large classes. At the same time, Bani and I settled into a cozy, two-bedroom apartment close to the campus. We started making new friends—not to mention a new addition to our family.

I was happy at the prospect of becoming a father, although I was also worried about our finances. The University failed to inform me when I joined that my new health insurance would not cover the cost of childbirth for nine months, or until May 1963—two months too late for Bani's March due date. For the normal delivery of a child in those days, the doctor's bill, including all the checkups before and after delivery, hovered near $1,000. The cost of the four-day hospital stay was an additional $400. Somehow, I figured I'd manage to cover the hospital cost, but the doctor's charges were too much. I had no idea what to do.

Financially ready or not, on March 1 at 11:30 on a wintery night, I rushed Bani to the hospital when her labor started. Once registered, Bani was transferred to a wheelchair. Her attending nurse waited for me to kiss her goodbye before taking her to the delivery room. The nurse waited and waited. But because kissing in public was not a part of Indian culture, I did not lean forward to kiss Bani. And since Bani did not expect me to do so, the impasse continued for what seemed like an eternity. Finally, in exasperation, the nurse wheeled Bani away. As the doors swung shut behind them, I overheard the nurse saying to my wife, "You are going to have a baby and your husband didn't even kiss you goodbye? Honey, get rid of that lousy guy!"

I went to the waiting room, which I had chosen to call *the heir-port*, the term my parents used for the room where I was born at home. I sank into an easy chair as millions of random thoughts started rattling my brain. "The first child is always a girl in the Mittra family," I reminded myself, "so I'm sure we are going to have a daughter. But what will the experience of raising children be like in America? And what do I have to do to avoid the mistakes American parents typically make?"

I flashed back to my first experience seeing up close how Americans raise their children, which occurred back at the UF when I did a summer job at the UF bookstore and the manager, Jack DeMint, invited me to his house for dinner one evening. Jack and his wife Jane had a happy family and were proud of their two children. When we sat down at the dinner table, I thanked them for inviting me and remarked how lovely everything looked. Jane thanked me and asked how my family was back in India. I expected that this would be the start of a pleasant conversation. But before I could respond, we heard a yell from the second floor.

"Mom! He kicked me!" a girl's voice bellowed.

"No, I didn't. She's lying!" a boy's voice responded, equally emphatic.

I had never been exposed to a situation where children felt comfortable speaking that way, especially when they knew a guest was in the house. I had no idea how to respond.

Jack looked up toward the staircase and shouted back, "Bobby, Kimmy, both of you come down, *right now!*" Within a minute, both children tumbled down the stairs and stood before their father. Bobby looked to be about 11 and Kim about 13.

"Bobby, tell me what really happened *from the very beginning*," Jack said.

"Well, it all started when she hit me *back*."

"Oh, I see, so that's how it all began, did it? Kim, tell me, what did Bobby do to you."

"He kicked me real hard, and it hurt," she replied.

"No, I didn't," Bobby retorted. "She's exaggerating. I just touched her with my foot." At that point, Jack seemed more amused than angry. He did not scold his two children, nor did he apologize to me.

"Kids, go back to your rooms and close your doors," he told them. "And no TV or music tonight for either of you. Do you understand?"

The children did not accept the punishment lightly. "You're being mean! Why can't I watch TV? I didn't do anything wrong!" Bobby protested.

"Bobby kicked me and I am being punished?" came Kim's retort. "Why are you doing this to me?" The fight would have gone on, but dinner was getting cold and Jane realized that I was being put into an uncomfortable position.

"All right you guys, go upstairs and leave us alone. We will talk about it tomorrow," she scolded. That settled it.

In India, while children did not always obey their parents, they were taught never to contradict their elders in public or in the presence of outsiders. In a way, that was bad because Indian children failed to learn the difference between disagreeing and being disagreeable but nevertheless, that's how it was. So I didn't understand what Jack was trying to say when he mumbled something about the challenges of parenting. I failed to recognize that what I experienced that night was *normal* for many American families.

Now in the hospital waiting room, about to become a parent myself, I wondered how different our experience would be from the DeMints. Exhausted, I soon fell asleep. At dawn, the nurse awakened me to announce the birth of our first child. True to the Mittra custom, we had a girl.

On March 2, 1963, Dr Robert Jeremiah delivered our baby daughter, Rita. Dr Jeremiah had earned the reputation of delivering thousands of healthy babies, and he always wore the most reassuring smile. I liked him immensely. Bani loved the good doctor.

A month later, I took Bani for her first postnatal checkup. After gleefully announcing that Bani was doing great, Dr Jeremiah invited me into his private office. When I sat facing his desk, he smiled and said in a soft voice, "Professor Mittra, I am thrilled by how well Bani and Rita are doing. I hope that both you and Bani are enjoying your first baby. Remember, if you have any questions—I mean any questions at all—be sure to call me, day or night." Those were most comforting words for an overwhelmed new father.

The doctor paused for a moment and then continued, "And now let me make a personal suggestion. I am aware that your current insurance policy does not cover the cost of delivery. As you may have noticed, I have not yet billed you for my services. I suggest you give me a personal check, dated, signed, and payable directly to me. Just leave the space for the amount blank, and I will fill it in."

Despite his apparent kindness, I was suspicious of the doctor's suggestion. I did not know him well, and I had no idea how much money I would need to put into my account to cover the check. But I did what he asked, hoping desperately that he would not choose any amount higher than $1,000.

Every day I watched the mail anxiously, and finally, when the next bank statement arrived, I took a deep breath and thumbed through the canceled checks. When I came upon the check payable to Dr Jeremiah, I jumped with astonishment. For all of his services, many of which were beyond what we had any right to expect, Dr Jeremiah had not billed me $1,000. He charged merely $50. Since that day, I have always treasured that canceled check. I will be forever in Dr Jeremiah's debt.

‿

Although we were now a happy family of three, the immigration issue still loomed. Fearing that UD's sponsorship would fall apart, in desperation, I visited the US Immigration Office in Detroit on May 13, 1963. After waiting for more than two hours, I was directed to a cubbyhole where an officer was waiting. I had a bad feeling as soon as I laid eyes on this officer. He looked like a professional football player, totally misfit for his small office. He seemed bored with the thankless job of handling the immigration problems of foreign nationals. He did not even ask me to sit down in the chair facing his desk. I sat anyway as he opened a file placed in front of him with little expression.

"Your name?" he asked in a tired voice.

"I am Sid Mittra, and I am here to get some help on my visa problem," I answered sheepishly.

"What kind of problem?" he asked, still looking uninterested.

"My student visa allows me to work for only 18 months." I took a breath before I continued. "The University of Detroit, where I am teaching now, is ready to sponsor me for a permanent visa. But they have been told that the Indian quota is overfull and chances are nil that I will be granted a green card before the 18-month period is over. I am here to find out how I could continue teaching at UD until I have my permanent visa. I would like to stay in this country permanently."

"You and 18 million other foreigners," said the officer facetiously. "Every foreigner wants to stay here permanently. But the answer is *no*. We can't allow you to stay here after your training period is over."

I sat there petrified as the officer reshuffled the papers in my file. Suddenly, with no prodding from me, he blurted out, "Was your daughter born here?"

"Yes," I answered, hoping that would make some difference. It did.

As soon as he learned about Rita, the officer warmed up to my efforts. His voice mellowed as he noted that by virtue of being born in the US, Rita was automatically a US citizen. At the same time, he emphasized, as I already knew, that the quota for Indian nationals was backed up for many years and was getting worse. But he did offer me a way out.

"Your only viable option is to find a job with an international organization like the International Monetary Fund or the United Nations," he said sympathetically. "If you succeed, then we will allow you to work for that organization and stay in the US." Unfortunately, he did not know how to go about finding a job with an international agency. I left the Immigration Office baffled and discouraged. I drove home disconsolately.

A week later, still fearful of deportation, I received a letter out of the blue from a man named Dr Edward Holland, who invited me to join the economic consulting team of Simulmatics Corporation for two years. The responsibility of our team, the letter explained, would be to create a large-scale computer simulation model for Venezuela, acting as consultants to the Venezuelan government. It would require spending two years in South America.

I had no idea who Dr Edward Holland was, and I had never heard of Simulmatics Corporation. But the salary he offered me was more than twice what I was making, teaching at the University. Even more surprising was that the letter had coincidentally been drafted in Boston about the time I was returning from my visit to the Immigration Office in Detroit. Lady luck was smiling on me.

Excited about the opportunity this offer had created, I applied for a two-year leave of absence from UD. The University agreed to grant me the leave, provided I made a written commitment to return to the University for at least one year, following the conclusion of my assignment in Venezuela. I readily agreed.

With the leave of absence from the University in my pocket, I rushed to accept Dr Holland's offer by phone. As I would later discover, the project was financed by the US Agency for International Development in Washington, D.C. The immigration authorities were not about to create visa problems for someone the US government wanted to hire.

I still had one more hurdle to clear. While the letter of appointment authorized me to *stay* in this country as long as that employment lasted, the prevailing immigration rules did not permit me to *return* to the US from Venezuela (or from any other foreign country) if I left the US during the course of the appointment—a confusing mess.

In the end, however, the Immigration Department solved my visa problem by granting me a *parole* visa, one generally granted to criminals, which I was told would authorize me to return to the US after completing my Venezuelan project. The solution seemed a strange one to me, but who was I to argue with the US government?

One year passed after Bani, Rita, and I left the US for Caracas, Venezuela. Then we flew back to America so that I could comply with the terms of my parole visa, which had mandated that after an absence of one year, I must return to the US for at least four weeks. When our flight landed at JFK, we headed for the US immigration entry gates. One was for the US citizens, while the other was for foreigners. We waited in the second line until the immigration officer examined our papers. His expression grew more bewildered as he shuffled through our paperwork.

Each of us was carrying a different type of entry permit. Our daughter Rita had a US passport and so did not need a visa to enter her own country. Bani was an Indian citizen, but since she was born in Ceylon, her entry into the country had to be charged against the Ceylonese quota. In the 1960s, the Government of Ceylon prohibited its citizens from migrating to the US, so the American government's quota for granting permanent resident visas to people from Ceylon was wide open. This meant that Bani had been able to successfully receive the all-important green card. She was authorized to enter the country as a permanent US resident. But my situation presented a notorious wrinkle—my parole visa did not pass the smell test. The immigration officer felt that I should be treated as a persona non grata and refused entry.

What followed was a nightmare at the time, but now looking back on it, it seems comical. A poker-faced immigration officer, wearing a permanent snarl, snatched Rita away from her mother and handed the then-screaming baby over to a female immigration officer standing nearby. When Bani panicked, he explained that as a US citizen, Rita *had* to enter the country through a specially designated red-carpeted gate. Bani, on the other hand, would need to enter through the gate earmarked for non-US citizens. Once mother and child had legally entered the US, he explained as he signaled Bani through the proper portal, Rita would be immediately returned to Bani.

"Mr Mittra," the officer then said to me in an authoritative voice, "We do not let parolees enter the United States of America. Period."

I tried in vain to point out that I was not a criminal and explained to the officer why it was that I had a parole visa. But everything I said fell on deaf ears. It actually seemed that I might be deported while my wife and daughter would be allowed to remain in the US. My luck, it seemed, might finally run out in the airport where I had first set foot on the American soil.

At the end of his patience with me, the red-faced officer finally agreed to call the Immigration Department in Washington, D.C. Fortunately, some soul there finally confirmed that I indeed had legitimate papers to enter this country legally. At first, the officer refused to accept that verdict. He continued belligerently arguing that he had never heard of a parole visa being recognized as an entry permit, and hence he needed to speak to a higher authority. When the voice at the other end of the line told the officer that he was indeed speaking to a *higher authority*, identifying himself as the chief immigration officer and giving the airport immigration officer his badge number, the man acquiesced. He let me in—but he did so without glancing at me even once.

My visa problems, however, were not over. The US government had granted me the parole visa for one year only, not to be extended for any reason. But because I was working on a US-government-financed contract, Simulmatics was successful in twisting the arm of the Immigration Department to get me a one-year extension of that same parole visa. So I knew when I left that I would be able to return to Caracas after the required four-week stay in the US without fear of being denied reentry. But I had only a one-year contract to teach at UD waiting for me upon my eventual return. I knew it would take longer than that to get my green card. So if I could not find an institution that would be willing to sponsor me for an indefinite period, I would have to secure yet another position with an international organization—or risk being deported. Under the circumstances, I had little choice but to hope for the best.

I returned to Venezuela in the summer of 1964, and along with my teammates I became involved with the creation of a computer simulation model that would help accelerate the Venezuelan economic growth. But I never put the visa issue out of my mind. I was determined to solve the problem—I'd come way too far and worked too hard to just turn around and admit defeat.

After returning home from work one Friday, I sat down on our balcony facing the bustling city of Caracas. I closed the door to the living room behind me so that Bani wouldn't interrupt my thoughts, and started mulling over all my visa-related options. It was a beautiful sunny afternoon, with specks of white clouds floating in a gorgeous blue sky. From the second-floor balcony of our *Los Palacios Grandes* (The Grand Palaces) apartment, I had a grand view of scores of families out shopping and enjoying themselves, and *porpuestos* (taxis) clogging up the narrow streets, creating dreadful traffic jams.

But none of that managed to interrupt me that afternoon, as my focus remained glued to my intractable visa problem. I was unable to shake the feeling of doom and gloom. It seemed pretty unlikely that I'd be able to connect with an international organization, such as the UN or the International Monetary Fund in Washington, D.C., while living in Venezuela.

Suddenly, I thought of something that gave me a glimmer of hope. Maybe when the project in South America was finished, I could find a job with a branch of the UN in another part of the world outside the US. That would allow me reentry to the US whenever I wanted it. It would give me more time for the green card to come through. Even though the chances of finding such a position seemed remote, I had to try. Yet I couldn't figure out how to go about it.

After agonizing for several months about how I might accomplish such a feat, I finally went to see Dr Jorge Ahumada, the Director of El Centro de Estudiosdel Desarrollos (The Center of Development Studies or CENDES in Spanish). This was the Venezuelan organization we were working with closely. I wanted to explain my visa predicament. Dr Jorge Ahumada was a Chilean citizen, hired by the Government of Venezuela because of his expert knowledge of economic problems facing South American countries. But he was mindful that he was not a Venezuelan. So he made a special effort to be kind and helpful to all CENDES employees.

After listening to my story and showing concern for my plight, Dr Ahumada suggested I contact the Asian Institute for Economic Development and Planning in Bangkok, a UN institution. He even volunteered to provide me with the name of the director who, much to my surprise, turned out to be none other than P.S.N. Prasad. He was the head of the research department I worked at the Reserve Bank in Bombay—the man who had recommended me for the Fulbright Fellowship years before! Could it be that some higher power lifted up Prasad from Nigeria, where he had until recently been working as a UN representative, and put him down at the Bangkok Institute just so he would be there when I needed him? I am convinced that's really what happened.

When I had contacted Prasad and expressed an interest in joining the Asian Institute as a consultant, he remembered me and worked his magic. In just a few short weeks, I received a project appointment letter from the United Nations (UN). Although the consulting job was of short term, he explained that along with the appointment, I would receive a UN identification badge. He told me that, although he could give me no official assurances, he believed that immigration would look at my entry back into the US more favorably. It would be less inclined to deport me simply because I would have a UN stamp. This might give me just the final break I needed to obtain my permanent residence status.

As miraculous as this offer was, there was one catch. To accept the appointment with the UN, I would need to be in Bangkok at the end of May 1965, which was a full six weeks before my contract in Venezuela would be up. Fortunately, I was able to obtain an early release from my sympathetic supervisor. I left Caracas with my family by the third week of April.

∽

Instead of heading directly to Thailand, however, we first spent three weeks vacationing in Europe and India. We started out flying to Belfast, Ireland, visiting with my brother Braj for a few days. This was followed by some sightseeing in London. While there, I realized my Indian passport would expire not long after I arrived in India, but because Indian citizens experienced considerable delays in getting passports renewed in Delhi or Bombay, I thought it was wise to get my passport renewed at the Indian Consulate in London.

From London, with my new passport in hand, I flew to Bombay with Bani and Rita. We enjoyed a few exciting days with our extended family. At that point, we decided that, since the UN had arranged for me to stay in a Bangkok dormitory not meant for family use, Bani and Rita would stay behind in Bombay while I went on alone to Bangkok. Once the UN assignment was over, in less than three months, I would then return to Bombay. Then Bani, Rita, and I would finally return to Detroit so I could finish my one-year contract with the UD.

Everything worked out as planned, and I indeed returned to Bombay after completing the UN assignment in August. But because we did not yet have a place to stay in Detroit, we decided I would return to the US alone, and my family would join me once I found a suitable apartment for us.

On the way back to Detroit, I stopped in London for a few days. While checking my travel papers on the night before my departure for the US, I was horrified to discover that my new passport, issued only four months previously by the London office, was missing. Without a valid passport, I could not be admitted to the US, UN identification badge or no. Because I had recently obtained a new passport at the Indian Consulate in London, I feared that reporting a lost passport now would raise suspicion. I sank into my chair, unable to believe what was happening.

All night long, I tossed and turned. I decided to visit the Indian Consulate the next day and tell them the truth. Early the next morning, I arrived there baggy-eyed, emphasizing to the receptionist that the matter was urgent because I had a plane to catch in the afternoon. Even so, I was made to wait for two hours before I was called in to talk to an officer.

The mid-level officer suspected skullduggery. The officer began asking pointed questions. I was given an affidavit form to fill out to swear that my passport was in fact lost and to acknowledge that I would be prosecuted if foul play were discovered. Another officer subjected me to even more questions. Finally, when I was exhausted and could take no more, he told me that a new replacement passport would be issued in 24 hours.

Although I had to miss my original flight, the next day I indeed flew to Detroit with my new passport and my UN badge. I was admitted into the US without incident. It was not nearly as colorful an entrance as my previous reentry, but I was not complaining.

I returned to the UD in the fall of 1965, and Bani and Rita joined me soon afterward. We happily settled back into the university community, but I had been worried about what would happen when my one-year contract with UD was up. I yearned for some semblance of stability in our lives, and I desperately wanted to find an institution that would offer me a multiyear contract with permanent visa sponsorship.

In January 1966, I heard about an opportunity at Oakland University, a state school 30 miles north of Detroit in Rochester, Michigan. Robbin Hough, chairman of Oakland's Economics Department, told me that the University wanted to expand its department, which currently had only four faculty members. Specifically, he was looking for someone with expertise in money and banking, as well as in international economic development—which matched my expertise. Although I had never heard of Oakland University before this opportunity presented itself, Robbin told me that Oakland aimed at becoming the Harvard of the Midwest, which sounded good to me. I later learned that the provost, who had been a Fulbright scholar, had earned both his master's and his PhD from Harvard.

Robbin set up a meeting with me, and the instant I set foot on Oakland's 1,600-acre campus with its picturesque rolling hills, I fell in love with it. Robbin sweetened the pot by promising that Oakland would give me the liberty of creating my own courses and the freedom to develop a new teaching style, if that's what would keep me excited. But best of all, after listening to my visa situation, he told me he felt that he would be able to talk to the powers that be and offer me not the usual one-year contract, but a three-year faculty position—*and* he felt the University would be willing to sponsor me for a permanent visa. I returned home that afternoon believing in miracles.

True to his word, Robbin sent me an informal appointment letter on January 19, which I received four days after our meeting. Final confirmation would come within the next few months. Could it finally be that the baby born under crossed stars in Banaras, the dunce who was caned constantly in Calcutta, the high school student who misspelled *science* in his final exam and then graduated late after nearly dying of typhoid, the clerk for the Reserve Bank in Kanpur who was trapped in a dreary dead-end job, the research assistant in Bombay who fumbled the Fulbright, the foreign graduate student who was thrown in a rural jail by a formidable Georgian cop, had somehow grown into the man whose dreams of earning a PhD and permanently settling down in America were about to come true? Dare I believe it?

The answer to that question came four months later on a Saturday afternoon in May, just after my 36th birthday. I was sitting on a lawn chair, reading a *Time* magazine article on how to think big and watching Rita play on our front lawn. The mail carrier stopped and handed over what seemed at first like a bunch of junk mail. Leafing through it, however, I noticed an official-looking letter from Oakland University.

As I eagerly slit open the envelope, I couldn't help remembering opening another envelope on another continent almost nine years previously—an envelope that would, like this one, change my life forever.

"I am pleased to inform you," the letter from Oakland Provost Donald D. O'Dowd began, "that the Board of Trustees at its meeting on April 21 approved your appointment … from August 15, 1966, until August 15, 1969." The letter also said that the position offered was not an assistant professorship, which I had initially expected, but an associate professorship. In academia, it normally takes six years to go from assistant professor to associate professor, and then eight to ten years or more after that to become a full professor. So this was an amazing offer indeed!

But the letter also contained some alarming news: By the time my three-year contract was up, I had to earn tenure, or my contract would not be renewed. I knew that would be difficult. I'd have to work hard to satisfy the tenure committee. But knowing this was the final step to being able to stay in the US, I was ready.

I couldn't have known it on that glorious May afternoon, but, by the time that first three-year contract was up in August 1969, two momentous events would have occurred—events that at one time had seemed not merely improbable, but impossible. One of them would alter the history of mankind, and the other would alter the history of my life: Astronaut Neil Armstrong became the first man to walk on the moon, and I, Sid Mittra, PhD, became not just an associate professor as had been expected, but a full professor with tenure—*and* holder of a green card.

Finally I was home at last, and this time for good.

Epilogue: Life's Lessons

Bani and I arrive in Florida and begin our new lives together, eventually moving to Michigan so that I can take a job teaching at the UD. But I soon discover that at the expiration of my student visa, I will be permanently deported. Thus begins a musical-chairs-like series of adventures with the US Immigration Service, involving my obtaining both a job with an international organization and a parole visa, which actually causes more problems than it solves. One example: The first time Bani, our US-born daughter Rita, and I attempt to reenter the US after my first assignment out of the country, Bani is directed to enter the immigration portal through a gate for non-citizens, a screaming Rita is handed to a female immigration officer because regulations require that she enters through a specially designated red-carpet gate, and I am denied entry altogether until I can convince the belligerent immigration officer to call the US Immigration Department in Washington, D.C. My problems are eventually solved when I get an assignment with the UN in Thailand, obtain a UN badge and permit, and can then legally return to the US without being branded as a criminal.

As I look back, I marvel at the twists and turns of my life's journey, from being born into marginal circumstances with discouraging prospects to working for the UN and settling down in the US as a distinguished professor and revered financial planning expert. Seemingly impossible? Indeed. But like the bee that really never should have been able to fly, I recognize that I have met every improbable, frantic, and often hilarious challenge with unswerving determination, sheer will, and optimistic grace.

The following Four Ps' list identifies the P(s) that I have covered in this chapter:

[X] Persevere with passion.
[X] Pursue professional, family-oriented, social, and spiritual goals.
[X] Persuade family and friends to help.
[   ] Promote a culture of giving back.

13

MY ACADEMIC LIFE: FAILURES AND ACHIEVEMENTS

To teach is not a transitive verb. It is a reflexive verb.
—Dr John Hart

Thank God for the United Nations.

I returned to the US from Thailand in 1965 through the back door. I used a UN passport that I obtained as a result of my acting as a financial planning expert. And since I had a contractual obligation to return to the UD for one year in the fall of 1965, I arrived in Detroit. But I was still seeking a home. That opportunity presented itself. I learned that the Economics Department of Oakland University in Rochester, Michigan, what I hoped would be the "Harvard of the Midwest," sought a faculty member with the special skills I acquired in Venezuela and the UN. I arranged an interview, hoping that all of my problems would be over.

Someone must have cracked up at my naïveté.

During the interview, I learned that Oakland would sponsor me for a permanent resident visa but with a condition: publish or perish within three years. I was on a probationary, three-year tenure track appointment. I had to establish a substantial publication record to gain tenure. I accepted the offer with guarded optimism, recognizing these myriad challenges.

I arrived at the campus of Oakland University in 1966, hoping to settle in this sleepy university town known as Rochester. This was the end of the first phase of my life and the beginning of another. The first phase was characterized by endless challenges and disappointments, coupled with occasional glimmers of hope and sunshine. Fortunately, now that I had secured a regular faculty appointment, had a family, and was about to be granted my permanent resident visa (the elusive green card), I could put my volatile past behind me and embark on a new life in America. But I forgot that I would have to move again if I was denied tenure.

Before sharing with you my varied experiences as an academic professional, I would like to make a confession. Despite successes in my early academic life, I met numerous challenges both in areas of teaching and research and suffered many failures. For instance, my book on the working of the major central banks of the world, accepted for publication by a highly prestigious publishing house, never saw the light of day because the editor got fired and the publisher reneged on his promise (I self-published it later). The course I developed based on my experience as a consultant to the UN was never approved by the university-designated teaching committee. The personal financial planning (PFP) program I launched at Oakland was never given the respect it deserved. My grant application to the National Science Foundation for a undeserving grant was turned down with a condescending note underserving of such an august body. My superiors at the University chided me for being much too demanding a professor, thereby negatively affecting the impressive growth in the student population the University was experiencing. Academic freedom notwithstanding, the University argued that it could ill-afford that outcome. And some business school faculty accused me of branching off into the area of personal finance because I couldn't succeed in the traditional field of finance (even when I was the only faculty member in our School who published a highly successful investment text with Harcourt Brace, a reputable published company). The list goes on and on and on. Fortunately, I found the courage and had the wisdom to endure all of these failures, challenges, and criticisms with silence as well as with grace.

Reverting to the main theme, I should have diligently started preparing for the three courses I was assigned. But I couldn't. Bad memories plagued me. I kept searching for a way to become a distinguished professor. One day I recalled my mother's advice which in the past I had ignored: "There are only one of three ways you can make a mark in this world: Be the first, be the best, or be *different*." (I learned much later that John Templeton, the investment maverick, made similar points when establishing his famous investment philosophy. "It is impossible to produce a superior return unless you do something different from the majority," said Templeton as recounted in the book *Investing the Templeton Way*.) I decided then that I would strive to become a different kind of teacher, with an academic career that would underscore that point.

When I began teaching a basic course as a graduate student I was also influenced by Dr John Hart, Dean of the School of Business at the University of Florida.

"To teach," he explained, "is not a transitive verb. It is a reflexive verb."

Puzzled, I asked what he meant.

"Sid," replied Dean Hart with a smile, "teachers have a tendency to transmit knowledge to their students and test them on how well they remember what was transmitted to them. That results in memorization. But you *educate* when students can reflect upon the information you presented, then digest it, and, if found useful, internalize it. Only then do you become an effective teacher."

Notwithstanding the sound advice, I began teaching with an embarrassment that I would never forget.

My first class in economics at Stetson University in DeLand, Florida, was scheduled to begin at 10 am. I had been preparing for that class for weeks and had my first lecture memorized. So I was convinced that I would deliver an outstanding lecture.

Just before class, I went to the restroom to freshen up. But when I emerged from the restroom, a pretty blonde girl walked up to me and said, "Professor Mittra, don't be nervous. We are well-behaved students and won't create any problems for you. Promise."

I was offended by her condescension and wanted to tell her what I thought. So I responded angrily, "What makes you think I am nervous? I can assure you that I am fully prepared for the class and am not fearful."

"Oh really?" she replied. "If you are not nervous, Professor Mittra, then why the heck did you just come out of the ladies room?"

Nervous or not, I delivered a good lecture on the first day, which was followed by well-prepared and comprehensive lectures the rest of the semester.

At the end of the semester, the department conducted the traditional, confidential student evaluation. It was sent to my chairman, who shared it with me. I learned then that while students liked my teaching style and appreciated my letting them participate in class discussions, they also found me stiff and too demanding. But since I was new to this process, I again requested Dean Hart to advise me how to overcome my deficiencies. Once again, the Dean obliged: "Sid, I have one piece of advice: Don't demand less, but smile more." When asked for clarification, he explained that an effective teacher should relax and "have fun," but just to have an easier time he should never demand less of students in terms of rigor and sophistication.

Those two lessons—recognizing that to teach is a reflexive act and remembering to smile more without sacrificing rigor—have been the cornerstones of my teaching, and helped me win over students both in and out of the university classroom.

∽

Even before I joined the faculty of Oakland University in Michigan in the fall of 1966, remembering my mother's advice, I had decided to become an effective teacher by being *different* and taking the road less traveled. I used my participatory teaching style when I joined Oakland. Owing to the large size of the class and the rigid structure, I couldn't use my participatory style in the introductory courses. But I did use this somewhat risky teaching style in the upper level and graduate courses.

For example, in the Investment Analysis and Portfolio Management course, on the first day of classes I would lay down the four basic rules of how the class would proceed:

1. At the beginning of each lecture I would write down on the black board a number of topics pertaining to the chapter assigned for that day. Each student would be free to pick one topic, stand in front of the class and explain it to the fellow students.
2. Those who did not voluntarily choose a topic would be required to explain topics I selected for them.
3. If the explanation needed further clarification, other students would get a chance to provide information, or I would help.
4. If there was still time left, I'd share stories unrelated to the course material which contained life lessons.

Understandably, many students complained to the chairman and the dean about this unorthodox teaching style, and for a while my class enrollments dwindled to the point of great concern and anxiety. But I persevered, partly not only because of only my firm belief in the lasting value of this teaching style, but also because the University's academic freedom policy prohibited administrators from interfering with my freedom to use my own teaching techniques.

Here's how in my upper Investment Management course a dialog took place between myself and a student named Ted Bugenski. After picking DJIA as his topic, Ted explained to the class that DJIA, or Dow Jones Industrial Average, was the average of 30 industrial stocks in the index.

"Do you mean DJIA is the *average of the prices* of 30 industrial stocks in the index?" I asked.

"That's correct," answered Ted with confidence.

"Do you know by any chance where the DJIA closed yesterday [January 8, 1987]?" I asked.

"I sure do," replied Ted, "yesterday for the first time it closed above 2000, or to be precise, at 2002.25."

"Congratulations, Ted, for being so well informed. But you know, I still find something quite puzzling. If DJIA is an *average of prices* of 30 industrial stocks, as you point out, then the *average* price of each stock would have to be as high as $2,002. Ted, have you ever heard of any stock selling for $2,000?"

Ted was stunned by that question, and so were the rest of the students in the class. Everyone knew what the Dow Jones was, but none had a clue how the average price of 30 stocks in that index could be that high. When I sensed uneasiness in the class, I challenged the students to solve this puzzle on their own before our next class.

Notwithstanding the value of my teaching method, at first it was rough going. Most students did not want to talk in front of the class. But after a few years, the word got out that, even though I was a demanding instructor and my teaching method was rather painful, students learned a lot in my course. From then on, my upper level and graduate classes enjoyed full, and frequently overfull, enrollments. (Lower level courses were always full regardless of who taught them.)

Teaching, for me, was serious. But there were instances when it was also quite amusing. Here are two instances.

Once at Oakland, I was teaching Economics 202 in a theater-style classroom. As usual, the class was full (90 students) and without looking at my notes or the textbook, I was lecturing on the theory of comparative advantage. Explaining the theory, I stated that, strange though it might seem, both Mexico and the US tended to gain if each country specialized in activities in which it had comparative advantage. Hearing that, one student asked what the gross domestic products were for America and Mexico. I didn't remember the exact numbers, so I decided to look them up in the text. But since I never brought my textbook to the class, I walked over to the front row and extended my hand to a girl student who was holding the textbook in her hand. But I was startled when she didn't make any gesture to handover the book to me.

"Hey, I am not stealing your book, just want to borrow it for a moment," I said somewhat put off. I practically yanked the book out of her hands.

I shouldn't have been so reckless.

When I glanced at the book, the following handwritten script jumped out of the open page: "Prof. Mittra stinks."

The other incident was trickier, but far less painful.

At Oakland, to prevent cheating or plagiarism, professors were required to proctor exams. But I told my students that I trusted them and did not proctor the exams.

But one time that trust got me into serious trouble.

I discovered that at an exam in economics, there were two identical answers to an *essay question*. That presented a dilemma: How to detect the cheater and turn him over to the academic conduct committee for appropriate action? Both students denied cheating, and I failed to identify the culprit.

Fortunately, my student assistant had a sharper eye than me. He pointed out that in one part of the essay one student had written, "I don't know the answer." The second student, who was busy plagiarizing, copied, "I don't know the answer, *either.*" For me, that saved the day.

In 1966, I joined the Economics Department at Oakland. All of my teaching assignments came from that department. As observed earlier, over time I became more interested in teaching courses in finance, and also began publishing in that discipline. Finally, in 1990, long after I was granted tenure, got promoted to the rank of full professor, and succeeded in publishing three books and many articles in finance, I formally requested the University to switch me from the department of economics to finance. But just as I had experienced so many disappointments in the past, my request for making this change was flatly denied. Here is an excerpt from a letter I received from the dean of School of Business in 1990 that attests to the difficulties I encountered to achieve my goal:

August 20, 1990
To: Prof. Sid Mittra
From: Ronald M. Horwitz, Dean
School of Business Administration
RE: Your note of August 7, 1990

I have given your request to be placed in the finance field on a full-time basis much thought, and, by necessity, have discussed it with the chairpersons of the two departments which would be affected, Buck Dillon and Ron Tracy. We are unanimous in our conclusion that it would not be in the best interests of the School of Business Administration to grant your request [of changing your designation from Professor of Economics to Professor of Finance].

While I fully appreciated the Dean's position, I was discouraged by his negative response. But unwilling to give up, with renewed vigor, I continued teaching and publishing in the field of finance. I hoped that eventually the University would give in. In the end, I got lucky, as can be seen from the following notification I received from Oakland six years later.

OAKLAND UNIVERSITY
Office of the Vice President and Academic Affairs
Rochester, Michigan 48309-4401
BOARD ACTION
June 6, 1996

The Board of Trustees at its meeting on June 6, 1996 took the following action: Approved the appointment of: Mittra, Sid, **Professor Emeritus of Finance**, effective August 15, 1996.

One of my greatest pleasures as a faculty member was to encourage my students to reach their full potential. That was certainly the case with Travis Nobel, although it happened in a convoluted manner.

In the fall of 1974, in my Economics 200 class, Travis Nobel was one of the 90 students, so it was not possible for me to get to know him personally. But I did notice that occasionally he was absent, and he rarely participated in discussions. That was, of course, a common practice among students in a basic economics course. So Travis' behavior did not concern me.

The grading system I developed for this basic course was different: Instead of basing the final grade on mid-term and final exams, I used the weighted grade average from three one-hour exams, a term paper, and class participation.

I had noted that Travis had received only 1.2 in the first-hour exam, well below the minimum passing grade of 2.0. I routinely offered special help to students receiving a failing grade during the first exam, but only if they took the initiative to seek my assistance.

Travis did show up in my office one day to discuss his grade, but the encounter suddenly became nasty.

Travis informed me that he was receiving the university's scholarship for black students, and for it to continue he *had* to get a passing grade. But to my dismay, when I offered to help him improve his performance, he refused.

"Look Professor Mittra," Travis said in an irritated voice, "this course is too hard for me, and I don't think I can improve my grade by studying differently. But since I am black and must receive this scholarship to continue my studies at Oakland, I want you to give me a 2.0 in this course."

I was stumped.

"Travis," I said, "your color makes no difference to me. I am black, too, but no one gave me any breaks for that reason. If you want to get a 2.0 in this course, you'd just have to work harder. I *will not* make an exception in your case just because you are black."

Travis retorted, "Dr Mittra, you are not the right kind of black so you don't deserve a special treatment." And before I could respond, he startled me by barking: "Aren't you scared of getting hurt?"

I was petrified, especially because no student had ever physically threatened me before, and it did take a few minutes for me to get hold of myself.

After recovering, I replied: "Don't kid yourself, Travis. Like everybody else, I'm petrified by the thought of getting physically hurt. But I have taken a vow to treat every student fairly and with respect, and no threat can make me violate my sacred academic commitment. So, your threat won't change my decision. I will do my best to help you improve your performance if that's your wish, but I will not give you a grade you don't deserve."

Travis stomped out of my office. And I dreaded the thought of getting hit by a stone or a bullet when I left the building. Fortunately, that night I returned home safely, though exhausted and frightened.

Travis did not show up in my class for a week, which made me afraid that he was up to something nasty. Then one day, I was surprised to see him walk into my office. I was relieved to notice then that he was not carrying a gun.

Travis sat down on the chair facing me, looking somewhat somber yet nervous. After a long pause, he started mumbling, "Dr Mittra, I don't know quite how to say this. You are the first person who has treated me not as a black but as a person. At first, I was angry because you refused to give me the grade I demanded. But later I realized that you wanted me to develop self-respect as a human being and not get everything the easy way just as I am used to."

Travis paused for a moment and then concluded, "If you can forgive me for threatening you and still want to help me, I will study the way you want me to and earn a passing grade."

This story has a happy ending. Travis got a 2.2 grade in Economics 200, and underwent a profound change in attitude. He became a serious student at Oakland and continued to perform well in other courses. Eventually, he graduated from Oakland with a 3.1 average, a decent grade for someone who once thought he was destined to fail.

After he got his undergraduate degree from Oakland, I encouraged Travis to get a master's degree from a more prestigious school. He promised to pursue his graduate studies after he saved up the money.

I lost touch with Travis for several years. Then one day I opened an envelope that contained a handwritten note. It read,

> Thanks for your friendship, Dr. Mittra
> Dr. Travis Nobel, **Ph.D.**
> Your Friend

The opportunity to help a student reach his full potential presented itself in a different way in the case of John Locke, who was a senior in my investment class. John earned a 4.0 point in my course and received his undergraduate degree in Management with high honors from Oakland University.

Normally, that would have been the end of my association with John. But soon after graduation, he set up an appointment to discuss his future.

It was a beautiful sunny afternoon when John and I sat down. John said that he wanted to pursue graduate studies and asked me if I would mind writing a letter recommending him for admission to Oakland's MBA program. Instead of replying him directly I asked: "Since you graduated from Oakland Summa Cum Laude, instead of going to the same school shouldn't you plan on getting an MBA from the University of Michigan, which has one of top business schools in the nation?"

"How can you say that, Dr Mittra," replied John, "when you know it is extremely difficult for Oakland graduates to get admission to Michigan's MBA program? I hate to play such odds. I would rather seek admission to Oakland's program where I know I'd get in."

I was disappointed with John's response, and my demeanor must have showed it. Noticing my disappointment, John suddenly asked: "Do you think I should try Michigan first, even though the chances of my getting in are virtually nil?"

"If you're convinced that you can't get into Michigan," I said, "then I doubt it if you would succeed. But if you're determined to get into Michigan, and you are willing to do whatever it takes to achieve your objective, then I am convinced that ultimately you will succeed."

John left without saying another word but returned to see me the next day. I was pleasantly surprised to hear that he had decided to apply to Michigan. I was also encouraged when John sought my advice on how he could improve his odds to his getting into Michigan's MBA program.

John not only graduated from University of Michigan's prestigious MBA program with honors, but subsequently went on to obtain a couple of business-related certificates. He began working in finance and enjoyed a meteoric career rise. Currently, John is the managing partner of a prestigious firm, earning a high six-figure income and is overloaded with numerous fringe benefits and stock options.

When I joined the faculty of Oakland University, I dreamed of becoming an outstanding teacher in the classroom. But my student evaluations consistently revealed that I was a good (a 3.5–4 rating on a 1–5 scale) but not an outstanding professor. One day I read in the campus newspaper that a professor in Art Department had won the University's Best Teacher Award two years in a row. So I decided to seek his guidance on how to get to his level of teaching excellence.

"Sid," said the learned professor when I met him, "your reputation as a dedicated and a demanding teacher precedes you, and I have nothing to add there." He paused for a moment and then added: "But you still need to learn how to make your lectures a *fun* experience for the students. You can learn that in one of two ways: Keep trying until you learn it or invite a few professors from your School of Business to observe your teaching by sitting in your classes and then provide the inputs you need to help reach your goal."

I returned to my office enthused and, I must confess, somewhat scared. I saw great value in making this a standard business school policy so all professors could benefit from regular visits to their classrooms by their colleagues and offering them valuable advice. However, I also recognized that this was uncharted territory, and unquestionably it flew in the face of the University's highly revered academic freedom policy. Anyway, after reflecting on it for several days, when I was convinced that in this case benefits far exceeded the cost, I made an appointment to discuss this sensitive matter with the dean.

The dean's response was ambivalent at best and dismissive at worst. He did recognize the benefit of helping faculty members to become better teachers. But he also raised more important issues, such as favoritism, nervousness created by having *foreign* visitors, unwarranted complications arising from these visits, and much, much more. In the end, without even trying to find a workable solution to the problems he anticipated from officially acting on this plan, he dropped the matter.

And with that, my grandiose plan for helping the University by making my colleagues more effective teachers went up in smoke.

One of my greatest joys in teaching came from sharing stories with students after the day's lessons were covered but before each lecture ended. Of all the stories I shared, the following philosophical piece by Margo LaGattuta was the most popular among students.

SEVEN MAGIC ELEPHANTS EXPLORING THE PROCESS OF CREATIVITY

It's a new year, and we are given another chance to start our lives anew. We want to be better this year, more creative, more productive. The problem is getting started. Whatever we want to create in our lives can happen if we follow seven easy concepts.

This idea came to me years ago when I saw an ad in a magazine for "Seven Magic Elephants." For only $3.98, I could have my every wish come true—wealth, health, romance, and happiness. These seven ivory elephants, the ad said, would bring luck to the person who possessed them, so I decided to look for a series of seven elements (or elephants) of the creative process. This way I could remind myself how to be creative when my ideas dry up. Here are the seven empowering concepts I discovered:

Concept 1—INTENTION

Creativity begins with a wish and a plan. There must always be a longing combined with intent to begin any creative idea. Holding the elephants in our hands allows us to begin to name the possibilities. We begin with small choices and a bit of magic. This is the brainstorming stage, the "What do I want in my wildest dreams?" elephant. It's the blank page or canvas, but it needs a concrete place to begin. So begin by writing down an intention. What do you really want to create?

Concept 2—TIME

The next elephant is time, an obvious but rarely honored ingredient in creativity. We make time for nearly everything visible in our lives, but this is the invisible. It is the time before any measured outcome. Often we try to take our creative time from what is left when we have accomplished the necessities of life. But we then discover, there is no time left. It helps to commit one day a week, or one weekend a month, for incubation and creative projects, and stick to it. Even if you spend the afternoon staring out the window and doodling, taking the time gives focus, and soon you will have begun.

Concept 3—LOVE

Love, particularly self-love, is an elephant of empowerment. It is difficult because with anything that is bold or new there is always risk. The voice of the critic in our head says, "Who do you think you are?" Creativity takes an act of audacious authority, which can only come from self-esteem. There must also be the desire to make something happen, the love of the idea itself. Believing in ourselves and what we are doing is a paradoxical dance of amazement, a kind of love/fear mambo. It is what drives us on to face the elephants to come.

Concept 4—ENERGY
This elephant is the firecracker that explodes a project into motion, the leap of faith that overcomes all obstacles. It comes in a burst of electricity or a quiet urgency. It is the red cardinal to a bird watcher, who must sit very still to notice its presence. It's a zoom, a flash of insight, a theatrical drum roll, and should be seized and honored.

Concept 5—FEAR
Once we've processed all the other elephants, this is the big challenge. Fear of failure (or worse, fear of success) can stop any idea cold: This elephant says, "Give up," and triggers any fear that lingers in the memory bank of loss. This is where most of us stop. Standing up to it takes digging in our proverbial heels. Yet, in this stage of the birth process, the doorway to the delivery room, there is no turning back, no easy way out, and no one else can help. The only way out is through.

Concept 6—LETTING GO
This is the nothing elephant—the time when it seems like we've failed for sure, and we don't know what to do. It's the time of total surrender to the process. If we think we had control before, we are now certain we have none. We need to meditate or clear our mind of all thoughts, let go of all agendas. This is a very secret place, where something we never expected can come in. This is where a creative leap can take place. We can make a change that makes it work.

Concept 7—BIRTH
The brand new elephant resembles its parents, yet has the look of an original. The idea in its infancy still trembles. We need the nothing element to become still enough to even recognize this elephant. We rejoice and stand in awe. The birth of any new project is as painful as it is joyous. And there is hard work ahead, involving wish, time, love, energy, fear, and letting go. The circle of elephants goes on into infinity. What a gift to know we hold them all in the palms of our hands.

At Oakland, in 1969, the new Business School used a typical business curricula, and our Economics Department was moved from the School of Arts and Sciences to the Business School. For the next two decades, our school grew by leaps and bounds with the department of finance frequently stealing the show. During this entire time period, Personal Financial Planning (PFP) was assumed to lack academic rigor (because it was assumed to be the domain of stockbrokers and insurance salesmen) and, hence, was never considered to be an integral part of the common body of knowledge needed to earn a business degree.

By the time I earned my certified financial planning (CFP) diploma in 1982, and joined the CFP Board three years later: I became thoroughly convinced that PFP provided an excellent pedagogical laboratory for professors in business schools. Once I came to that realization, I moved swiftly to create a detailed proposal to include PFP into our business curriculum and submitted it to our School's Curriculum Committee. Not surprisingly, my hopes were quickly dashed when the Committee pointed out that since my proposal had failed to provide hard evidence to make my point, it had little choice but to reject my proposal.

Once again, I decided to continue this fight by following a circuitous route. First, as part of Oakland's Continuing Education Department (separate from Business School), in 1985, I established a comprehensive PFP program (which is still alive in 2015). I also created a prestigious Board of Advisers, consisting of financial planning practitioners and academic professionals to help the program mature. Simultaneously, I started working on a textbook that would clearly establish a close relationship between theory and practice of PFP courses. The result was one of my proudest moments in my academic career. In 1990, I published *Practicing Financial Planning: A Complete Guide for Professionals* by Prentice Hall. In my "Personal Message," I wrote: "It is not merely a collection of facts or a collage of practice-oriented ideas.... Throughout the book important financial planning theories and concepts have been inter-woven with practically-oriented planning strategies ....." Commenting on the book, Cynthia Foreman of the prestigious College for Financial Planning wrote: "The financial planning industry has been waiting for a book like this. Sid Mittra has succeeded where others have failed. The information is comprehensive and well written; the planning strategies are practical and right on target." When I read that note, I felt vindicated.

There was another dimension to this text that also became a trendsetter. Recognizing that a book of this complexity and magnitude in an ever-changing financial world could not be developed only by me, in a highly unorthodox fashion I accepted technical contributions from a large number of highly reputable financial planning practicing professionals. I continued this practice as the book went through 11 editions (2012). This approach, invented more than two decades ago, still represents a novel experiment while enriching the readers with the contributions of a wide variety of nationally recognized professionals, a privilege they would not have any other way.

On numerous occasions during my academic career, I challenged the status quo. I prevailed on the University, and made serious attempts to improve the currently prevailing practices. Still, in one instance I failed miserably.

Once I attended a seminar on the role of economics in public policymaking in which the highly sought-after speaker began by saying: "Ladies and gentlemen, today my task is to speak and your job is to listen. Let me know if you finish before I do." Everyone laughed at that remark as did I. But I also noticed that the speaker used humor to keep the discussion alive and enjoyable. Afterward, I privately met with the speaker who eloquently made the point that people (and by inference, college students) retain a lot more if the lessons are delivered in an enjoyable way but without sacrificing rigor.

Energized with that newfound knowledge I returned to my class, determined to use that technique in teaching my courses in economics and finance.

I failed.

It didn't take me long to realize that while the idea was good, it was the *effective execution* of that idea that was at the heart of its success. So, after experimenting with this idea a little longer, I decided to abandon it for good.

That did not mark the end of that novel idea, however.

When I was hired by the University, it was clearly explained to me that, as a member of the faculty in good standing, I had to demonstrate satisfactory performance in three areas: teaching, research, and university and community services. After I was granted tenure, as part of my community services, I chose to present public seminars on PFP. Now, with this newfound knowledge, I decided to use humor to spice up my public seminars.

It worked beautifully. In essence, I literally transferred my new technique from my university classroom to these seminars and achieved great success. Here's one story I frequently shared with the audience that was always a great hit with them.

Once Bob and Jack decided to use a hot air balloon to travel without a break all the way from Los Angeles to Bangor, Main, and have their achievement listed in the Guinness Book of World Records. One day, they arrived at the launching pad, got in the balloon waiting for them, bade good bye to the media, and took off.

About a half hour into the air, they were engulfed by thick fog and started floating aimlessly. Their communication equipment did not work which frightened them terribly. Then, after sometime, the fog disappeared miraculously. Both could see that they were floating over an empty field and there was someone standing on the field. Anxious to find out where they were, Bob leaned over and asked the person: "Where are we?"

Instantly, the man replied: "You are in a hot air balloon, Sir."

Hearing that, Bob turned to Jack and remarked: "Gee, I never thought that I would see a financial counselor standing on an open field."

> Jack retorted: "That's hogwash. The man is standing so far away that I couldn't even tell if it is a man or a woman. So how could you know that he is a financial counselor?"
>
> Bob replied: "The man did four things that gave away the secret."
>
> "What four things, Jack barked, totally unconvinced."
>
> Here's how Bob responded:
>
> First, he spoke without thinking.
>
> Second, he answered correctly, but only as far as it went.
>
> Third, he was *outstanding* in the field.
>
> Fourth, the answer he gave us didn't do us a damn bit of good.

In retrospect, I admit I failed to effectively use this novel technique in the university classroom. But I can say without equivocation that I had noted success both in public seminars and in the conference rooms dealing with my financial planning clients.

As a finance professor, schooled in theory, logic, and analysis, I believe that for every financial problem there is only one *best* solution. But that's not the way it always is in the world outside of academia. As an adviser, I found that for a client with a problem the best solution was the one acceptable to the client, even if it was not quite accurate, or even theoretically sound. That certainly shook my foundation, but there was more. I also learned that clients didn't care how much I knew until they knew how much I cared. And since I remained convinced that my success as a financial counselor was tied inextricably to enlightened clientele, I had little choice but to transform my knowledge-based academic classroom into a more personal, care-based teaching conference room.

The best decision I ever made was to transform my financial counseling conference room into a teaching classroom.

Once I came to this realization, I pursued my goal with passion. And, over time, I became an effective teacher of my clients.

In those days, it was customary for financial planning clients to move from one counselor to another, depending on what promises—real or imaginary—were made by various counselors. I rejected that. I only accepted clients who promised to make a long-term commitment to our practice. I understood my success rested on my ability to develop a new and effective way of educating clients so that they would not be blinded by the latest fad or outrageous promises of unscrupulous salespersons. As the philosopher Immanuel Kant eloquently said, "The best government was the one that taught people 'to govern themselves.'"

As I started experimenting with my novel teaching technique, valued clients found one aspect of this new teaching method scary, which required them to grade me on the test I took in their presence. Here's how that test was structured.

Following rigorous analysis of the comprehensive planning questionnaire by our client, John and Jane Smith, I would set up a Goals and Objectives Interview (GOI). During the interview, I would learn much about the Smiths: their individual personalities, hopes and fears, risk tolerance, major concerns, understanding and past experiences with investments, feelings about security, ability to trust their counselors, dreams for the future, and more.

Once the GOI was over, I would present the highlights of our interview in an organized manner. I would request John and Jane to grade me (choose between an A and an F grade). Naturally, I would receive an A grade if they were convinced that I now had a thorough understanding of their financial affairs, their psychological makeup, and what they wanted to achieve in their financial life. If not, I would receive an F.

Fortunately, during my 25 years of running a financial counseling service, I never flunked a GOI test.

The educational process began when the financial counseling began. It continued as long as the client–counselor relationship remained in place. I met with my clients regularly, upgrading their understanding of various financial concepts and theories, ensuring that they remained informed. And the fact that, except for death or relocation, I never lost a client suggests that clients appreciated the value of placing teaching at the core of my financial consulting services.

And so, by making the risky decision to *be different*, and taking to heart Dean Hart's advice on teaching, I became an effective teacher and an educator, both in the classroom and in the conference room. By adopting this unorthodox method, I did face numerous challenges along the way. Still, I enjoyed the ride far more than I would have, had I remained a traditional teacher.

∽

Actually, in academia I faced a bigger challenge. Instead of offering me the regular seven-year tenure track, Oakland required me to become tenured in three years or lose my service. That implied, in essence, that I had to establish a substantial publication record in that short period, a virtual impossibility as I saw it. Still, not willing to give up, I decided to have my PhD dissertation published quickly by a noted university press. But once again, my initial efforts to become a published author in a short period of time ran into a road block.

I sought the advice of Robbin Hough, chairman of Economics Department, on how to meet my goal. And as if he didn't know it, I reminded him that publication of one major book was a prerequisite for my getting tenured at Oakland. I assured him that my PhD thesis was practically ready for publication. I was looking for a publisher willing to publish it as a scholarly book.

Robbin's response was disturbing.

"Frankly," said Robbin, "the way you are going about it, I'm afraid you will never make it. I suggest you invite an established professor to become the senior author and you become the junior coauthor of the book. Only then will you succeed in achieving your goal." Then, as if to console me, Robbin added, "But don't worry. Once you become a published coauthor, you'd have a much easier time publishing books and articles on your own."

I found Robbin's advice unacceptable. It seemed both deceptive and immoral. Besides, I didn't accept his premise that I couldn't publish a book myself just because I was an unknown author. So I remained silent.

When Robbin noted my silent disapproval, he knew what was going through my mind. So, after a brief pause he continued: "Sid, I don't blame you for feeling disheartened. But that's the real world for you. In fact, I'd bet that if you send your thesis to a publisher, he will return it to you without even opening it."

Robbin's prediction turned out to be right on the money. In fact, when challenged that he did not even read the manuscript, one publisher went so far as to send me the following condescending note: "You don't have to eat the whole egg to find out it was rotten."

Fortunately, that rotten rejection only strengthened my resolve. Within three years, as a *sole author*, I succeeded in publishing three books. First, I published my doctoral dissertation through the Asia Publishing House. The next one on money was published by Random House. And the third one, in the field of money and banking, was also accepted for publication by Random House, but was in press when my three-year tenure term ended. This episode had a happy ending: My early successes in authoring several books and articles coupled with my unorthodox teaching style significantly helped my academic career. Within three years of my initial appointment, beating all odds, I received the following note from the University which I still hold as a souvenir.

OAKLAND UNIVERSITY
Board of Trustees
To: Sid Mittra
At its June 30, 1969 meeting the Board recommended that
Sid Mittra be granted tenure.
The Board also recommended that Sid Mittra be **promoted to Full
Professor of Economics, effective August 15, 1969.**

And now, by way of summing up my experiences as an academic professional, I can say without equivocation that regardless of the difficulties I encountered, I always persevered, remained focused on my goals, and approached every task with deliberate passion. And that brought results.

In the area of teaching, my unorthodox teaching method, coupled with my desire to expose students to life's important lessons set a new trend at Oakland, and that still remains my proud pedagogical achievement. In fact, I recall with great satisfaction what Ted Bugensky, my former student shared with me years later: "That experience in your class taught me to dig deeper and discover for myself the *real meaning* behind everything I learned in your class. But what I value even more is your sharing of life's important lessons which taught me so much about life. To be honest with you, Sid, I never expected that from a finance professor, and I don't recall any of my other professors ever doing that."

That was music to my ears.

In the area of research, I faced many new challenges, some of which proved to be insurmountable. Here again, I persevered and established a respectable track record. During my academic career, as a sole author (except in one case) I published more than a dozen books, all through prestigious companies such as Harper & Row, Harcourt Brace, Prentice Hall, Random House, and Irwin-Dow Jones. I also published over 100 articles in professional journals, and presented technical papers and seminars in professional meetings all over the world.

I would like to conclude by saying that while I am generally pleased with my publication record, what excites me most is the following passage. In the foreword to the 11th edition of *Practicing Financial Planning for Professionals*, Harold Evensky (former chairman of the CFP Board and a Hall of Fame inductee) wrote: "The Eleventh edition that you hold in your hands speaks eloquently of the quality of [Sid's] leadership . . . as a result of the enormous respect the profession has for [the book, Sid has] managed to corral contributions representing the best-of-the-best in many of the critical areas of financial planning. As a result, this edition not only represents the authors' enormous wealth of knowledge, it incorporates the intellectual capital of an amazing array of other respected professionals."[1]

This, indeed, is the souvenir I would value for the rest of my life.

Epilogue: Life's Lessons

After completing my assignment at the United Nations I return to the US and join Oakland University in Rochester, Michigan, as an associate professor on a special three-year tenure track. My contract specifies that I would be granted tenure in three years only if I develop substantial research base during that time period; if not, my contract would not be renewed. Fortunately, based on my success on the publication front as well my impressive teaching and service records, at the end of the three-year period I am not only granted tenure, but am also promoted to the rank of full professorship, a rarity for the University.

In order to distinguish myself as an outstanding teacher, I develop a participatory teaching style and invent a novel way of sharing with students inspirational stories drawn from real world experiences. It works very well, both for me as well as for my students.

Buoyed by my success in the teaching area, I venture into the risky path of changing my research orientation from economics to finance. I regularly publish articles and books in the area of finance and at one point in my career seek to change my official title from Professor of Economics to Professor of Finance. Initially, my request is categorically rejected by the University. Subsequently, however, based on my substantial publication record and scholarly activities in the area of finance, the University cheerfully grants me the title of Professor of Finance.

As part of my commitment to be of service to the society, in an unconventional manner I inspire students—both mediocre and brilliant—to reach their full potential in life. I do so not out of duty but because I feel obligated to return something meaningful back to the society that offered me so much.

There are two other areas in which I achieve noted success by following nontraditional paths. First, for ethical reasons I categorically reject the highly recommended approach of embarking on a joint-publication plan (with established professors with no connection to my research) to get my foot in the door and then publish as a sole author. Despite suffering from many initial rejections,

I prevail and ultimately succeed in publishing a dozen scholarly books with top-rated publishers. Second, following my newly-developed publication interests, I clearly shift my focus from economics to PFP. I achieve noted recognition by joining the prestigious Board of Certified Financial Planners and publish arguably the first theoretically sound textbook on personal finance entitled, *Practicing Financial Planning: A Complete Guide for Professionals* (currently on the 11th edition).

The following Four Ps' list identifies the P(s) that I have covered in this chapter:

[X]   Persevere with passion.
[   ]   Pursue professional, family-oriented, social, and spiritual goals.
[X]   Persuade family and friends to help.
[   ]   Promote a culture of giving back.

Note

1. Sid Mittra et al. (2012). *Practicing Financial Planning for Professionals*, American Academic Publishing, Eleventh Edition.

14

ON THE ROAD LESS TRAVELED:
RISKS AND REWARDS

Two roads diverged in a wood, and I—
I took the one less traveled by,
And that has made all the difference.
—Robert Frost, "Mountain Interval"

As I began my academic career, I seemed to be destined to remain an economics' professor forever in Rochester, a sleepy little Michigan village. And yet, I often wonder if what transpired soon after I joined Oakland University is a figment of my imagination.

In the spring of 1969, less than three years after I began teaching for the Economics Department, a businessman and a benefactor approached Woody Varner, chancellor of Oakland University, with an interesting proposition. "Have one of your business professors produce eight half-hour television shows on personal finance for broadcasting on NBC's Channel 4 in Saginaw, Michigan. And in return, I will make a substantial contribution to your university."

At the time, the University did not have a school of business. Our Economics Department faculty, part of the School of Arts and Sciences, had only four professors. I was one. Personal Finance was not part of our economics or business curriculum. None of us had any expertise or interest in the subject. Chancellor Varner might have been aware of this situation. However, since he did not wish to turn down such a generous offer from an important bene-factor, he asked George Matthews, Dean of Arts and Sciences, to find a qualified faculty member to produce the shows. He, in turn, approached me to do it because I specialized in Money and Banking.

My response was direct, and possibly impolite. I noted that I had no knowledge of what constituted personal finance. Besides, I felt uncomfortable appearing before a TV camera. For these reasons, I suggested that the dean look elsewhere.

My resolve was considerably weakened, however, when Chancellor Varner bypassed the normal protocol and personally appealed to me to assume that responsibility. As he put it, "Oakland stands to reap substantial benefits from this deal, and God knows we desperately need the money."

As I weighed Varner's request against the difficult task that lay ahead, I realized there were weighty arguments on both sides. On one side was my debt to the University. In many ways, Oakland had been kind to me. The University had already sponsored me for obtaining a permanent resident visa. There were distinct signals that Oakland would soon change my probationary status to the rank of a tenured professor. The University had permitted me to build an attractive tri-level home on a half-acre lot in the university-sponsored faculty subdivision. Finally, the department chairman had assigned me courses I enjoyed teaching while still leaving plenty of time to conduct research and perform university services. Oakland had made it possible for me to achieve every-thing I wanted. I felt duty-bound to honor Chancellor Varner's fervent appeal.

On the other side, the thought of mastering the esoteric subject of personal finance in a relatively short time with the sole objec-tive of producing eight half-hour shows for TV terribly scared me. As mentioned, I had never been trained in the discipline of per-sonal finance. I was petrified by a TV camera, broadcasting my live interview to thousands of viewers all over the country.

In the end, my desire to return the favor to Oakland trumped everything. After reflecting on it for a week, I accepted Chancellor Varner's invitation, albeit with trepidations. I continually blamed myself for not sticking to my original conviction.

For the next few months, I directed my energies almost entirely toward learning about the subject of personal finance. I found the process daunting and frequently intimidating. But after months of intensive study and suffering, I felt that I was as ready as I could ever hope to be.

During the summer of 1959, the University arranged for weekly trips from my Rochester home to the television studios in Saginaw, Michigan. There, over a period lasting four weeks, I recorded eight TV shows on budget planning, investment, taxes, estate planning, insurance, retirement, educational planning, and finally, financial independence planning. Frankly, I never had the opportunity to learn either the professional quality of the TV shows I produced or the reception these received from the viewers. But I did indeed feel good about helping the University financially. I naively convinced myself that eventually I would establish myself as a budding television personality.

Fortunately for me, my dream of becoming a TV celebrity never materialized. But by undertaking this project I did indeed benefit in a roundabout way. My efforts to learn about personal financial planning planted the seeds for a supplemental career path for me. However, it was not a straight path. I was on a road that took false starts. But it also included several unexpected strokes of luck. It spanned a long period, perhaps a decade or more.

While preparing for the TV shows I realized that the personal finance discipline provided a valuable *real-life laboratory* for testing traditional financial theories. Coincidentally, in the early 1970s, personal finance began emerging as the fastest growing component of the financial sector, generating considerable interest among professionals active in the financial services industry. Judging from that rapid growth, I concluded that personal finance would soon become a mature business. That, in turn, encouraged me to take appropriate steps so that eventually I would be recognized as an expert in personal finance.

Over the next few years I studied hard, learned a lot, and started changing my focus from my traditional discipline of money and banking to personal financial management. And, with the publication in 1976 of my text, *Personal Finance: Lifetime Management by Objectives* by Harper & Row, I was officially recognized as the University's resident expert on personal finance.

I should have found that recognition fulfilling, but I did not. The problem was this: Although the personal finance text I published was conceptually sound, and demonstrated my knowledge in all the major financial planning topics, the text nevertheless lacked the sophistication that could only come from a *practicing financial planner* with real-world experience. Once I realized that, I decided to gain significant experience before attempting to write an advanced book. That seemed like a great idea. But as I would soon discover, that was easier said than done.

In 1977, I arranged to have lunch with my friend, Ken Peterson, President of Oakland Financial Group, a prestigious financial planning firm in Birmingham, Michigan. During the meeting, I asked him if he could arrange for me to gain practical experience in personal finance. I still remember Ken's response, and my embarrassment. "Sid," said Ken, "I will help you, but only if you make two significant changes in your fashion taste. Stop wearing your maroon polka dot tie with a green checkered jacket, and get rid of your bright yellow Maverick car with a black stripe on both sides. Neither exudes confidence in financial planning clients."

Despite his critique of my fashion sense, in the end Ken turned out to be the answer to my prayers. During the 1978–1979 academic year, I took a sabbatical from Oakland and joined Ken's financial planning practice as an apprentice. I didn't have the necessary licenses to practice, so I was precluded from directly dealing with his planning clients. But I did get a year of experience. This meant that I could become a bona fide Certified Financial Planner (CFP) once I obtained the necessary credentials required by law.

I returned to Oakland in the fall of 1979, determined to establish a legitimate financial planning practice. I learned then that before I could legally provide planning services to the general public, first I would need to pass several planning-related exams and fulfill a myriad of fiduciary and certification requirements. These included, but were not limited, to the following: (a) A six-part CFP exam; (b) Series 7 and Series 63 exams as required by the National Association of Securities Dealers (NASD); (c) exams to qualify for a variety of state insurance licenses; and (d) a number of other exams, depending on the specialized services, such as retirement and estate planning, that I intended to offer my clients. I felt dizzy merely looking at that long and confusing list.

But the list was just the beginning. Besides passing exams and obtaining necessary licenses, there were more daunting obstacles blocking the way. As I would soon discover, the university rules did not allow faculty members to establish a private consulting business. And even if I could persuade the authorities to bend the rules for me, I couldn't attract planning clients without formally advertising my private services. That, too, was prohibited by the long-established university rules.

Once I fully understood the seemingly insurmountable challenge I faced, I had to admit that if I still wished to establish a privately owned financial counseling practice, I had little choice but to give up my academic career. For me, that constituted an unacceptable choice. As a tenured full professor, I was sitting in an ivory tower, with a guaranteed job *for life* (no compulsory retirement age for tenured professors). I had already established an impressive publication track record. That allowed me to put my professional life on cruise control and *go golfing*. I was well recognized in the academic community, which provided me with respectability and a high level of comfort that I valued immensely. For these and other reasons, quitting the university job and starting a full-time financial planning career with an uncertain future was hardly a viable option.

So, after thinking through everything I breathed a deep sigh of relief and gave up the idea of establishing a planning practice altogether. That should have been the end of that dream, but it was not meant to be. This *idea of defeat*, as I viewed it then, did not sit well with me. As was true so many times in the past, I became frustrated and restless, and could not concentrate on my academic career. I had to do something, but I did not know what or whom to turn to for help and guidance.

One chilly evening in the fall of 1981, still upset and restless, I went to my campus office in Vandenberg Hall. Recalling Blaise Pascal's famous comment, "Men's miseries derive from not being able to sit in a quiet room alone," I locked my door, turned off the office lights, sat down on a chair, and closed my eyes in a meditative style. Suddenly, I remembered that once before I had experienced grave doubts about myself. In 1949, after getting my undergraduate degree, I became totally depressed when I felt I had to look forward to nothing but a condemned life. What had saved me then was a relentless dual between two inner voices, one defeated and the other one upbeat. The latter voice won. Buoyed by that thought, almost three decades later, I summoned my upbeat and sound inner voice to help me understand why I was getting so restless even when everything was going great for me.

"Is it glamour of money and fame that is attracting you to the financial counseling business?" asked my inner voice.

"It is neither," I answered. "I feel as though I am missing out on the opportunity to teach finance to a much wider audience."

My inner voice threw a loop around me.

"If you believe that teaching is your calling," asked the voice, "then why don't you continue teaching at Oakland and establish a financial counseling practice that is education-based? That way, you'd have the best of both worlds."

The naïveté of that response irritated me. So I responded angrily: "You don't seem to recognize that, as you are suggesting, the university rules don't permit me to have it both ways. If I want to become involved with financial planning on a full-time basis, I'd be forced to resign from my university job. I *absolutely* refuse to do that."

There was a long pause as I waited for a response. Suddenly, my inner voice spoke again.

"Maybe not," said the voice. Then, after a pause, the voice continued: "You *need to convince* the University that by getting involved with financial planning you are merely extending your classroom to your counseling conference room. This exposure would give you a real-world experience, thereby making you a much more seasoned professor. Also, don't forget to make the argument that the University would also reap the benefits from your engaging in financial planning activities."

"How so?" I asked impatiently.

Answered the inner voice: "I'm merely repeating what you've already figured out. As an academically oriented financial planner, you would be able to charge a fee for public speaking and financial planning seminars. You could specify that all of these earnings would be donated to the University so it could provide educational grants to deserving School of Business students. And since this real-world experience would eventually make you one of the most sought-after professors in business school, the university administrators would view this as a win-win situation, and that would ultimately persuade the University to bend the rules in your favor."

That conversation with my inner voice, partially supported by my independent thinking on the subject, gave me the courage to forge ahead. I spent a restless night, formulating and reformulating my next move. And when I woke up the next morning, my mind was made up. The disturbing process reminds me of a piece that Confucius had written in the Analects: "The Master said, no vexation. No enlightenment. No anxiety. No illuminations."

That fateful morning I wrote the following letter to President Joseph Champagne. I believe that this letter captures my determination to launch a financial planning career without sacrificing my tenured position at Oakland University.

November 2, 1981

To: Joseph E. Champagne, President
From: Sid Mittra, School of Economics and Management
Subject: Meeting on November 10, 1981

In order to maximize the gains I could derive from our proposed meeting, I am jotting down a few points for your consideration.

Basic Observations
I am enclosing my vita for your perusal. It will give you an idea of my background, interests, and activities.

1. Since coming to Oakland in 1966, my major efforts have gone toward publishing a variety of books. I have now reached a saturation point and have decided to become less active in the publishing world.
2. I am still under contract to publish a second book on Personal Finance. My "real-world" activities include financial consulting for individuals and businesses. My long-term objective is to become a highly visible financial planner and consultant who is a well-established faculty member at Oakland University.
3. Already there are signs that suggest I am making Oakland visible. I serve on the Board of Financial Institute of America. I have also been elected to the Board of Directors of the International Association of Financial Planners. I have been invited to present a paper and chair a session on financial planning at the International Atlantic Economic Conference. These examples could be easily multiplied.
4. Since I became active in the real world, I believe I have become a much more effective teacher. In fact, on a one to five scale, students consistently rate me at around 4.5 (as opposed to the previous rating of around 3).

Major Goals
1. I would like to continue my present activities as described above and improve the quality of my work. WJR has approached me for a feature on money to

> be broadcast regularly on their radio. The Birmingham Eccentric is also discussing the possibility of my writing a regular column for them. I would like to be able to provide financial advice to our faculty and staff on a consistent basis. In fact, I developed all the slides for our tax seminar which was presented by the School of Economics and Management. Perhaps you could consider this to be a fringe benefit for the faculty in the contract negotiations next year.
>
> 2. I would like to organize, every summer, an Institute on Personal Finance for the general public. This would certainly provide a valuable service to the community and enhance the visibility of Oakland.
>
> 3. I would like to offer brief seminars for the staff members of major corporations. This might result in our obtaining funds from these corporations.
>
> *Major Problems*
>
> It is obvious that for me to be able to achieve any of the above goals I would need: (1) an understanding and appreciation of these goals, (2) adequate support for these activities, and (3) above all, encouragement. At a time of severe budget crunch I wonder whether any of my needs can be fulfilled. Hopefully, we can discuss these and other related matters on Tuesday.

Miraculously, this letter worked like a charm. I received more support for my financial planning activities than I had expected. President Champagne's support virtually changed my career. Indeed, subsequently he also served as the honorary member of the Board of Advisers of my financial planning practice. And to cap it off, on January 5, 2014—some three decades later—I received the following note from Dr Champagne: "Sid, it is my complement to have opened a door at Oakland that expedited a portion of your career and success. Congratulations again."

The year was 1980. It was a beautiful summer afternoon when my phone rang at the University. On the other end of the line was Tuck Brubaker, president and owner of Mutual Service Corporation (MSC), a prominent brokerage firm in Detroit.

"Hello, Dr. Mittra, this is Tuck Brubaker. Several years ago as president of the Michigan Chapter of IAFP (International Association for Financial Planning), I invited you to speak at our annual convention. Since then, I have read your Personal Finance textbook and have followed with interest your activities in the financial planning field."

"Hello, Tuck," I replied, "what a pleasant surprise. I remember you very well. How nice of you to call."

"I am glad you remember me," Tuck continued, "and here is the reason for this call. I have decided to add a financial counseling department to my firm and am looking for someone to head that department." Tuck paused for a moment, and then concluded: "If you are interested in pursuing this matter, I would love to discuss the project with you over lunch."

I had just completed a year working as an apprentice for K.P. Associates, a financial planning firm owned by my friend, Ken Peterson. I wondered how I could use my newfound knowledge in financial counseling. And as has been the case so many times in the past, suddenly there was a wonderful opportunity.

The opportunity Tuck provided was unparalleled. But unknown to him, it was also loaded with seemingly insurmountable road-blocks. Taking on a second job while continuing my full-time position at Oakland was impractical. But as I would discover, simultaneously working on both assignments presented me with a logistical nightmare. Still, I was so taken by Tuck's lucrative offer that initially I missed all of these road blocks, but not for long.

I lived in Rochester, a northern suburb of Detroit, and Oakland University, my place of work, was only a 10-minute drive from my home. But Brubaker's office was in the Renaissance Center (called RenCen) in downtown Detroit, which was 45 miles away. I soon discovered that during the morning rush hour it would take me an hour and a half to drive to the RenCen office, plus another 15 minutes to walk from the parking lot to the office building. Then I would ride the elevator to the 39th floor offices of MSC.

The alternative was to take a bus and avoid the drive. But to do that, I would have to catch the 5 am bus in downtown Rochester and endure *a two-and-a-half-hour bus ride* to reach the RenCen. Then, after a full day's work, I would have to repeat the ride in the evening. I would arrive home around 8 at night. That is only if the bus ran on time, which was frequently not the case.

Given the commuting time, it seemed impossible for me to work in Detroit while simultaneously maintaining a full schedule of teaching, research, and administrative duties at Oakland. Something had to give if I chose to accept Tuck's offer while devoting to each profession the attention it deserved.

Fortunately, at that time I had one thing going for me. During the fall semester, I was teaching all of my classes only on Tuesdays and Thursdays; so I could work the rest of the weekdays at RenCen. Initially, Tuck was not too pleased when I made that counter offer. But ultimately he acquiesced because there was no other alternative if he wanted me on board.

Once I settled the issue of working three days a week for Tuck, I turned my attention to the next big challenge: finding the time to prepare for my lectures at Oakland and also maintain quality research and publication activities. Clearly, the three days I worked at RenCen offered no free time. By the time I arrived home and had my dinner, I could barely keep my eyes open even for an hour of TV.

I thought long and hard about the problem but couldn't find a solution. I knew that soon my dean would recognize that I wasn't pulling my weight, ending my new financial-counseling career.

After thinking about it, I came up with a possible solution that could only be called preposterous.

A city bus ran between Meadowbrook Mall near my home in Rochester and the RenCen in Detroit. But to use that facility I would have to leave home around 4.30 in the morning to arrive at the bus stop in time to catch the bus at 5, arriving at RenCen around 7.30. The same bus would leave RenCen in the evening at 5.30, arriving at the Meadowbrook Mall at 8. I figured the five hours on the bus each day would give me sufficient time to do research and prepare lectures.

This appeared a workable plan except for one minor hitch. I realized that it was dark outside when I rode the bus in the morning and in the evening. The driver routinely turned off the interior lights so that passengers could nap. It was impossible to do any academic work on the bus. But that did not deter me. I improvised.

My plan consisted of bringing a small flashlight with rechargeable batteries, a head band, and my reading material. Each day, I would position myself on the corner of the last seat of the bus. Then I would put on my head band, stick the flashlight under the band, and turn it on. The light on my head freed both my hands and provided sufficient light for me to work on my teaching and research activities. Other passengers sitting nearby looked at me as if I was a weirdo, and occasionally made nasty comments, but I chose not to pay any attention to them.

I was pleased with the progress I made by following this routine, but soon realized I needed to become *more creative*. During these long bus rides, I had plenty of time to prepare lectures, develop quizzes and exams, and even grade exams and term papers. But the cramped bus seat made research impossible. There was insufficient space to spread out research material. By then, I had established an impressive publication record at the University. I was convinced that a slowdown in my publications would be blamed on my involvement with external activities unrelated to my university position, something I could ill-afford.

Once again, I became creative. I found a solution by dividing the process. On Tuesdays and Thursdays—my university days—I would conduct research in my office and take copious notes. Then, while riding the bus, by referring to the notes I brought on board, I would use a portable dictaphone to dictate the text for an article or a book. Once done, I would ask my department's secretary to transcribe my tapes. As a final step, while riding, I would edit the transcribed material, producing a publishable version of my research.

I confess that my dictating the tapes while riding the bus did not sit well with my fellow passengers, especially since they were trying to snooze. I could feel that they were put off. To ease the tension, I always made an effort to sit as far away as practical from other riders. Fortunately, to my great relief, people did not complain to the bus driver about my strange behavior or disturbing the peace. So, I could conduct my research, albeit in a weird way.

I still shake my head in disbelief when I recall that I used this technique for dictating the first draft of an entire investment book. Subsequently, in 1982, this book was published by Harcourt Brace Jovanovich (a prestigious publication firm) under the title, *Investment Analysis and Portfolio Management*. When the book arrived in the mail, I noted with amazement that the material I dictated while riding on the bus covered a whopping 782 printed pages!

Sometimes, facts turn out to be stranger than fiction, don't they?

During the two years I ran the financial planning department of the MSC, I learned about dealing with clients. What intrigued me, however, was that, for a given problem, for a client the right solution was not necessarily the one that was technically accurate; rather, it was the one with which the client was most comfortable. Soon I realized that if my solution didn't appeal to a client, he or she wouldn't act on it. That's regardless of how good or appropriate that solution was. Yet another valuable lesson learned was that clients didn't care how much I knew until they knew how much I cared.

But what frustrated me was that, despite my PhD and years of university teaching experience, I could *not* effectively communicate with clients. I was used to delivering lectures. I failed to realize that effective client communication depended as much on listening as it did on speaking. The light bulb finally went on when I heard a convention speaker make the following remark: "Ladies and gentlemen, today my job is to talk and yours is to listen. *If you finish before I do, please let me know.*"

My work at MSC was going very well. I was beginning to settle down. But my fate intervened once again, turning my life upside down.

One day, without giving me prior notice or establishing a clear agenda, Tuck Brubaker invited me to his elegant office. Judging from the serious look on his face, I feared he wanted to complain about something or tell me that I had offended him in some way. However, I found my fears were wrong. Tuck surprised me.

There were a few awkward moments of silence when I arrived at Tuck's office and sat down on the chair facing him. After some time, in a soft but deliberate voice, Tuck complimented me for running a fine financial planning department. Suddenly, his voice firmed up as he struggled to inform me that he needed to take his financial planning department to the next level. Delivering his final message Tuck said: "Sid, I have started to look for someone with marketing skills and anxious to make a *full-time commitment* to our planning department."

Having delivered his message in such a forthright manner, Tuck quickly assured me that he wanted to be fair with me. Therefore, he decided to keep me on his payroll until I found a new assignment with another firm. He also told me of his decision to appoint in my position Walter Kerrigan, an established financial planner and someone eager to join MSC on a full-time basis.

By the time Tuck was through, I had already concluded that I would not try to convince Tuck to reverse himself. So I took the high road. I told Tuck that I was grateful for giving me the opportunity to gain financial counseling experience. I also told him that his offer to let me stay on his payroll revealed his caring personality.

I stopped a moment, collected my thoughts, and then said: "Tuck, I would like to make a counter offer. Instead of offering me money without work, which is against my principles, I request that you continue teaching me the lessons I haven't yet learned about financial counseling practice. In return, I will establish my own financial counseling firm and demonstrate that I am worthy of the confidence you have placed in me."

That was one of the best decisions I made in my life. After leaving MSC, Tuck and I remained close friends for a very long time and he beautifully played the role of a caring mentor.

When I left Tuck Brubaker, I was determined to establish my own financial planning practice. Then no one would ever be able to lay me off, especially when I least expected it. As a first step, I passed the Series 7 exam conducted by the National Association of Security Dealers (NASD). That satisfied the statutory requirements for running a financial counseling practice. But if I was also going to be involved with handling investment products for clients, then I would also have to be associated with an established broker-dealer firm. This was, of course, a no brainer for me: I quickly became a registered representative of MSC, of which Tuck Brubaker was the president. What a small world, I said to myself, as I completed that formality and got ready to open my doors.

Next, I rented space in an office complex that was a 20-minute drive from my home. It was a small office in an unimpressive office building, but the rent was affordable. Still feeling the financial burden of starting a business, I bought used furniture and equipment for this office and hired a part-time secretary. Finally, having become an entrepreneur, technical expert, marketing director, bookkeeper, and bottle washer—all wrapped up under one title—I proudly hung outside my office the following sign: COORDINATED FINANCIAL PLANNING.

And with that, along with my title of a Full Professor with tenure at Oakland University, and with the permission of the university authorities, I became a licensed registered financial counselor. Surprisingly, however, the fact that my career path was never meant to turn out that way totally eluded me.

Setting up the planning practice turned out to be the easy part. Getting people through the door to seek our services and pay for them, however, continued to remain elusive. University's rules prevented me from making cold calls or advertising my services in any form. And I had not yet set up a mechanism for presenting organized seminars to the general public, so for me that too was not a viable option. The result was scary: Since I had just launched my practice, the few clients I had did not generate enough revenue to cover the overhead. So after reviewing my few options, I took two actions that I believed would solve my marketing problem without violating university rules or costing me a bundle.

My first major action involved taking the step to present myself as an expert financial counselor. My academic position at the University and impressive publication record helped me become a weekly finance columnist for the *Eccentric Newspapers*, which had circulation in Detroit and its suburbs. Simultaneously, with the help of friends and acquaintances in surrounding communities, I began receiving invitations to speak on various aspects of personal financial planning at the Chambers of Commerce, Community Houses, and Rotary and Kiwanis Clubs. These efforts produced dramatic results. That's because I presented myself as an educator, interested in both educating and helping people achieve long-term financial objectives.

And so, in the fall of 1982, a boutique financial counseling practice, Coordinated Financial Planning, was born. The name was subsequently changed to Mittra & Associates to reflect educational philosophy as the cornerstone of my practice. From its inception, until the practice was sold a quarter of a century later, my motto remained unchanged: Accept clients for life, educate them until they become enlightened, and serve them with such passion that they, too, would make a lifetime commitment to my practice.

Once my planning practice began, I discovered that a CFP's designation was recognized by the general public as the only qualification for offering financial planning services. That meant I had to earn that designation tout de suite. But to my consternation, the existing rules did not offer anyone the choice of quickly earning the diploma. To earn the CFP designation a candidate had to pass six separate exams, but no more than one exam could be taken during any given quarter. That meant that even if I could pass each exam on the first attempt—an outcome not guaranteed—I'd need at least a year and a half to earn the CFP designation. That was unacceptable.

I contacted the College for Financial Planning which administered the CFP exams. My initial request to take all the six exams in one sitting was instantly rejected by the college on the grounds that it violated the college's rules. Not willing to accept their refusal as the final answer, I challenged, arguing the rule was arbitrary and untenable. Fortunately, after review, the college made an exception. It allowed me to take all six exams in two installments. I seized that opportunity. I took three exams at the end of the fourth quarter of 1982 and the rest at the beginning of the first quarter of 1983. And so, literally in two weeks (instead of the regular 18-month period) I earned CFP, a designation I still hold (2015) with great pride.

Ironically, three years after I earned my CFP designation, I received a surprise phone call. It was from Dr William Anthes, president of the College for Financial Planning, who once turned down my request for taking all six CFP exams in one sitting. After exchanging a few pleasantries with me, Dr Anthes informed me that on the basis of my academic achievements and publications in the field of personal finance, he wanted me to join the prestigious Board of Examiners of the International Board of Certified Financial Planners (IBCFP). This Board, he explained, was charged with the responsibility for designing a new, totally integrated, CFP exam, comparable in form to the Certified Public Accountant (CPA) exam. I immediately accepted. And, by doing so, my colleagues and I on the Board became the architects for the single, integrated exam that all financial planners must pass today to earn a CFP designation.

Not everything I did as a boutique financial counselor turned out to be pleasant, however. There were instances in which I committed grave errors, and I paid painful price. Here's one instance that was difficult and embarrassing.

My planning practice was about three years old when an advisor, who I was informed by my staff was a CPA, brought one of his clients with him to consult with me. This CPA, whom I had never met before, sought my advice on how to improve the insurance portfolio which he had independently created for his client. After an examination of the portfolio I became angry, criticizing the insurance agent who loaded his client with a bunch of *unsuitable* insurance policies. I could have disagreed with the portfolio selection without being disagreeable, but I had not yet learned that skill. The meeting ended when the CPA thanked me and left with his client.

When I came out of the meeting, my secretary handed me a note which revealed that the advisor in my office (who my staff had told me was a CPA) was in fact the insurance agent involved with selling the policies and creating the portfolio. So, as is true with any professional, when the agent had doubts about his product selections, he wasted no time in seeking my professional advice. But instead of complimenting the insurance counselor for his professional and laudable conduct, I belittled him in front of his client. And by doing so I literally proved to them as well as to myself that my PhD designation could well stand for *Pizza Hut Deliverer.*

Making judgmental errors was not the only obstacle I faced in running my counseling practice. Almost continually I had to endure employee management problems. Once, in the late 1980s, they reached a breaking point.

In those days, I had a stable base of high net worth clients. Our office was spacious, lavishly decorated, and located in a prestigious office complex in Birmingham, Michigan. I had three associate planners and a secretary, and each person had the freedom to play a significant role in the practice.

One day, when I entered the office, something was out of place, and the employees seemed reserved and withdrawn. And even before I settled down, one of my associates entered my room and requested that I meet with all of my employees without delay. When we sat down in our conference room, one person spoke up: "Sid, you have a well-established practice, and we believe we are the ones who do most of the work. That's why we feel each one of us should get an immediate 50 percent raise in salary."

I was blown away by that outrageous request. When I regained my composure, I asked: "And what would you do if I did not give in to your demand?"

The instant response was unequivocal. "Sid, you don't have much of a choice," said the spokesperson, "and if we don't get what we deserve, we will all quit."

"You have made my job easy," I responded with as much gravity as I could muster.

"Then you agree to our request?" asked the associate.

I responded facetiously, "I agree to the second part of your request which stated that you'd quit if you don't get what you deserve." Then, after pausing for a moment, I continued: "I do not like anyone intimidating me. You have made a great judgmental error by threatening to quit. And by doing so you have left me with no choice but to request that you turn in your office keys, clear your desks, take whatever belongs to you, and leave this office by lunch time." And before the employees could recover from their initial shock, I stood up, shook hands with each one, wished them good luck, offered to help them find a suitable job, and walked out.

I returned to my office and drafted a letter to all of my clients which stated: "For personal reasons all of our employees have quit the practice and I have hired a temporary secretary to handle the workload. I will remain fully engaged and will ensure that our services are not disrupted in any way." Once I finalized the letter, I came out of my office and asked the secretary to send it out to all of our clients before leaving the office. Then I returned to my office, sat back in my chair, took a deep breath, and reminded myself of the famous words of King Solomon: "This, Too, Shall Pass."

Fortunately, that ominous moment did pass, but not before permanently implanting a black spot on me as an entrepreneur. In my arrogance as a business owner, I neglected to recognize that by instantly firing all the employees I imposed a heavy financial burden on them and their families. And even the idea of keeping them on a payroll for a little while in order to ease their financial burden a little totally escaped me.

I still carry this deep psychological scar with me, even though three decades have passed.

ᔐ

My first test as a veteran financial counselor came in a roundabout way. One morning in the early 1980s, as part of my university's community service as a specialist in financial planning, I presented a seminar for the benefit of a number of key benefactors of Oakland University. In the audience was Jeff Steinbach (name changed to maintain privacy), president and chief executive officer of a Fortune 500 company. He served as a member of Oakland's Board of Advisors. After my seminar, Jeff surprised me by the following question: "Sid, in your hypothetical illustration when you predicted that the couple was going to have a comfortable retired life, you were not serious, were you?"

Somewhat startled and puzzled by that expression, I asked, "What makes you say that?"

Jeff went on to say that his personal situation was quite similar to that of the couple in my illustration. And yet, a nationally recognized, prestigious financial planning firm located on the east coast, which developed a comprehensive financial plan for him at a cost of $5,000 (an astronomical figure in those days), had clearly predicted that, unless something drastically changed to prevent that outcome, he would run out of money in 20 years, or more precisely, a few months before his 77th birthday. Jeff challenged me to analyze his financial situation and then tell him whether or not I agreed with the conclusion of his original planner. I accepted Jeff's challenge, albeit with some reservation.

Six weeks later, I met with Jeff and his wife Judy in my office. I opened the meeting by pointing out that my sole objective was to create a financial plan for the Steinbachs and develop an effective plan. I took pains in emphasizing that, consistent with our firm's established policy, I had not concerned myself with the other plan and had no interest in critiquing someone else's work.

Next, I projected my findings on the screen so that the Steinbachs could get a clear picture of my findings. I meticulously covered the highlights of my plan, ensuring that the couple was comfortable with every aspect of these findings.

When I finally reached the Summary Page of the plan, I paused for a moment, looked straight at them, and presented my basic conclusion: If the Steinbachs followed my recommended action plan, then at no point in their life would they ever run out of money. In fact, I predicted that, over the next 25 years, instead of running out of money the Steinbachs would in fact amass substantial wealth and need a sophisticated estate plan to solve their horrendous estate tax problem.

John and Judy were virtually speechless. When they fully recovered, Jeff asked me if I would be willing to give him a copy of my plan so that he could compare it with the one he had before coming to any definite conclusion.

"It would be my pleasure," I responded with a grin, as long as you do not ask me to critique the other plan. And then I added as an afterthought: "Please remember that I will always stand by my findings. I have to, because each time I develop a plan for a client, I put my reputation on the line."

At that point, something unusual happened. Judy Steinbach got up from her chair, walked up to where I was standing, and gave me a hug. I stood there, stunned, as Jim stared at us with a look on his face that bordered between shock and disbelief.

As a financial counselor, that was the highest compliment I ever received from someone who was not even my client.

Jeff and Judy Steinbach soon became my most highly valued clients and stayed with me until I sold my practice.

Running a successful financial planning practice alongside my academic career brought affluence to the family that was beyond our fondest expectations. But there was also a dark side of this affluence of which I am not very proud. All my life I had lived frugally and avoided financial waste. But as our affluence grew, so did our sloppy behavior, and sadly I had consistently indulged in wasteful activities.

One day I realized that we had eight television sets, two high density boxes, four DVD players, two VHS machines, nine cassette players, and seven stereos.

We had 18 remote controls, most of which were not even used.

We had three computers (HP, Toshiba, and Epson), four printers, two of which did not run, and two fax machines. We had two phone lines, two cell phones, and two answering machines.

We had 382 dishes, bowls, cups, saucers, mugs, and glasses even though we only occasionally invited friends home for dinner.

We had 506 CDs, cassettes, iPod, vinyl, and eight track recordings. But we mostly listened to only a few of the favorite ones.

We had expensive and gorgeous hand-carved, especially designed, and imported Indian furniture in the living room that was rarely visited by guests.

We had 230,000 frequent-flier miles on five airlines, three of which had long disappeared from the face of the earth.

I had 23 suits, 39 shirts, 29 pairs of shoes, and 18 especially-designed dresses from India. But many of them didn't fit, and I wore only a few of my favorite ones.

We had eight full-size table radios and four portable radios, but we spent only 60 minutes each day watching the ABC news on TV and rarely listened to the radio.

And that was not all. There were so many artifacts, dolls, spoons, and expensive handicrafts collected from all over the world that we didn't have space to display all of them. We had three cars, but only two drivers.

And just when I think I have said it all, I recall that only the two of us lived in a 5,300 square-feet European-style home where each room had a window and a beautiful view. In this house, we also had a 40-gallon hot water heater and three 16.3 cubic feet refrigerators.

We rarely remembered that our two children were long gone. Bani and I were empty nesters, and we enjoyed living in this cozy place all by ourselves.

But there was hope. We were convinced that someday both of our children with their families would choose to visit us at the same time. When that happened, if ever, we would have a full house, and our large home would be put to good use. But it wouldn't surprise me if on such an occasion one of the grandchildren complained, "Gosh, there is no room in this house, and how come there is no *real* food in any of the three refrigerators?"

Besides friendship, for some clients I took responsibilities that went beyond handling their financial affairs.

For example, in the late 1980s, Mary Curtis came to my office with her aunt Betty Skipper. She sought financial counseling. Mary was only 19 years old then, and had inherited $2 million when both of her parents died in an accident. Aunt Betty was uncomfortable engaging any unknown financial planner or a stockbroker to manage such a large sum of money. But when she learned that I was a tenured professor of Finance at Oakland University and also owned a boutique financial counseling service for the affluent, she decided to find out if I was worthy of her trust.

The first meeting was anything but routine. I learned that, besides finding an astute investment counselor, Betty also wanted the counselor to act as Mary's financial guardian. I would be a mentor, ensuring she lived within her budget and cautioning her against squandering money.

Mary also had her own agenda, which appeared convoluted and bizarre. She wanted the advisor to *hide* all her money from public view, so that boys interested in her wouldn't be able to find out that she was superrich. Mary was afraid that if a boy got wind of her money, then he would be interested only in her bucks, creating havoc in her life. Under no circumstances, she explained, would she embark on such a risky venture.

At first, I didn't want to get involved with such a convoluted and unorthodox scheme. But after agonizing for several days and obtaining an assurance from Betty that she would not interfere in my management responsibilities, I finally accepted. It was a risky proposition at best and downright arrogant at worst.

My experience of dealing with Mary Curtis turned out to be extremely challenging. For more than a decade, I was her investment manager, her guardian, her confidant, and even her advisor in personal matters. Mary fought with me like a teenager does with a father when I refused to give her additional money. But she also shared with me stories about her dates and complained about her difficulties in concealing her wealth from her roommate. She asked my advice on what college courses to take. Yet she showed little interest when I explained how her investments were performing. During this entire period, Mary never insulted me, nor did she reject my advice, no matter how much she hated it at the time.

Then one day she brought me the exciting news: Bill Collier, her steady boyfriend, had finally proposed to her. Although she was madly in love with him, she still asked my permission to marry Bill. For some time, I had known about Mary's feelings toward Bill. He was a moderately successful attorney, and I was certain that he had no knowledge about the extent of Mary's wealth. He seemed a perfect match.

After marriage, I invited Bill and Mary to discuss their financial affairs. Bill was shocked when I disclosed Mary's wealth and was intrigued by the techniques I had used to conceal her money.

Today, Bill and Mary are happily married with three beautiful children. And to my great relief, I no longer have to deal with Mary's financial needs or fight with her whenever she wishes to squander her wealth.

∽

Bob Burns, a valued client and my regular racquet ball partner, suddenly stopped in the middle of a game. And since he had the nasty habit of doing so anytime he was on the losing side, I warned him not to disturb the momentum that was clearly in my favor.

"No, Sid," said Bob, "I have a serious financial problem, and I believe only you can help me. Please hear me out, right now."

Bob presented me with a challenging problem. His son, Dick, 18, was earning good money mowing the lawn and shoveling the snow, but was blowing it all away on electronic equipment, clothes, and entertainment. Bob had tried, but failed, to convince Dick to put away as little as $2,000 (he was earning around $6,000–7,000 every year) into an Individual Retirement Account (IRA), or tax-deferred IRA. Dick vehemently rejected his dad's plea, arguing that it was his money and he should be allowed to do with it whatever he damn pleased. And since Bob had learned from me how tax-deferred investments could exponentially grow over time, he wanted me to *force Dick* to change his mind.

That was certainly a strange request, at the middle of a racquet ball game no less. So I countered Bob with another question: "What makes you think that an 18-year-old would listen to a total stranger, especially when he refuses to listen to his own Dad?"

"I don't know," replied Bob, "but I've heard that you are a miracle worker, so let's see if you deserve that title."

For reasons I can no longer remember, I accepted that challenge but agonized over Dick's problem for weeks. Then one day I came up with a solution which I thought just might work. So, I invited Dick to have breakfast with me. He was reluctant at first, especially since he sensed that I was going to ask him to do the same thing his dad had been trying for so long. But when I assured him that I would only share a story with him and nothing more, he accepted my invitation.

At a breakfast meeting, over six layers of pancake, hash brown potato, sausage, and a large cup of coffee (Dick's breakfast, not mine), I presented Dick with the following story.

Sam and Tony, both 18, are good friends. They make good money but never save a penny. One day Sam's dad advised him to invest each year $2,000 into an IRA. And since he knew nothing about investing money, dad directed him to put the money into an Index Fund that mimicked the stock market.

Sam accepted dad's advice but only on one condition: Each year he would faithfully invest $2,000 into an IRA but would quit investing when he turned 24, six years later. He argued that by then he would graduate from college, find a full-time job, get married, and start a family. Hence, he would no longer have any money left for investment.

Tony had a similar discussion with his dad. He, too, decided to invest $2,000 into an IRA. But he said that he wouldn't start investing until he turned 24. By then, he would have graduated from college and found a suitable job. That would be the right time for him to start investing $2,000 a year into an IRA.

At this point, I posed Dick the following question: According to the story I just presented, Sam would invest $12,000 into an IRA ($2,000 a year for six years). If he then left it untouched, he will have a big chunk of change in his IRA account when he turned 65. If at the age of 65 in his IRA account Tony also wanted to have approximately the same amount of money as Sam would, then after he begins investing $2,000 a year at the age of 24, for how many years would Tony have to keep investing before he could stop? I also repeated that in our story Sam intended to stop investing after only six years.

Then, by way of a little help, I presented Dick two additional pieces of information. (a) I cautioned that since Tony didn't start investing until the age of 24, clearly he would have to continue investing for *more than 6 years* if at the age of 65 he wished to have the same amount of money as Sam would in his IRA. (b) Both Sam and Tony could assume that their Index Funds would generate an annual return of 10 percent [which was true when this illustration was presented].

Dick reflected on this story for some time while still eating his 6,000 calorie breakfast. Suddenly, he stopped eating, looked straight into my eyes, and blurted out: "You said that Tony would have to keep investing for *more than six years*. But since Tony waited only six years before starting to invest, I would say that after starting to invest at the age of 24, he could quit in, say, 10 years so that both Sam and Tony will have the same amount of money when they reach the age of 65."

I remained silent.

Feeling somewhat uneasy, Dick asked impatiently, "Am I right or what?"

I seized that perfect moment to respond.

"Dick," I said, "If the market continues to behave the way it has during the last 80 years (that is, provide the historic 10 percent annual return that was true for that period), *Tony will never catch up with Sam*, not even if Bill continues to invest that amount of money every year *for the rest of his life*."

The next day I got an unexpected phone call from Bob.

"Sid," Bob said with a bit of surprise in his voice, "Dick came to see me this morning and surprised me by asking how to open an IRA Index Fund Account." Then he added, "I hate to admit it my friend, but in my books you have definitely earned the right to be called a miracle worker."

Is there a better way to end this chapter of my life that should never have been written in the first place?

Epilogue: Life's Lessons

A string of unexpected events create an opportunity for me to embark on an entirely new discipline of personal financial planning and management. At first, my involvement is strictly limited to producing a set of eight programs for broadcasting on an NBC-affiliated TV station. Once I accomplish that, however, I get deeply immersed in that discipline: first by acquiring the CFP designation, then by publishing a book and several articles in that field, and finally completing a year-long internship assignment in that discipline.

What happens next defies imagination. With the blessings of Oakland University, where I hold the position of a full professor, I obtain all the necessary licenses to begin a boutique financial planning business named Coordinated Financial Planning. Shortly thereafter, I join the International CFP Board and publish arguably the first theoretically advanced, real-world-oriented textbook entitled, *Practicing Financial Planning: A Complete Guide for Professionals*. And with all that behind me, the University enthusiastically changes my title from Professor of Economics to Professor of Finance.

Once I am recognized as a sophisticated financial planning professional, I use that opportunity to help scores of people: by helping individual families achieve their financial objectives in a non-traditional manner and by using this service as a way of giving something of value back to the society.

The following Four Ps' list identifies the P(s) that I have covered in this chapter:

[X]   Persevere with passion.
[X]   Pursue professional, family-oriented, social, and spiritual goals.
[X]   Persuade family and friends to help.
[X]   Promote a culture of giving back.

15

GIVING BACK TO SOCIETY: REDEFINED CONCEPT OF SUCCESS

From what we get, we can make a living; what we give,
however, makes a life.
—ARTHUR ASHE

What do Azim Premji, Shiv Nadar, G.M. Rao, Ronnie Screwvala, Nandan Nilekani, Kiran Mazumdar Shaw, and Ratan Tata have in common? Not much, except that each has promoted a culture of giving back to society in a significant way. By the latest official count, in a *single year* each has donated anywhere from ₹310 crore to ₹8,000 crore to charitable causes. God bless these *multi-crorepatees* (multi-billionaires) and other like-minded philanthropists.

Convinced that in life I am destined to always remain an ordinary person with limited means, but still wishing to make a small difference in this world, early in life I *redefined* the concept of success. Without realizing it at the time, I embraced the philosophy immortalized by Ralph Waldo Emerson:

[Success is] to find the best in others; to leave the world a bit better, whether by a healthy child, a garden patch or a redeemed social condition; to know even one life has breathed easier because … [I] have lived.[1]

As I learned over time, redefining success to suit myself was easy. Implementing it in real life was not. But when I had serious doubts about my ability to achieve my objective—and in all honesty I had plenty—I confronted them by reminding myself of Helen Keller's classic comment: "I am only one, but still I am one. I cannot do everything, but still I can do something. And because I cannot do everything, I will not refuse to do the something that I can do."[2]

In keeping with my modified definition of success, what follows are my multidimensional and largely uncoordinated efforts to *make a difference*. While my actions were all over the map which often did not involve making *financial* contributions, I feel they were nevertheless consistent with my idea of giving something meaningful back to society.

I am one of the very few fortunate ones who could remain active in two continents, totally separated by geography, history, religion, culture, social attitudes, and stage of economic development. And I could seize this unique opportunity by solely following my inner compass and remaining focused on my modified definition of success.

During the first 27 years of my life, I was embroiled with my fight for survival and could not even entertain such noble thoughts as giving something back to society. Then in the fall of 1957, soon after I arrived on the University of Florida (UF) campus in Gainesville, as part of my orientation, I visited Dr Ivan Putman, director of the Foreign Students Office. The suggestion I received from him created an opportunity for me that was far beyond my wildest imagination. "Sid," said Putman in a commanding voice, "from now on you will be our *unofficial Indian Ambassador* to America. You will carry the privilege and the responsibility for enlightening us about your culture, your religion, and your social beliefs, so that someday we all will have a better understanding of your country, your culture, and your people." I accepted that challenge with delight, albeit with predictable reservations. Sadly, during my first academic year I became so consumed with my studies and adjustment on campus that I had little choice but to keep my nose to the grindstone. I postponed all nonacademic activities until I was ready.

Once I received decent grades for all of my first-year courses, I felt comfortable participating in a number of key *cultural activities*. Before I share my achievements in this area, however, it is apropos to make an important point. What appears next might lead you to believe that everything I got involved with turned out to be a great success. I must caution you that nothing could be further from the truth. I experienced multiple failures, numerous false starts, many disappointments, and fierce opposition to my efforts, from my own countrymen no less. And yet, because of what I truly believed in, I endured, and fortunately in the end, prevailed.

As a start, with the help of our advisor, I helped the International Student Organization (ISO) transform into a vibrant, forward-looking, and progressive organization. Next, acting as its leader, I developed a number of programs designed to achieve our objective of improving an appreciation of the diversity in different cultures.

As time passed, I slowly turned into a catalyst. Under my direction, supervision, and encouragement, a number of programs were staged. Each focused on songs, dances, costume shows, and culinary samples of a selected country. The idea caught on. Indeed, by the time I left Florida, after graduation in 1962, these colorful programs had become synonymous with ISO.

Once ISO was established as a bona fide *international* organization, I reverted to my original role as an unofficial ambassador from India. I got involved in a number of diverse activities: Appearing on a local television to explain the complexities of Indian religions and the nuances of our Hindu caste system; broadcasting on WCGG-TV a special program demonstrating the complex patterns of Indian classical and modern music; staging a costume show depicting diversity of dress styles prevailing in India, and much, much more.

During the 1959–1960 academic year I was elected the *Commissioner of Foreign Affairs*. In that capacity, I coordinated all foreign student activities conducted on campus, including orientation and problems associated with acclimation. Subsequently, I was elected the vice president of the Organization of Asian Students (OAS). In that capacity, I began publishing a weekly column in the university's student newspaper. It dealt with the contributions of foreign students to the enrichment of the American culture. I also accepted numerous speaking invitations from schools, churches, and civic organizations. And in that capacity, I carefully brought to light the important role foreign students played in improving the understanding between themselves and the American community.

In the fall of 1961, I capped my role as an unofficial ambassador from India, a role I played with great delight and passion. I did so by presenting on WUFT-TV a special program on Indian music. In this program, my wife Bani performed as the lead vocalist and I accompanied her on tabla. We explained to the audience how Indian classical music was improvised by the vocalist according to a melodic form called raga, a cluster of notes. The tanpura generated a continuous hypnotic drone, thereby creating the basis for establishing the selected raga. This live performance of Indian classical and modern music indeed turned out to be a novel experience for the viewers. To our delight, rave reviews were published in the local newspapers commenting on the uniqueness and sophistication of Indian classical music, and we were touched by the invitations we received from other cities to broadcast Indian musical programs on live TV.

Shortly before my graduation, Dr Ivan Putman, our foreign students advisor, who had initially challenged me to assume the unofficial Indian Ambassador's role, published a report on my extracurricular activities in Florida. The report, which I have treasured all my life, concluded: "S. Mittra... has made a varied contribution to cultural life and student activities on the campus, *perhaps the greatest such contribution made in the past ten years by any foreign student.*"

∽

In 1966, after I joined the faculty of Oakland University and settled down in Rochester, Michigan, Bani and I decided to spread our rich Indian musical and social culture among the American public. With that objective in mind, we started making live presentations on stage, on the radio, and on television. We also established *Sangeet Bani School of Music* and began training both Indian and American students in vocal and instrumental (tabla) music. To our singular delight, under our direction these students began performing on stage, thereby sharing our rich musical heritage with a larger American community.

A natural extension of our social activities was our decision to use Indian music as an entrée to raising charitable funds for financing a variety of social activities. It soon dawned on us, however, that to reach our goal we needed to formally create a powerful musical group, train its members in vocal and instrumental music, and ultimately choreograph and orchestrate each stage presentation to suit the tastes of the respective potential donors. The result was the formation of a musical group called *Navrang* (nine colors). Soon Navrang became a widely acclaimed music group, and for over a quarter of a century we used this group extensively to raise funds for numerous well-deserved charitable activities.

One of our capstone programs involving Navrang was the production of an hour-long musical extravaganza entitled, *Musiculture of India*. This was the first program of its kind that included authentic songs, dances, and instrumental music from India, and more importantly, all the participants in this program were non-professionals living in Michigan. In 1974, this lavishly produced musical program was aired on the PBS (public broadcasting stations) TV all across the US. To our delight, the broadcast received rave reviews from the press and we were invited by PBS to produce another program for broadcasting at a later date.

There was yet *another first* in our repertoire when Bani and I were invited to air a monthly hour-long program on Indian Music on WDET-radio, the radio station owned and operated by Wayne State University in Detroit. For this airing, we painstakingly produced specially designed programs on Indian music that we believed would be intelligible and enjoyable to the Western listeners. In addition, to make our program even more interesting, we requested Western musicians with an appreciation for the Indian music to explain to the Western listeners the nuances of our music which they found difficult to comprehend. Our program on WDET radio turned out to be a highly popular one, and it was broadcast for a very long time.

Not all of my activities were associated with popularizing Indian music and culture in America, however. Recognizing that redeeming social conditions was also defined by Emerson as an integral part of being successful, once I got involved with solving an Indian social problem without realizing what I was getting into. The going was indeed rough and occasionally I thought of calling it quits. But I prevailed and in the end I felt vindicated.

In the summer of 1993, I met Ram Jain at a marriage party in the US. He was a physicist in India and at the top of his profession. I discovered by accident that his wife was permanently disabled and he had virtually no family life. But Ram was also proud of making a number of bold decisions even though these required him to make great personal sacrifices.

When Ram married years ago, he looked forward to a successful family life and a bright professional future. They had two beautiful children—a boy and a girl—and he continued to make steady progress in his profession. Then one day, his wife Maya was diagnosed with an incurable mental illness, requiring round-the-clock nursing care. And with that prognosis, Ram's personal life came crashing down. However, running out of options, he decided to raise his children by himself. At the same time, he was also a male nurse for his mentally-challenged wife.

After sharing with me this tragic personal story, Ram asked if I agreed with the way he had decided to handle his domestic crisis. Assuming that he wanted my honest opinion, I responded: "Ram, if financially affordable, it's best that you have your wife admitted to an established nursing care facility."

Ram looked perplexed. "Don't you realize," he argued, "that society would severely criticize me for throwing out my wife?"

I replied: "On the contrary, you would be providing her with the *best possible medical service*, something she is not getting at home now. Look at it another way. You are only in your mid-fifties, and you have a long, highly productive life ahead of you. Besides, you still have two young children to raise, and they definitely need a father *and* a mother."

I concluded our meeting by suggesting to Ram to do the follⁱlowing: (a) recognize his wife's permanent loss of memory, get her admitted to a reputable nursing home; (b) after getting his children firmly on his side, officially arrange for a divorce; and (c) find a life partner eager to accept the dual role of a wife *and a mother*, get married and permanently reestablish a happy family life.

Ram's reaction to my suggestions was one of total disbelief. "How could you make these suggestions," he retorted, "when everything you say is contrary to Indian customs and beliefs?"

I felt Ram's pain and predicament and chose to remain silent. Surprisingly, this episode ended in a way that was beyond my fondest expectations.

After returning to India and reflecting on our conversation for over a year, Ram followed my suggestions to the letter. He put his wife in a prestigious nursing home, obtained a legal divorce, remarried, and finally settled down in his new life. His extended family and friends criticized him severely and many of them severed all connections with him. But he stood his ground and eventually prevailed. Initially, Ram's children were ambivalent about this marriage. However, over time they accepted his new wife as part of the family.

Today, Ram is well settled in his life with his new wife. Both of his children are now married and are living with their spouses in various parts of the world. He visits his former wife on a regular basis and makes sure that she is fully taken care of. She is oblivious to her surroundings and has no idea that she is now divorced and her former husband is remarried. And Ram often wonders how his life would have turned out had I not encouraged him to take the steps that were at best preposterous, and at worst totally unacceptable to the Indian society. And, as for me, I finally do feel vindicated and am very happy for Ram's family.

৵

Of all the many ways I helped getting the Western audiences soaked with Indian music and culture, none is more newsworthy or sensational than my association with two visiting Bollywood legends: Lata Mangeshkar and Mukesh Chandra Mathur. In the summer of 1976, this team presented 10 musical concerts in America and Canada. And good fortune smiled on me when for all of their concerts I was invited to act as the Master of Ceremony as well as the co-manager of the musical team.

Incidentally, in my modified role, by privately associating with the two superstars and their musicians, I learned a great deal about the key aspects of their diverse personalities that were largely unknown to the general public. What follows, therefore, reflects a mixture of my personal impressions of these superstars, and by design goes *far beyond* what I would normally be expected to cover in this space.

Let me begin with a rare encounter I had with Lata Mangeshkar early on during the concert tour.

The year was 1976 and the place was the Vancouver International Airport Terminal. As Lata and I were slowly walking down the corridor leading to the departure lounge, she startled me by asking: "Mittra Ji, do you have a PhD degree?"

For a moment, I thought I was hallucinating. Could it possibly be that such a strange question came from none other than Lata— the reigning musical queen of all times? After all, who can deny that the legendary Dilip Kumar lamented how he could never adequately describe the incredible musical talent of his *little sister* and that, the unconquerable Mukesh boldly predicted that she could never be persuaded to embark on a musical tour of America, and by performing on stage, *Aye Mere Watan Ke Logon*, she literally brought tears to the eyes of the attending prime minister, Pandit Jawaharlal Nehru?

Anyway, Lata's question literally froze me in my tracks. But after regaining my composure, I answered by merely nodding my head affirmatively.

Lata quickly cleared up the mystery. Even though almost four decades have passed since then, I literally remember every word she uttered that day (spoken in Hindi and translated into English here):

"Mittra Ji, I presume once you were awarded a PhD, you earned that title for life. Right? But *each time* I step up to the mike, be it in a recording studio, on stage, on TV, or during a musical tour, I am asked to pass a new PhD exam. This is so because every song I sing is closely scrutinized, and that too by people of all ages, musical orientation, of diverse backgrounds, and speaking many different languages. That is the *constant* challenge I face, and I can never let it out of my mind."

That brief encounter I had with Lata almost four decades ago clarified in my mind two critical issues that help define her place in history: Why she reached the top of the musical world and remained there for more than three generations, and how she managed to set the bar for other singers so high that it became virtually impossible for any other singer to reach it, let alone cross it.

Lata Mangeshkar is a unique human being, regardless of how you size her up. She is many things, all wrapped up into one larger-than-life personality. She is a professional singer, a social thinker, a charitable-minded person, creator of a new dimension for Indian musical performances, an inspiration to generations of people, holder of the exalted Bharat Ratna title, and much, much more. To use a metaphor: She is like a kaleidoscope where different-sized glass pieces of multiple colors are randomly placed inside a cylinder. When we peek into the kaleidoscope, we see one fixed structure radiating in dazzling colors. But as we rotate the cylinder, we see these shapes and colors changing and bursting into a whole new variety of shades of gorgeous colors. You can now imagine why it is virtually *impossible* to adequately describe the multidimensional personality of this lady. So, as the next best *alternative*, let me share with you a few personal encounters that highlight the key aspects of her venerable life.

Let me begin with those momentous words: "Are Babaaa, *Shor Naheen, Sooor, Sooor, Sooooor*."

What in the devil's name is that? Or more importantly, who is delivering such a nonsensical order, to whom, when, and for what reason? And don't think that just to tease you I am making this all up. I am not. In fact, I was there when this incredibly funny incident took place, on a public stage and in front of a packed auditorium no less.

Some four decades ago these words, by a guru aiming at his *shishya* (disciple), were spoken by the venerable Mukesh attempting to teach none other than—are you sitting down?—the one and only Lata Mangeshkar. Equally unbelievable, that expression brought the whole auditorium down with a thunderous applause as Lata couldn't control her emotion bursting into a sustained laughter and Mukesh looked on with a mischievous grin on his face.

As you are no doubt aware, in the Bollywood classic movie *Milan,* produced in 1967, using those famous words on the screen, Sunil Dutt scolded the gorgeous actress Nutan (with Lata's on-stage impromptu laughter missing). Reliving that scene on stage in front of a capacity crowd by the two famous playback singers demonstrated the incredible synergy that existed between them. In fact, the selection of Mukesh as her singing partner for the 1976 tour reflected an important dimension of Lata's penchant for identifying both the quality and camaraderie of this legendary singer.

My first encounter with Mukesh was in Vancouver in 1976, prior to the starting of our musical tour. Even though I was the selected Master of Ceremony, I had not yet been formally introduced to the team, and by default the task of introducing myself to the singers fell upon me. That was an awkward moment for me, but I had little choice but to somehow manage the situation.

So, when I first met Mukesh, just to impress upon him how much I admired him as a playback singer, somewhat facetiously I blurted out: "Mukesh Ji, many years ago at the Kardar-Colinos musical contest in Bombay I sang your very first recorded song, *Dil Jalata Hai To Jalne De Ansoo Na Baha Fariyaad Na Kar.*" I also boasted that I won the best singer contest and still had the trophy to prove it.

I wish I had a camera to capture the bewilderment and disbelief reflected on Mukesh's face: "What? You singing? In the prestigious Kardar-Colinos contest? Oh p-l-e-a-s-e, give me a break!!" But it is equally amusing to note that Mukesh also inadvertently made me famous. Once, when I finished as an emcee, with a serious expression on his face and a *gotcha* tone in his voice, Mukesh blurted out: "*Ye Mittra sahab ne jo angreji me bola woh adha samajh me aya aur adha samajh me nahi aya*" (I understood only half of what Mittra sahib said in English). Those mischievously spoken Mukesh's famous words (I speak bad English fluently) are a part of the now-famous 1976 Musical Tour Record Album.

Let me now share with you a sense of how deep an impact each of these two legendary singers had on the audiences during the 1976 musical concerts in America and Canada.

It was not very often that Washington's Indian community had visiting performers of the stature of Lata and Mukesh. So, in honor of these visiting *dignitaries*, the Indian Ambassador to the US arranged for a gala luncheon party.

We arrived at the embassy shortly before 12 and were greeted by the ambassador, other embassy staff members, and a number of prominent citizens. None of the attendees had personally met these two popular playback singers before, so it was a special treat for them.

Then something unexpected happened. During the social hour, a distinguished-looking gentleman shocked everyone by openly requesting Mukesh to sing for the whole group. A stunned silence followed. With no advance notice, no traditional accompaniments, and no microphone available, no one would make such an incredibly dumb request to a singer of his stature. I feared Mukesh would lose his temper and blurt out something he would later regret.

I was wrong. Dead wrong.

Mukesh responded softly: "I *never* deny any of my listeners, and today I will be happy to sing for you." He then stood up, folded his hands, and sang an entire song while the audience looked at him in total amazement. Standing virtually next to him, I watched him in disbelief and was so mesmerized that I can't even remember anything else about his impromptu performance that has since been lost to history.

Because of that incident as well as others I came to witness during this concert tour, I have to come to believe that because of his generosity, civility, and respect for his listeners, throughout the world Mukesh Chandra Mathur has achieved incredible success in spreading much more than the rich Indian musical culture.

Moving now to Lata, the incident I wish to share is equally impressive. Anyone familiar with Lata–Mukesh concerts knows that, as the organizer of the show, one of Mohan's outstanding achievements was to carefully select those auditoriums that were both *cozy* (as opposed to large stadiums) and *elegant*. But once he picked a hall that created an unexpected problem for the performers.

The concert hall I am referring to was the famous *Front Row*, located in Cleveland, Ohio. Both cozy and elegant, it had a *revolving stage* which allowed everyone in the audience sitting around a circle to have a *front row view* of the stars. This feature was perfect for American-style concerts. But because of the nature of our performance and the unfamiliarity of the musicians with revolving stages, our singers were petrified and expressed deep concerns about performing under such conditions.

The impasse would have continued indefinitely with disastrous results; fortunately, Lata's professionalism saved the day. She overruled everyone by pointing out that it was us who selected the hall, and it was too late to change the venue. So, despite the discomfort and uneasiness she and others felt about the revolving stage, she directed the show to go on as planned. She then stepped on to the revolving stage and delivered one of her best performances of the entire tour.

But something else happened that night that truly defined Lata's enduring quality as a performer. After the show, I walked over to the auditorium to greet a family I had personally invited to attend the show. Surprising everyone, their six-year-old daughter, Ritu, blurted out: "I want to talk to the lady singer. Can you take me to her?"

I knew Lata never liked to meet anyone after her performance. But since this little girl made this unusual request, I felt I had no choice but to try. So I went backstage and asked, "Lata Ji, a little girl named Ritu wants to meet with you personally. Should I tell her you are too tired to meet anyone?"

"Mittra Saheb," responded Lata politely, "I want to meet her too. Please bring her to me."

As soon as Ritu arrived backstage, Lata came forward, put her hand on Ritu's chin and asked in a sweet voice, "Bitiya, kya naam hai tumhara?"(What is your name, my child?)

Not understanding what Lata asked her in Hindi (Ritu spoke only English and Bengali), she replied: "I liked your songs v—e—rrr—y much."

Let those momentous words coming from a six-year-old, born and brought up in America, and having rarely been exposed to Indian music, be the ultimate tribute to a remarkable lady we all reverently and lovingly call *Lata Ji*.

The concerts presented by Lata and Mukesh did more to spread the rich Indian *musiculture* in America and Canada than any other Indian musical concert presented in the US up to that point. So, it is nothing short of a cruel twist of fate that the series ended in a total disaster no one would have predicted even in their wildest imagination.

The day was August 27, 1976. It was a gorgeous summer day in Detroit, and the air was filled with hope and excitement. That evening we were scheduled to present our final—and unequivocally the most extravagant—musical performance of the entire US–Canada concert tour. After all, Detroit was the hometown of our promoter Mohan Deora; it was also the city which Lata had fondly called her second home.

I was also excited because Bani was going to be in the front row of the audience. From her childhood days, and even after she came to America, got married, and settled down here, through the medium of radio and TV, CDs, and stage performances, Bani had continued to popularize Lata's songs. Among her most favorite songs were: *Ayega Aanewala, Yeh Zindagi Usiki Hai, Mohe Bhool Gaye Sanwariya,* and *Aye Malik Tere Bande Ham.*

And that was not all. The organizer for the Detroit show was Narendra Sheth—an outstanding leader of our Indian community in the Michigan area. Not only was he the host of a popular Indian radio program called Geetmala, but he was also a perfectionist to a fault. As an example, for that evening he had made special arrangements to install a 300-pound silver gate on the back of the stage. To the amazement and delight of the audience, at a precise time that gate was designed to open so that Lata could walk through the door and step on to the stage. He made numerous other arrangements to ensure that this show would be nothing short of an extravaganza. This thought, too, was getting me very excited.

I arrived at the Ford Auditorium shortly after 4 pm. I watched the crew members and the musicians arrange the furniture and musical instruments, and get ready for the show. The excitement continued to build in me, and I silently rehearsed the speech I would deliver before the capacity home crowd. By 5:30 pm the stage was all set, so I went backstage, ready to welcome our legendary star performers Lata and Mukesh, and also to greet the musicians as they arrived from the hotel.

At 6 pm out of a clear blue sky, suddenly the atom bomb was dropped on us, literally devastating our entire world. As I was waiting backstage, Mohan approached me, looking completely drained and washed out. In a husky, barely audible voice, he informed me that our beloved Mukesh had just suffered a massive heart attack and passed away en route to the hospital. He asked me to control my emotions because, as he put it, "You are the one who will have to go on stage to make this shocking announcement to the audience and then cancel the show."

Millions of disjointed thoughts started circling in my head, literally knocking me off my feet. "How could this have happened?" I kept asking myself, especially since I was just at the hotel where Mukesh was conducting his preconcert practice session. And how would I carry this devastating news to thousands of fans eagerly awaiting his arrival on stage? All these conflicting thoughts were too much for me to bear. I was frozen in my tracks, and stood there like a zombie, unable to move or act.

I don't remember how long I stood there before Mohan approached me again. This time, he informed me that Lata had directed her brother, Hridaynath Mangeshkar, to come on stage to make the announcement of Mukesh's death and cancel the show. Then he added that my job would simply be to announce that Hridaynath had an important message to deliver. I was greatly relieved.

That evening, by special arrangement, Air India flew the body of Mukesh from Detroit to Bombay. At the Bombay airport, millions of mourners, including the legendary actor Raj Kapoor, waited to receive the body and pay their last respects to the legendary singer, Mukesh Chandra Mathur.

Four decades have passed since Mukesh Ji passed away, but the legacy he left behind is just as live today as it was then. And even though now an octogenarian, the legendary Lata Mangeshkar is still vibrant and actively continues to enrich our world.

For as long as I can remember, one of my cherished goals has been to make a special effort to bring together the rich cultures of India and America. This goal was based on the valuable lesson that I had learnt from my mother: "Always remember where your roots are, but never let the past dictate your future." What follows are my efforts toward reaching that long-term goal.

Almost six decades have passed since I left India for America, carrying with me only a lofty dream. During this long period, almost everything has changed. The world has become flat. Most third-world countries have emerged from their internationally-created cocoon. Emerging nations have begun vying for world stage. The computer age, loaded with smart phones, Skype, twitter, Facebook, Google, and a 24-hour news blast on CNN, has produced a new paradigm, more powerful than the world has ever experienced.

By the middle of this century the human race will have expanded in ten thousand years from less than ten million to nearly ten billion people. Some of the billions alive today still live in misery and dearth even worse than the worst experienced in the Stone Age. Some are worse off than they were just a few months or years before. But the vast majority of people are much better fed, much better sheltered, much better entertained, much better protected against disease and much more likely to live to old age than their ancestors have ever been. The availability of almost everything a person could want or need has been going rapidly upwards for 200 years and erratically upwards for 10,000 years before that: years of lifespan, mouthfuls of clean water, lungfuls of clean air, hours of privacy, means of travelling faster than you can run, ways of communicating farther than you can shout. Even allowing for the hundreds of millions who still live in abject poverty, disease and want, this generation of human beings has access to more calories, watts, lumen-hours, square feet, gigabytes, megahertz, light-years, nano-metres, bushels per acre, miles per gallon, food miles, air miles, and of course dollars than any that went before. They have more Velcro, vaccines, vitamins, shoes, singers, soap operas, mango slicers, sexual partners, tennis rackets, guided missiles and anything else they could even imagine needing. By one estimate, the number of different products that you can buy in New York or London tops ten billion.[3]

Admittedly, this is a parochial view. During the same period, we have simultaneously had massive challenges. These include exponential population growth, explosive political turmoil around the world, unprecedented demands for higher living standards in all countries, rapid depletion of the world's resources desperately needed for survival, and above all, a distrust among people that is shaking the foundation of the world body we call the United Nations.

Against the background of such an earth-shattering revolution in the world, I often wonder how my country of birth has *really* changed during the last 60 years. A parallel question that also keeps popping up in my mind is: Do *I* still have the capacity to bring about a better understanding between the peoples of India and America?

A quick review of the developments in India over the last six decades leaves me both excited and somewhat disappointed. On one hand, after decades of torpor, India's economic activities have accelerated to the point that by the end of this century, it could become the envy of the world. And a visit to the cities of *New Delhi, Bangalore, Hyderabad, Ahmadabad,* and *Mumbai* could convince even a skeptic that, in terms of economic and social development, in time India is most likely to surpass China. Despite occasional setbacks, India's economic growth, which parallels that of China, appears to be for real. India's middle class is swelling, governance is improving, and the society is gearing up to meet the increasing demands of the affluent middle class.

Perhaps the most important development since gaining independence was the Indian general election completed in May 2014. With 815 million people eligible to vote, this was the largest-ever election in the world. The BJP, winning 51.9 percent of all seats in Lok Sabha (lower house), became the first party since 1984 to have a mandate to govern without the support of other parties.

The euphoria of the landslide election has subsequently unleashed two distinctly divergent sets of emotions. On one hand, reflecting the difficult challenges facing India, Montek Singh Ahluwalia, Deputy Chairman, Planning Commission said:

First, it [the government] must ensure a sound macroeconomic environment, reversing the fiscal deficit rise that took place from 2008 onward. Second, we need to rapidly step up investment in infrastructure from public sources and public–private partnerships. This is the single-biggest supply-side constraint for India's growth and competitiveness. Third, we need to bring our energy prices in line with global prices through a gradual transition. Fourth, the goods and services tax (GST) will be a major step forward in indirect taxation. Finally, we need to improve the ease of doing business, where India's ranking is too low.[4]

On the other hand, citizens of emerging India applauded the newly elected Narendra Modi's steadfast commitment to accelerate high levels of investment, especially in infrastructure. This also includes establishing a business-friendly environment, instituting accelerated economic and tax reforms, and promoting an inclusive growth process. It would be one in which all sections of the society could participate in the country's accelerated economic growth.

The EY's 2014 survey underscored high expectations for India's bright future, assuming the government successfully meets its myriad challenges. The survey revealed that by 2020 India is expected to be among the top three economies of the world, particularly for economic growth and manufacturing. The survey concluded that the strengths—such as a burgeoning middle class, growing domestic consumption levels, and a skilled workforce— are supporting it in the global marketplace.

The country has not experienced such optimism among the general masses for a long time, if ever. But the challenges the country faces are weighty and the nation's democratic/bureaucratic machinery moves in slow, often in reversible, motion. For these reasons, it is best to be hopeful but vigilant. After all, stories of large swaths of the country not fully participating in the unprecedented growth are rampant. Age-old bureaucratic problems are unaddressed. And a new, vibrant, and progressive educational system for the entire country has yet to be instituted; one that would make it one of the leading countries of the world.

And so it appears that by the end of the twenty-first century India could conceivably achieve its goal of becoming a dominant world-class player. But for that to happen, all sections of the country must begin sharing in the economic growth and the country's infrastructure. And its educational system must match or surpass that of a fully developed nation.

Although of a different nature, problems facing America are no less challenging. Fortunately, the American press is completely open about the problems this country faces, so the problems surfacing even in the remote village of Jewell, Oregon, for instance, are instantly flashed on TV screens in the little town of Numazu, Japan. As a result, the whole world can see the complex problems that Americans currently face. And, for a variety of reasons, the solutions continue to be difficult, if not elusive.

Transcending these myriads of problems, the single most troubling issue revolves around America's declining power on the world stage. While new questions continue to raise their ugly head, the country officially claims that the two major wars in Iraq and Afghanistan are winding down. Equally important, America shows great reluctance to restore the world order by interfering in Syria, Egypt, Libya, Iraq, Ukraine, and North Korea. The result is predictable. In the eyes of the world, America is no longer viewed as the superpower it once was.

In fact, with perpetual deadlock in Washington, D.C., and constantly facing intractable social and financial problems, the world is becoming progressively more convinced that the US is unable to effectively address even its own domestic problems. America, the world now screams, is permanently doomed. What a shame that it has finally come to this!!

Everything I just said about America is true. Polls indicate that people think that America is on the wrong track. This could lead one to be rather pessimistic about the country and about its direction as a nation. That, however, is at best a parochial view. It fails to look at the bright side.

First, in the not too distant a future, America is poised to change its status as a net importer of huge amounts of oil and gas from unfriendly nations. It will become a net exporter of this valuable resource, the most significant economic and geopolitical event in our recent history. Second, America remains the place where breakthrough ideas, and the products they help develop, are still being generated in the world of commerce and technology.

As a proud American puts it: "We remain the place where 'Facebooks' are created and Apple's pipeline of personal technology thrives." And that does not happen by accident. American culture handsomely rewards individual creativity. It provides the opportunity for those who fail to keep up their quest until they find elusive success.

Third, in the area of medicine, which typically represents by far the largest expenditure of all industrialized nations, America continues to develop medical breakthrough devices and wonder drugs. These ultimately help improve the lives of millions of people around the world. Fourth, American businesses and investors are awash with liquid funds. They continue to look for the next opportunity. As this nation frequently boasts, "The risk takers and entrepreneurs are at the starting line awaiting the gun." It is no stray accident that the gross domestic product (GDP) of America is three times the size of China's GDP while its population is one-fifth that of China.

Given the misunderstandings about each other that currently exist both in the US and India, I believe I can *make a difference* by accentuating what is best in each of these two great countries. And since we live in a digital world, I note with some satisfaction that I have already started relying primarily on digital means. These include posting a blog on a website, using Facebook, starting an international group via e-mail, publishing articles electronically for the national media, and relying on other rapid means of mass communication. I realize that, since I am only one person, my progress is likely to be painfully slow and uneven, and my efforts would have at best a limited impact. Yet I am determined to vigorously continue my pursuit of promoting mutual understanding. I hope that by accentuating the positive, someday I will achieve success by narrowing the gulf existing between our two great nations.

〜

The most emotionally, spiritually, and philosophically satisfying activity relating to the idea of giving back to the society in *financial terms* began many years ago. The decision to get involved with fund raising activities was easy; however, deciding which activities to fund was not. For one thing, long time ago I had embraced Walt Disney's philosophy, "It's a small world after all," which encouraged me to raise funds to help charitable causes both in America and India. For another, I suspected that success in raising charitable funds required the efficient use of techniques that significantly differed from the ones I understood.

After a great deal of soul searching and discussions with professional fund raisers, I took two significant steps. I decided to create a tax-exempt foundation in India to support (mostly) educational opportunities for the economically underprivileged people. I also established a charitable [Section 501(c)(3)] foundation in the US to improve the quality of financial education in this country. Needless to say, I was nervous about plunging into this uncharted territory. I had no experience in fund raising, and my new venture seemed destined to fail. But to allay my fears, I reminded myself that I had faced impossible tasks before, but that did not stop me from trying.

On December 20, 2000, almost at the beginning of the new century, I created a charitable foundation in India and financed it with personal funds amounting to ₹18 lakh ($30,000 at the then-prevailing exchange rate). At that time the *size* of the contribution by an average person like me living in the US to an Indian foundation was incomprehensible. But I made this personal contribution (rather than publicly raising the fund) merely to avoid total failure of my newfound passion.

But I did not just stop there. During my trip to India in the winter of 2005, I made a special effort to visit Vrindaban and pay my respects to the holy city. Almost a quarter of a century ago, having fulfilled all of her family duties, my mother had renounced the world and settled down in this holy city. It was here that in 1974 she was laid to rest. Since then, I have treated Vrindaban as a holy place.

During this trip, I visited Ramakrishna Mission about which my mother had often spoken with great fondness and reverence. Prior to my visiting the Mission, I had discovered that the Math and the Mission are the two key organizations. These direct the work of the socioreligious Ramakrishna Movement influenced by the nineteenth-century saint Ramakrishna Paramahamsa and shaped by his chief disciple, Vivekananda. Also referred to as the Ramakrishna Order, the Math is the movement's monastic organization. Founded by Ramakrishna in 1886, the Math primarily focuses on spiritual training and the propagation of the movement's teachings. By comparison, the Mission, founded by Vivekananda in 1897, is a humanitarian organization which carries out medical, relief, and educational programs.

During this visit, I had the distinct pleasure of meeting Swami Suprakashnanda, the general secretary of the Mission. A middle-aged saint with an engaging smile and a pleasing personality to match, I connected with the Swami almost instantly. I learned from him that Vivekananda proclaimed renunciation and service as the two-fold national ideals of modern India and the Mission strives to practice and preach these ideals. The service activities are based on the message of *Jiva is Shiva* from Vivekananda's message of *Daridra Narayan* to indicate that service to poor is service to God. The principles of Upanishads and Yoga in Bhagwad Gita reinterpreted in light of Ramakrishna's life and teachings are the main sources of inspiration for the Mission. The motto of the Mission is *"Atmano Mokshartham Jagadhitaya Cha"* or "For one's own salvation, and for the good of the world."

During the course of my conversation, I mentioned to the Swami that my mother, who lived as a widow for some 37 years, had spent her final days in this city and had often spoken to us about the great work the Mission does for the needy. Hearing that, the Swami proudly explained that the Mission operated a nursing school which (at very little out of pocket expenses by the students) graduated widows and battered women abandoned by the society as trained nurses. The total cost for room, board, tuition, and all other educational expenses for a three-and-a-half-year training program was a minuscule ₹168,000 ($2,800 at the exchange rate of ₹60=$1 prevailing in June 2015; this exchange rate is subject to change with time).

The operation of the Mission's nursing school certainly piqued my interest. So, with the Swami's permission and blessings, I carefully examined the nursing school's accounting records in order to convince myself that the total cost figure the Swami spoke about was in fact accurate and that it was based on acceptable accounting principles. I then spent one more day learning about a number of other Mission's activities and then bade the Swami goodbye, promising to keep in touch.

After returning from India to America, I did get busy with my professional activities, but couldn't get the nursing school out of my mind. So, I spent another year researching various aspects of the nursing training program. Fully satisfied with the value the school was creating, I finally decided to raise a significant amount for financially supporting the school. The amount I selected was $100,000, equivalent to ₹60 lakh, an amount that appeared to be coming out of a fairy tale.

On October 1, 2006, I launched the Capital Campaign, 2006: North American Capital Fund Raising Campaign to Benefit Ramakrishna Mission Sevashrama, Vrindaban, India. On that day, as the chairman of the Campaign, I mailed the following letter (excerpt) to a large number of prospective donors:

After completing a two-year, in-depth investigation of all aspects of the Ramakrishna Mission Sevashrama, founded by Swami Vivekananda, we have decided to wholeheartedly endorse their efforts in Vrindaban, India. The depth and breadth of the humanitarian services being provided by the Mission are truly unparalleled, and the fact that these services are being offered virtually free of charge makes it a unique charitable endeavor. We are convinced that Ramakrishna Mission Sevashrama deserves and needs our large-scale financial support to continue its valuable work. You may see the Mission at work by visiting their website at www.rkmsvrina.org.

I have therefore accepted the Mission's invitation to become the Honorary Chairman of its 2006 Capital Fund Raising Campaign.

Sid Mittra

As has been true so many times in the past, for a long time the going was excruciatingly slow and very disappointing. In fact, that instituted in me the innate fear that this time I had indeed dreamed too big even for my own good and I was destined to fail. But somehow I found the strength to persevere and ultimately prevailed.

So, it is with deep satisfaction that I can say this: I feel gratified that after four long years of trying very hard, and frequently tumbling and falling flat on my face, the miracle that had eluded me for so long did in fact materialize. This can be seen from the following letter:

December 2, 2010

Ms Lisa Piner,
American Service to India
Costa Mesa, California 92628-2456

Dear Lisa,

Attached is a check for $7,000. This check represents the last installment of the series of checks I have mailed to you for financing the Nursing Program at R.K. Mission, Vrindaban.

This brings our total contribution to the Program equal to our original goal of $100,000, or ₹60 lakh in Indian currency.

Sid Mittra

I sincerely believe that on that auspicious wintery day, my efforts to give something meaningful back to the society came to a full circle. I do realize, of course, that thus far I have taken only the first step toward achieving success, and lot more has to come. But I also recall the famous words of Lao-tzu

(604 BC–531 BC): "A journey of a thousand miles begins with a single step."

Epilogue: Life's Lessons

Early in life I *redefined* the concept of success by embracing the philosophy immortalized by Emerson: "[Success is] to find the best in others; to leave the world a bit better, whether by a healthy child, a garden patch or a redeemed social condition; to know even one life has breathed easier because … [I] have lived." And when I had serious doubts about my ability to achieve my objective I confronted them by reminding myself of Helen Keller's classic comment: "I am only one, but still I am one."

As a start, at the UF, I helped the ISO transform into a vibrant, forward-looking, and progressive organization. Next, acting as its leader, I developed a number of programs designed to achieve our objective of improving an appreciation of the diversity in different cultures.

Of all the many ways I helped getting the Western audiences soaked with Indian music and culture, none is more newsworthy or sensational than my association with two visiting Bollywood legends: Lata Mangeshkar and Mukesh Chandra Mathur. In the summer of 1976, this team presented 10 musical concerts in America and Canada. And good fortune smiled on me when for all of their concerts I was invited to act as the Master of Ceremony as well as the co-manager of the musical team.

The most emotionally, spiritually, and philosophically satisfying activity relating to the idea of giving back to the society in *financial terms* began many years ago when I embraced Walt Disney's philosophy, "It's a small world after all." After settling down in Michigan in the 1960s, with the help of musical programs Bani and I along with our children organized many fund raising activities to help a variety of charities. Then, in 2000, I created a charitable foundation in India and financed it with personal funds amounting to ₹18 lakh ($30,000 at the then-prevailing exchange rate). At that time the *size* of the contribution by an average person like me living in the US to an Indian foundation was unthinkable.

But I did not stop there. After four long years of trying very hard, the miracle that had eluded me for so long did in fact materialize. In December 2010, I was able to donate a whopping ₹60 lakh for financing a nursing program run by the R.K. Mission in India.

I sincerely believe that on that auspicious wintery day, my efforts to give something meaningful back to the society came to a full circle. I do realize, of course, that thus far I have taken only a few initial steps toward achieving success, and lot more is bound to come. But I also recall the famous words of Lao-tzu (604 BC– 531 BC): "A journey of a thousand miles begins with a single step."

The following Four Ps' list identifies the P(s) that I have covered in this chapter:

[X] Persevere with passion.
[ ] Pursue professional, family-oriented, social, and spiritual goals.
[X] Persuade family and friends to help.
[X] Promote a culture of giving back.

Notes

1. Ralph Waldo Emerson (2009). *Quoted in the Essentials of Ralph Waldo Emerson*, Random House Publishing Group.
2. Edwin Osgood Grover (Ed.) (1909). *The Book of Good Cheer: A Little Bundle of Cheery Thought*, Kindle edition.
3. Matt Ridley (May 20, 2010). *The Rational Optimist: How Prosperity Evolves*, HarperCollins, Reviewed in Nature 465, pp. 294–295, DMF.
4. Montek Singh Ahluwalia, giving keynote speech at the Salwan Media OG13 Uniting Knowledge Communities Conference held on February 7–8, 2013, New Delhi.

16

CHALLENGES IN CREATING A FOUR-GENERATIONAL LEGACY

It doesn't matter what you do ... so long as you change something from the way it was before you touched it into something that's like you after you take your hands away. The difference between the man who just cuts lawns and a real gardener is in the touching. ... The lawn-cutter might just as well not have been there at all; the gardener will be there a lifetime.
—RAY BRADBURY, "FAHRENHEIT 451"

Growing up in colonial India in the 1940s, I was considered a weirdo at best and a dunce at worst. In fact, I was such a loner that no one ever thought I would ever be fit for a civilized society.

I was part of a large family. My concept of a family consisted of a mother, a father, and their biological children living together under one roof. I also assumed that in a family, it was always dad who went off to work, and it was inexorably foreordained that mom's destiny was to remain a homemaker and a mother. As I grew older, I further learned that family is the foundation of society. It's where we come into the world, are nurtured, and empowered with the tools to go out into the world as responsible citizens.

I carried this notion of a typical family for a long time. But something strange happened shortly before I was to leave for America, and that helped me embrace a *new definition of family*.

It was Thursday, August 2, 1957, a typical summer day in Kanpur: hot, humid, and sweltering. I was sitting with Mother on our porch, sipping on a cup of jasmine tea, saying goodbye to her before I set sail for America. For a while, Mother quietly sat on a chair, trying heroically to control her tears. I, too, was emotional. But in all honesty, after trying so hard for over five years to win a scholarship, now I was excited about going to America. Neither of us had any idea of how the new country was going to treat me, and more importantly, how long it would be before we saw each other again.

Suddenly, without forewarning, Mother blurted out: "I feel I am not going to be around when you return from America. So today let me share with you something that has been on my mind for some time."

Mother became quiet for a moment, as if she needed to take the time to collect her thoughts. After a few moments of silence, she continued: "As you know by now, we were devastated when you were only seven years old and your father had suddenly passed away. But even though at times I felt helpless, all my life I tried hard to provide help for each of you so you could become successful. It's no secret that we constantly struggled, but we never gave up. And now I believe each of us has succeeded."

Mother stopped again, so that I could digest what she had just shared, then spoke again: "Today I request you to continue our family tradition. *Before* you start a family, remember this: 'Do not give up until *you* have helped each one in your family—your wife and your children—to reach his or her *fullest potential*'." She paused again, this time to give me a chance to fully appreciate the gravity of her advice, and then continued: "But don't just stop there. Teach *your children* our new definition of a family so they, too, will remember to help their spouses and children achieve their fullest potential."

I sat there, dumbstruck. Just listening to her made me feel dizzy, if not downright nervous. But before I could say anything, Mother concluded: "I guarantee you sometimes the going will get rough. When that happens, remember that no matter how much you achieve, your life will remain unfulfilled until you have accomplished your mission."

I sailed from Bombay on August 10, 1957, nervous, unsure of my immediate future, and in no position to dream about a family. So for a long time, my mother's advice remained buried deep down in my psyche. But when I got married in 1961, Mother's advice miraculously surfaced. I felt then that since I remembered her advice at the start of my family life, I'd have an easy time following it.

It didn't take me long to realize that I was wrong, dead wrong.

Bani Mittra grew up in the large cosmopolitan city of Bombay (now Mumbai). By Indian standards, most people living in that city were progressive. But the culture prevailing in Bani's family was still traditional, where her father acted as the sole decision maker. So she grew up believing that her father always knew what was best for her and never felt the need to express her independent opinion. She also assumed that once married, her father's role would be transferred to her husband. That is precisely what happened after her marriage, and that had unpleasant consequences. Here is an example:

Once I was invited by the UD to interview for a faculty position. This was the first time I was leaving my wife alone in unfamiliar surroundings, so naturally she wanted me to let her know as soon as I safely reached my destination. But realizing that I was practically broke and couldn't afford to make a long distance call, on my arrival I decided (a shameful act) to make a person-to-person *collect* call and have Bani refuse to accept it. That would get the message across to Bani, but I would not need to pay for the call.

Well, the situation became muddied after I arrived at the dean's office. At the dean's suggestion, in his presence I used his phone to make a person-to-person (but *not* a collect) call, and that turned out to be a major embarrassment. When Bani answered, the operator announced that this was a person-to-person call for Bani Mittra. Speaking in a loud voice, and with complete confidence,

Bani answered: "Yes, I am Bani Mittra, but before leaving town my *husband instructed me* not to accept a collect call when he phones me from Detroit."

This embarrassing episode prompted me to help Bani break away from her traditional upbringing, and encourage her to rely more on her own independent thinking. That, I was convinced, would allow her to benefit from the freedom and opportunities available to everyone in America.

In the winter of 1961, when we began our married life in the sleepy little southern town known as DeLand (pronounced as Dee Laand), Bani had little, if any, understanding of the obstacles she would face as I pushed her to assume a new role. These ranged from modifying her deep-rooted Indian culture to getting acclimatized to the American language to adjusting to the prevailing social mores. But it didn't take long before she was simultaneously exposed to all these challenges, and more.

In those days, residents of DeLand had almost no knowledge of the outside world. No one in that town had ever seen an Indian lady before either in person or on TV. Most believed that all Indians were American Indians from New Mexico. So when Bani was first seen in public, walking down the street wearing her beautifully embroidered sari and Indian jewelry, traffic virtually came to a standstill. Everyone stared at her as if she was from outer space. It took months for people to feel comfortable seeing Bani.

Bani had to constantly face a challenging environment in order to survive and succeed. But that was not all. Her bachelor's degree was in Indian classical music, something no one at the University recognized. Despite numerous challenges, however, buoyed by my constant encouragement, she overcame her fear of failure and forged ahead, albeit taking small steps. Bani began making new friends and even adopted as her American god-mother the head of a girls' dorm on campus. Next, she enrolled in various classes at the University, including arts and crafts, foreign language (Spanish), and secretarial skills, such as typing and shorthand. These and other related activities laid the groundwork for later development.

The *real* test of my resolve to help Bani continue her progress toward reaching new highs came when our son, Robert, turned six. Until then, she deliberately limited her activities to taking classes at the University, entertaining the Indian community through TV and radio broadcasts as well as stage performances. She also raised funds for her favorite Indian charities. She believed that until our youngest child started school on a full-time basis, it was imperative that she remained a homemaker. Her decision was final, and not subject to negotiation.

In April 1972, when Robert turned six, I wasted no time in broaching the subject of her acquiring marketable skills. Bani's response was disappointing, but predictable. According to the old Indian tradition, she claimed that her life should be dedicated to her husband and children. Any attempt to carve out a niche for herself would be a gross violation of her traditional role, subject to severe criticism by the Indian community. And before I could counter that, she threw me a curve.

"Besides music," said Bani, "the only thing that interests me is teaching young children. But for that I'm sure I'd need a college degree in education from an American university (she had a degree in music from an Indian university) as well as a teaching certificate. I have neither, and don't have the smarts to earn them. So I guess that's the end of my teaching career."

I reflected on her objections for a while, eventually concluding that those were indeed valid. But instead of giving in, I let my hubris take over and decided to take action. Having convinced myself that her two roles as a homemaker and a school teacher were not mutually exclusive, I dismissed her first argument. Successfully tackling the second objection, however, took longer than I had expected.

Initially, when I started addressing the issue, I became overwhelmed by a series of disappointing news. I began by knocking on many doors, including those at the US Department of Health, Education and Welfare, the American Montessori Society, and the Education Department of the University of Michigan. Unfortunately, I did not receive even a glimmer of hope or encouragement from anyone. I even argued and pleaded with a number of college admission officers and counselors but always came away empty handed. Yet somehow I found the courage to persevere, refusing to take no for an answer.

In the end, I prevailed.

One day I accidentally learned that, even though it was in the field of music from an *Indian* university, Bani's undergraduate degree would satisfy the minimum educational requirements needed to qualify for earning a Montessori Teachers' Diploma. And after completing the necessary practical training in child education, she would indeed become a certified Montessori teacher for children.

"Mission accomplished," I said to myself as I savored the moment.

This story had a delightful ending. When I broke this exciting news to Bani, she became so ecstatic that her first objection to deal with the negative response from the Indian community totally escaped her. But instead of reminding her of a critical memory loss, I preferred to remain silent, whispering only to myself: "Impossible dreams like this come true only to those who persevere."

Bani came to America to get married, become a good homemaker, subsequently a mother, and finally settle down for life. And yet, due largely to my continually bringing up the unlimited opportunities that lurked on the horizon, eventually she became sufficiently inspired to follow her own dreams. So, without any fanfare, and still fearful of failing in her mission, in January 1973

Bani enrolled in the Montessori Center of Michigan's Teachers' Training Program in Drayton Plains, Michigan. And by doing so, she embarked on a career path that would have remained elusive for life.

Starting her educational program to become a licensed Montessori teacher was hardly the end of her challenges and frustrations. Bani had been out of a classroom for a long time. The rigorous training program took a toll on her. Even worse, almost instantly her fear of criticism by the Indian community materialized. Because of her preoccupation with the educational program, she had to be absent from most social and religious functions, a fact widely criticized by the community. Fortunately, Bani's pleasing personality and mild demeanor masked her fierce determination to ignore these criticisms. That saved the day.

Incidentally, during these trying times, I, too, suffered continuously, although my problems were of a vastly different nature. I was forced to become a live-in nanny for our two kids. This was a situation that I frequently botched, something both of my children strongly resented. But since it was I who insisted on Bani's starting a new career, I had little choice but to endure these frustrations. And even though on a number of occasions I entertained the thought of strangling the kids, in the end, all of us survived, although barely.

On July 1, 1974, having passed her exams with flying colors, Bani was awarded the all-important Montessori Teacher's License. And on that day, this traditional Indian lady, who was destined to remain a homemaker *for life*, proudly placed her prized license on a pedestal and lit a candle under it to celebrate her victory. When I witnessed that, I couldn't help but whisper to myself, "Is this the reason why perseverance and passion are considered to be the two most important ingredients for success?"

In the fall of 1974, Bani launched her teaching career by becoming the directress of the Heart of the Hills Montessori Center in Rochester Hills, Michigan. She never looked back.

As is true with so many immigrants, by launching her teaching career Bani had fulfilled her American dream. But she didn't realize that in America those dreams have wings. They continue to fly even after the initial dream had been achieved.

Not too long after she joined the Montessori school as a Directress, Bani started dreaming of starting her *own Montessori school*. At first, I resisted, fearing that owning a Montessori school would conflict with the scheduled launch of my financial planning practice. Upon reflection, however, I felt differently and acquiesced.

In the fall of 1977, with much fanfare, Bani opened her own school, *Meadowbrook Montessori Center*, renting space from a local church. The sharing arrangement helped both parties: The school would safely operate inside a public building and the church would receive additional revenues by renting the space they did not use during weekdays. Also, I registered the school as a tax-exempt, charitable organization so that she could give something back to the society that had been so generous to her.

Everything for Bani worked like a charm. The church's pastor was happy with the way we operated our school and expressed his unconditional support. Bani continued to perform admirably. Her reputation steadily grew as an outstanding teacher, and the Center was acclaimed as *the* private school in the Rochester area. Two years later, in July of 1979, as if to confirm that she was indeed entitled to live the American dream, Bani was awarded American citizenship.

The year 1982 turned out to be a fateful year, but not for the reason you might suspect. By then, my financial planning career, which was launched the previous year, had taken shape. I had signed a five-year lease with an office complex, and the business had started to operate smoothly. Our Montessori school had a long-term contract that allowed us to use the church facility for the next five years, so availability of rental space for the school was not an issue. As stated, Bani's school was growing steadily and gaining reputation in the process. Everything was working beautifully for both of us. We were silently dreaming of putting our respective careers on cruise control. Alas, as has been the case with me so many times in the past, that was not meant to be.

This was Valentine's Day in 1982, a day of special celebrations all over the world. It was also Bani's birthday so we were doubly excited. But suddenly that morning all that changed when I received an urgent request from the pastor to meet with him in his office. When I arrived, he delivered a stern message which blew me away.

"Sid," said the pastor with a grim face and in a barely audible voice, "the church has decided to start using the school space during weekdays. Therefore, I ask that you vacate our building at the end of the school year." (Later, the pastor privately confessed that religious bias was the main reason behind the decision.)

I was shocked and speechless, to put it mildly. From the day I received this *death warrant*, we would have only six months and 14 days to relocate ourselves. There wasn't another building in Rochester that could be converted into a school and properly licensed in a few months. And even if one were available, we wouldn't have access to it on such a short notice. It would be presumptuous of me to sue a prestigious church on the grounds of religious bias. Besides, we had neither the time nor the money to embark on such a risky venture. Worst of all, if because of a lack of operating facility we were forced to close our school for a year, we'd undoubtedly lose all our students. And that would certainly force us to close our doors permanently.

The situation seemed hopeless. I could see Bani's dreams going up in smoke. That's when my hubris kicked in, and despite insurmountable obstacles, I vowed to find a solution.

Closing the school for one year was certainly not an option. That meant that in six short months we would have to accomplish all of the following tasks:

> - *Locate a private residence in Rochester that is currently on sale.*
> - *Buy the residence immediately on affordable terms.*
> - *Find a bank or a mortgage company ready to finance the project.*
> - *Rebuild the residence completely, converting it into a public school after complying with all the local, state, and national laws and regulations applicable to schools.*
> - *Change the building's zoning from residential to business (school).*
> - *Obtain permission from each resident in the neighborhood to operate the school.*
> - *Have Rochester City Council authorize us to operate a public school in a residential neighborhood.*

The most optimistic estimate for completing these tasks was two years, not counting the time it would take to locate a suitable property. That night I went to bed totally defeated, *almost* ready to quit.

I spent a restless night tossing and turning, generating sufficient energy to move forward. So, I created a Super Committee named TIP (The Impossible Project) that would fight the battle on my behalf. Members included: a CPA specializing in school accounting, a real estate agent and a home builder, a Rochester City Council member responsible for making zoning changes, a senior officer in the city's fire department, a company president specializing in constructing barrier-free entries to business properties, a school inspector working for the state of Michigan, and a loan officer working for Michigan National Bank. I convinced each member that the church had inflicted great injustice on us (everyone reviewed our long-term leasing contract), and in Rochester there was a growing demand for the services we provided. Members of TIP worked tirelessly and in unison to get the job done in a timely fashion, reminding me of Tocqueville's *Democracy in America*, in which he pointed to private associations formed to solve problems that the government was unable to solve.

For the next several months, I witnessed the power of *pulling together* to achieve an *impossible* goal. And while I did my part in keeping the group moving, it was these outstanding, dedicated citizens who performed the miracle, refusing to accept any compensation for their services.

On September 1, 1982, precisely *six months and 15 days* from the day we received the eviction notice from the church, our school opened at our new facility. When the parents drove into our newly paved parking lot, they were dazzled by an oversized sign, painted in rainbow colors and decorated with flowers, courtesy of Bordines Nursery:

MEADOWBROOK MONTESSORI CENTER
1590 Walton Boulevard

And on the opening day, as the parents with children approached the front door, they were warmly greeted by the school's triumphant director, whom the children and their parents affectionately called, *Mrs Mittra.*

There is an old saying, "Prosperity demands its own price." That certainly proved to be true the year our school celebrated its best year since inception.

Toward the end of that school year, our teachers and staff casually requested a short meeting with me. And since it was our standing policy to have year-end staff meetings, this request did not come as a surprise. As I soon realized, however, I shouldn't have been so trusting.

The meeting, attended by all the teachers and staff members, started with a bombshell. As the leader of the group put it to me directly: "Since the school is doing so well, and *we are the ones* responsible for making it happen, we *demand* an across-the-board raise in salary of 25 percent." The spokesperson paused for a moment as if to catch her breath, then concluded: "Since this is practically the end of the year, we would like you to make your decision NOW so we can plan for next year."

I was blindsided by this demand, and by our trusted and highly respected teachers no less. I was certain that agreeing to this outrageous demand, coming out of nowhere as it were, would bankrupt the treasury and the school would go under. I was also keenly aware that Bani's entire professional life was embedded in her school, and abruptly closing the school would devastate her. I couldn't decide on the spot how to respond, so to buy some time I promised to have a response in 24 hours.

Still reeling from the devastating school meeting, that evening I asked Bani if next year she could run the school by herself working overtime, assisted by only one full-time teacher. Calculating the mandated teacher–student ratio, and doing a little additional math, she informed me that such an arrangement could work, albeit with some downward adjustment in student enrollment.

I was relieved.

The next day I met with all our staff members to announce that, effective the end of the current school year, services of all staff members would be terminated. But I also assured them that anyone willing to accept the current compensation package would be unconditionally rehired. I concluded the meeting by expressing my gratitude to all the staff members for their many years of loyal and dedicated service, and added that it was my hope that next year we would welcome all of them back.

Surprisingly, the crisis passed rather peacefully. Most (though not all) members happily embraced the new contract once they realized that their threat had not worked. And in the fall, our school reopened with more enthusiastic staff members than we had in the previous school year. Equally satisfying was the fact that even the few employees who chose not to return continued to maintain congenial (although less warm) social relationships with us.

～

Ownership of the Meadowbrook School and an active teaching role fulfilled Bani's professional dream. But her heart was also set on another dream which had remained dormant from her childhood days. Given her rigorous training in Indian classical music, her breadth of knowledge of other forms of music and her gifted voice, she had always dreamed of producing her own musical CDs. However, since after marriage she had permanently left India, her dream had remained unfulfilled.

In 1993, by capitalizing on the seeds of opportunity sown almost a quarter of a century earlier I *literally invented* a way to make her musical dream come true. Sometimes in my life, facts had been stranger than fiction. This case certainly fit that description.

In 1966, a nationally respected Indian composer and music director named V. Balsara was on an American musical tour. As a local sponsor of his Detroit show, I got to know the composer personally. Upon his return to India, we agreed to remain friends by communicating regularly.

Some years later, Balsara's sister was diagnosed with third stage cancer. The doctors prescribed for her a special medicine, at that time available only in the US. And that presented a problem: The then-existing India's stringent exchange control regulations prohibited the purchase of US dollars to pay for this medicine. As soon as I received Balsara's fervent plea, I purchased the medicine through a physician friend (it was a prescription drug) and sent it to him through a passenger leaving for Calcutta the same evening. The medicine was delivered to Balsara the next day, an impossible feat. He never forgot that gesture, and vowed to return the favor when I needed one.

Since then, we had remained in contact with each other on a regular basis. Then one day in 1993 he shared with me the most exciting news: He had been awarded D. Litt by the venerable institute, *Vishwa Bharati*. Simultaneously, in recognition of his long and distinguished contribution to the field of Indian music, Balsara had been appointed as the president of the prestigious *Sangeet Research Academy*. The honorable composer ended the note by reminding me that he was still waiting to return his favor to his *beloved brother*. I must confess that the gentle reminder of his offer made me think of Bani's long-lost musical dream.

When I broached the subject with Balsara a few weeks later, I was literally blown away by his response. Without giving it a second thought, he immediately took over the ownership of that project, promising to help Bani realize her dream. But as I would discover later, in his euphoria to return my favor, at the end of his promise Balsara neglected to add: *Mission Impossible*.

The project turned out to be far more complex and time consuming than any of us had imagined, especially since it involved coordinating multilevel activities taking place on two opposite sides of the world. It also required the use of nascent technology that fell short of the demands of a complicated task. Still, not once did Balsara waiver from his mission, leaving me only with the mundane task of handling the administrative chores.

The project took much longer than expected. In time, by conducting a full 30-piece orchestra, and using eight-track super tapes, Balsara recorded the orchestral music for all of Bani's musical selections and shipped them by special courier to our home in Rochester, Michigan. I then set up multiple recording sessions at a professional recording studio in Detroit to complete the task. During this period, Bani recorded all of her selected songs accompanied by Balsara's orchestral music. The result was phenomenal. It was as though Bani traveled to India to record her favorite songs in a Calcutta recording studio. A full 30-piece orchestra accompanied her, conducted by none other than the renowned music director, V. Balsara.

In 1997, Bani produced her first musical cassette (Parts I and II) appropriately entitled, *My Musical Dream*. And with its publication (she published many more since then), the life of this remarkable lady came to a full circle.

In March 1963, we celebrated the birth of our daughter Rita with characteristic enthusiasm. True I also had the normal fear of my impending fatherhood, but that was trivial when compared with the two ominous signs raising their ugly head. I had neglected to note that there was a nine-month waiting period for the childbirth clause of my university health insurance plan to kick in. And since the expected birth date was two months shy of the clause's effective date, I had to bear the entire cost of childbirth, an expense I could ill afford. But I also faced a far bigger problem. Rita's birth virtually coincided with the expiration of my 18-month work permit in the US, which implied that after three months, I would be compelled to leave America for good.

Well, guess what? In both the instances, a miracle of sorts did occur. In the first case, I expected to receive a S1,400 ($400 covering hospital stay and $1,000 representing the doctor's fees), which I knew was far beyond my capacity to pay. The hospital bill, of course, remained unchanged. But recognizing what I was up against, Dr Jeremiah, the pediatrician, graciously and quietly reduced his bill from $1,000 to a mere $50. This check, an irreplaceable gift, still represents the finest example of great human tradition of selflessly caring for a fellow human being.

The second miracle may sound like a concocted story, but believe me it is not. Desperate to find a solution to my immigration problem, on May 13. 1963, my 33rd birthday, I went to meet the immigration officer in Detroit. Thoroughly convinced that I was wasting his time and mine, he dismissed me by sarcastically pointing out that the only way I could stay in this country was to land a job with an international agency, such as the UN or the IMF. I left the Immigration office disillusioned and demoralized.

Then something miraculous happened. Out of nowhere I received a letter dated May 16, 1963 (exactly three days after the immigration officer pushed me out) from Dr Edward P. Holland, director, Simulmatics Corporation, New York. (I have saved this letter as a souvenir.) Simulmatics had been hired by the US government to study Venezuela's economic development program, and the company wanted to engage me as an economic consultant. Dr Holland further clarified that Professor John Enos of MIT highly recommended me for the consulting position, and the job was mine for the taking.

To confess that I was literally blown away by that letter would be a gross understatement. But there was more. When I called Dr Holland to explain my visa problem, he assured me that since the US government wanted to hire me, my visa would be automatically extended.

On May 27, I received the following letter from Dr Holland: "I am very pleased to learn that you will be joining our team for economic research in Caracas, Venezuela." It was, however, comical that the Immigration Department solved my visa problem by granting me a *parole* visa (reserved for prisoners, but I didn't care) that authorized me to return to the US after completing our Venezuelan project.

I attributed the source of my phenomenal luck to our daughter. And in return, I vowed to help her become the very best that she could be in life.

By the time we finally returned to the UD after having lived both in South America and South East Asia for two years, Rita was a two-and-a-half-year-old bubbly child. But she did suffer from a serious language problem (mixed up between English, Spanish, and Bengali), and Bani had to make amends to get her ready for kindergarten.

When Rita was ready for kindergarten, in order to give her the best possible education we put her in Brookside (associated with the nationally famous Cranbrook school system) located in Bloomfield Hills. Rita did extremely well in that private school. But because of our concern that she was losing out on the social front, finally we moved her to the Rochester public school system.

From the time Rita settled down in Rochester until she graduated from Oakland University years later, the pattern of her development remained both consistent and remarkable. Rita grew up always wanting to do everything in sight. While going to school and carrying full load of courses, Rita opted to take lessons in piano and voice. She became an important part of our Indian Music Group. She played xylophone in our PBS television program. She sang duets with her mom and also performed on stage. She accompanied us on accordion when her mom and I presented duets on stage. And she did it all tirelessly and with enthusiasm.

And there was more. Besides her studies, Rita became active in dancing, singing (both Western and Indian styles), art, and much, much more. Her boundless energy, willingness to try anything that crossed her path, and her gift of caring for others—all were a source of pride for both Bani and me. And even her decision to earn an engineering degree when girls literally shied away from that discipline was reflective of her commitment to become who she wanted to be regardless of the obstacles she faced along the way.

There is yet another trait which Rita has inherited from the Mittra family. She cares about people, and rarely wavers from lending a helping hand to her friends, her acquaintances, and even to the people she hardly knows. This has been evident throughout her life. Her friends told us that they could count on her for help with their studies, their personal problems, and even for their financial problems.

Eventually, Rita earned a bachelor's degree in Mechanical Engineering from Oakland University, followed by both a master's degree in electrical engineering from the University of Rochester and an MBA from Northeastern University. She landed a senior management position with Xerox Corporation in Rochester, New York, where her individual Summary Index Score reached an unprecedented 99 percent. Subsequently, she left Xerox, and after a stint at Hewlett-Packard, she joined the Harris Corporation in 2008 as an executive engineer.

A major source of our pride is her insatiable desire to give back to the society. Currently, Rita is active with volunteer work, including her position as vice chair of the Board of Directors for Community Place of Greater Rochester, a social services organization. A longtime member of the American Association of University Women (an organization that advances equity for women and girls through advocacy, education, and research), she is currently responsible for its fundraising activities as well. Recently, Rita also earned a Certificate in Non-Profit Management from the State University of New York at Brockport and plans to use it for managing nonprofit entities.

∽

What a huge difference a short three-year period can make in the life of a parent!!

Our son, Robert, was born in April 1966, three years after his sister Rita arrived. But during this brief period, our lives had dramatically changed. By now we were settled in life, our never-ending immigration problem was history, and our childbirth-related financial crisis seemed like a joke. And that was not all. I had come to believe that by now I had become a self-styled pro in handling babies. In fact, I got so carried away that I volunteered to assume full responsibility for Robert's midnight feeding.

I should not have been so confident.

On the first night, I prepared the milk bottle for Robert and carefully placed it in the refrigerator. I also set the alarm for 2 am before confidently retiring for the evening. Well, as ill luck would have it, despite my meticulous preparations, something totally unpredictable occurred. The alarm did go off right on time. But I was sleeping so soundly that the alarm failed to wake me up. I presume the alarm did wake Robert up, and that he did cry for his milk. But realizing that his crying was not going to get him anywhere, he stopped crying and went back to sleep. I did wake up at 6 am, realized my mistake, poured the milk into the sink to erase any sign of my dereliction of duty, and happily went back to sleep.

I continued to follow this *creative* routine for a whole month until it was time for Robert's monthly checkup. Well, fearing what I was up against, I made a quick trip to our Hindu temple, prayed for forgiveness, and promised never to repeat my unpardonable sin.

I sat at the doctor's office on pins and needles, waiting for my guilty verdict to be pronounced by the pediatrician. After about a half hour, which seemed like an eternity, Dr Jeremiah called me in and blurted out: "Congratulations, Dr Mittra, Robert is doing far better than his sister did when she was one month old. Keep doing whatever it is you have been doing with Robert. I am so pleased."

When I heard that I thought God must have heard my prayers. Or was it that in his optimistic brilliance Robert directed his body to remain healthy despite the unwelcome dieting routine he was forced to practice by his sleepy father. Either way, it was fine with me. I felt completely vindicated.

When Robert was ready to go to school, recalling Mother's advice about my helping every family member to be his best, I had him tested and learned that he had a high IQ and an aptitude for creativity. Based on that aptitude test, we enrolled him in Roeper City and Country Day School, a prestigious private school in Bloomfield Hills, Michigan, for gifted children. He did very well there but due to social considerations, subsequently we moved him back to the Rochester school system.

Robert's performance in school was, by our standards, unremarkable. That was disappointing. But recognizing his innate intelligence, we allowed him a lot of latitude, hoping that eventually things will improve by themselves. While that did not happen, Robert continued to show his creative (although juvenile) thinking power in uncanny ways. Here's is an example.

One day, at the age of six, one morning Robert decided to play hooky. At that time, Bani and I were upstairs getting ready to go to work. Robert quietly slipped into the kitchen and called his school. When the secretary answered, he said: "Robert is sick today so he can't come to school." Hearing a child's voice and realizing what was going on, the secretary decided to lead him on and asked: "I agree that Robert should not come to school but should stay in bed. May I know who is calling?"

"My Mom," was the creative answer.

Robert did graduate from high school on time. But his grades were nowhere near where they needed to be to get admission into the prestigious University of Michigan. I offered to send him to Oakland University where I was a professor, but his heart was set on the University of Michigan. So he fought for it. His tenacity paid off, and ultimately he was admitted to that university.

But that was just the beginning. Once in college, Robert *exploded* in all directions and never looked back. He earned Bachelor of Science degree with *highest distinction* and with *High Honors in Cellular and Molecular Biology*. He also received the *James B. Angell Scholar, 1986–1987 Award* and *Membership in Golden Key National Honors Society*. And to top it off, he won the *Suma cum Laude Award* and was admitted to the *Phi Beta Kappa* honor society, the dream of every college graduate in this country, from the prestigious University of Michigan no less.

Robert's pursuit of an enviable scholastic record at Michigan did not stop him from excelling in other nonacademic areas. His passion for music, which he had developed in school, continued through college. He also learned to play tabla, the Indian percussion instrument, and took up golf later in life.

When Robert graduated from college, he had applied for admission to the University of Pennsylvania Medical School, America's oldest and one of the most prestigious medical institutions in the world. But to his utter disappointment and surprise, despite his spectacular scholastic achievements at the University of Michigan he was wait-listed for admission by the school with no assurance for a favorable outcome.

One day, after his patience had virtually run out, Robert decided to give up and informed me of his decision. My response to him was direct: "If you think you deserve to go to the University of Penn, then if I were you, I would continue to fight until you get the admission. Remember what Winston Churchill once said: 'Never, never, but never, give up.'"

I don't know if Robert found a way to challenge Penn or if he chose to patiently wait until the University made its final decision. But one day I found on my desk a letter from the University of Pennsylvania addressed to Robert. It read: "We are pleased to inform you ...."

Robert earned his MD from the University of Penn, where he developed an interest in ophthalmology and performed research at the Wills Eye Hospital. He completed his ophthalmology residency at the prestigious Duke Eye Center in Durham, N.C., where he was given the Edward K. Isbey Award for excellence in Clinical Care, Ethics, and Research. He completed a two-year surgical vitreoretinal fellowship at the Medical College of Wisconsin in Milwaukee where he was awarded a special teaching award by the residents. After completing his studies and fellowship programs, Robert ultimately became a partner in Vitreo Retinal Surgery, a medical practice located in Minneapolis, Minnesota, where he practices today.

Robert has been voted by his peers into the Best Doctors in America for every year since 2005. He has also received the Honor Award of the American Academy of Ophthalmology and also from the American Society of Retinal Specialists. Today, he is an internationally recognized eye surgeon and researcher. He is also an adjunct assistant professor of ophthalmology at the University of Minnesota. He lives in Minneapolis with his family and continues to do charitable work for eye patients, both in America and abroad.

As I recall, based on the trials, tribulations, and achievements of both of our children, two powerful thoughts come to mind. First, both of our children struggled throughout their lives to get to where they are today. They faced multiple challenges in their lives get to, and they met them head on and ultimately prevailed. Second, if Mother were alive today, she would be pleased to see that, as per her wish, we have successfully helped both Rita and Robert in reaching up to their full potential. Our children have also convinced us that while it is important for us to teach our values and philosophies to our children, it is the way we live as adults that ultimately convinces them that we truly believe in what we teach. In the end, our children will either succeed or fail *solely due to the good and bad decisions they make about how they themselves choose to live their lives.*

An integral part of Mother's advice was to encourage both Rita and Robert to assist their own children to reach their full potential. I believe they, too, are accomplishing that objective. As proof of that belief, I present here a letter I once wrote to our four grandchildren.

August 10, 2012

Dearest Rina, Markus, Rohan, and Ava,

Fifty-seven years ago to the day, I left Bombay for America, and Grandma followed me three and a half years later. We came to this country with a dream: to seek golden opportunities for ourselves, for our future children, and even for our grandchildren. I can certainly say without reservation that we, the members of the large and expanding Mittra clan, have achieved our individual and collective goals.

Now we are in the twenty-first century, and you are the next generation we dreamed of many moons ago. In this century, life appears to be shot through with wonder. Even the awesome achievements of the twentieth century—technological marvels, sophisticated communications, artificial intelligence, walking on the moon, deep probes of faraway planets, and most amazing of all, cloning life itself—pale in comparison. Now, in this new century, astronomers have discovered 50 new planets outside our solar system, one of them orbiting two suns! And scientists claim that subatomic particles have done the unthinkable by shattering the speed of light. If this claim ultimately becomes the new law of physics, it will redefine the word impossible.

Charles Kenny, senior fellow at the Center for Global Development, sums it up beautifully: "Never has there been a time in history when the average human could live so long, where food has been as plentiful, where newborns have a better chance of surviving. It's really hard to think of an important area where things aren't better—literacy, gender equality, the absence of slavery, the rights of minorities." Grandma and I are impressed that each of you is busy building a better you, and in the process, you are each preparing yourself for being able to make a difference in our vastly expanding universe.

Rina, at the age of 18, you have obtained a high school Regents Diploma with Advanced Designation, earning National Technical Honor Society and Character

Trait of the Month awards in the process. Active in gymnastics and varsity cheer-leading, you remain deeply involved in social and charitable activities, such as being a fundraiser event volunteer, a Listening Post volunteer (building relationships with senior citizens), a sleepover camp counselor, and a volunteer for Youth to Youth (a community drug-prevention and youth-leadership program).

Markus, at 14, you have established a record of academic excellence at school, athletic achievement in sports like hockey, prowess in the martial art of karate, and a keen talent for the arts (including dancing and drumming). Equally gratifying is that your charitable contributions include being a Karma Yoga Scholar at the Hindu Heritage Summer Camp and teaching the younger kids classes in karate. Your teachers in school and directors in various camps are impressed with your insatiable desire to lend a helping hand at every conceivable opportunity.

Rohan, when I was your age of 9, I hardly knew which end was up. But even at this tender age, you manage to be a diligent student in school and fill your life with other challenging activities. You are already an active hockey player and a golfer, and you also enjoy both swimming and sailing. We were also quite impressed when we attended your solo Suzuki piano concert. And we have noticed that at every opportunity, you listen when your papa talks to you about being helpful to others (such as assisting in the staging of your school's plays and similar events).

Ava, at 5, you are the angel of the family, vibrant and full of life. But we also see in you a desire to follow in the footsteps of your brother. Your teachers at MacPhail Center for Music have great hopes for you, and you are already showing a knack for fine arts and social activities.

So, dear Rina, Markus, Rohan, and Ava, with great pride and anticipation, we hereby pass on to you the torch of the Mittra family, which was originally lit by your great grandmother almost a century ago. It represents a simple philosophy: build a better you so that you can make a difference in building a better world.

We wish you every success, and at the same time, we hope that whenever you encounter life's inevitable setbacks and stumbling blocks that you will remember the paradox of the humble bumblebee, which easily takes flight right under the noses of all those aerodynamic experts who are convinced that there's no way it should be able to fly. If you can model that kind of faith and fortitude, we will indeed have achieved our lifelong dream of building a four generational legacy.

Yours affectionately,

Grandpa Sid & Grandma Bani

Epilogue: Life's Lessons

For a long time, I carried the notion of a typical family as consisting of a mother, a father, and their biological children living together under one roof. Then something strange happened shortly before I was to leave for America, and that helped me embrace a *new definition of family*.

It all began in August 1957, a few days before I set sail for the US. As I was saying goodbye to the family, my mother blurted out: "As you know, your father died when you were only seven. But even though at times I felt helpless, all my life I tried hard to provide help for you and your brothers so you all could become successful." Then after a brief pause, she added: "Today I request you to continue our family tradition. *Before* you start a family, remember this: Do not give up until *you* have helped each one in your family—your wife and your children—to reach his or her *fullest potential*. But don't just stop there. Teach **your** **children** our new definition of a family so they, too, will remember to help their spouses and children achieve their fullest potential."

That brief encounter changed my life forever.

In the winter of 1961, when we began our married life in DeLand, Bani's challenges ranged from modifying her deep-rooted Indian culture to getting acclimatized to the American language to adjusting to the prevailing social mores. She struggled for a long time to meet these challenges and at times it appeared that she won't be able to make it. But she surprised me and a lot of other people.

After passing an exam, she earned her Montessori degree and established a fully equipped and licensed Montessori school. Subsequently, she became the proud owner of the Meadowbrook Montessori School which came to be known as *The Private School* for small children in the city.

Ownership of the Meadowbrook School and active teaching role fulfilled Bani's professional dream. But her heart was also set on another dream: produce her own musical CDs. However, since after marriage she had permanently left India, her dream had remained unfulfilled.

Once the Montessori school began running smoothly, I found a way to fulfill her other dream. In 1997, with the help of several people living on both sides of the Atlantic Bani produced her first musical cassette (Parts I and II) appropriately entitled, *My Musical Dream*. And with its publication (she published many more since then), the life of this remarkable lady came to a full circle.

Finally, we succeeded in helping our children, Rita and Robert, and our four grandchildren begin their journey toward reaching their full potential. We are delighted that they are all engaged in trying hard to reach their respective goals.

The following Four Fs' list identifies the P(s) covered in this chapter:

[X]   Persevere with passion.
[X]   Pursue professional, family-oriented, social, and spiritual goals.
[X]   Persuade family and friends to help.
[X]   Promote a culture of giving back.

ABOUT THE AUTHOR

Sid Mittra is an Emeritus Professor of Finance at Oakland University in Rochester, Michigan, as well as a former partner and founder of the financial consulting firm Mittra & Associates. He is a former board member of the International Board of Standards and Practices of Certified Financial Planners and has many times been a presenter at the World Conference of the International Association for Financial Planning. Harold Evensky, a colleague of Sid (who himself was named as one of the five most influential people in the financial planning profession) has said of Sid: "He was one of the profession's pioneers. However, past tense does not fully capture Sid's contributions, for like the Energizer Bunny, Sid continues to lead."

Dr Mittra has written more than a hundred technical articles and 12 books on finance and economics, including *Practicing Financial Planning: A Complete Guide for Professionals* (originally published by Prentice Hall in 1990; the 11th edition was published in 2012 by American Academic Publishing), parts of which won a gold in Axiom Business Book Award in 2008. A few of Dr Mittra's other books include *Investment Analysis and Portfolio Management* (Harcourt Brace Jovanovich, 1981), *Inside Wall Street* (Dow Jones-Irwin, 1971), *Money and Banking: Theory, Analysis and Policy* (Random House, 1970), and *Dimensions in Macroeconomics: A Book of Readings* (Random House, 1971). Dr Mittra has also authored the longest running financial planning columns in *The Oakland Press* and the Detroit-area *Eccentric* newspapers, and has even hosted a regional television show called "Your Money" on personal finance.

This book *To Bee or Not to Bee* represents Dr Mittra's effort to introduce the public to a powerful concept entitled *The Four Ps Principles*. Details of these principles are articulated in the section entitled Prelude (see page xiii).